The Life of Trester

The Life of Trester
An Experience of Schizophrenia

Robert A. Harris

.:Virtual**Salt**
Publishing
Tustin

Copyright 2014 © Robert A. Harris

VirtualSalt Publishing
Tustin, California

www.virtualsalt.com

ISBN 978-1-941233-12-2

Introduction

This book consists largely of blog entries I made during several years of watching over my mentally ill brother, Trester Harris, Jr., taking him his weekly groceries and then going to lunch and shopping with him.

During this period, he wrote his thoughts on 3-by-5 and 4-by-6 note cards, accumulating thousands of them. Many were what he believed to be news headlines, while others were ideas for commercial products, foods, and so forth. I have included entries from some of these cards here and there in order to give a sense of what was on his mind. When his handwriting was illegible, I have either offered my best estimate (marked by a bracketed question mark) or given up (and entered a bracketed "illegible").

There are so many cards that order or organization by time is impossible. However, Trester did number them by various series and sequences, and I have kept those numbers for reference. Transcriptions from the cards are set off by the lightning bolts, as shown below.

⚡ ⚡ ⚡

45.1 Tindall attack won't end here —- & two others
45.2 Kennedy is invading Baja overseas again now
45.3 P.O. Box Headlines: Mail box blew up with bomb here
45.4 Petri dies in Hail of Gunfire & young [?] one who had same name also— not real one upstairs—
45.5 Headlines: Bombers hit islands over here just now—
45.9 Mac-Ro killed or injured up north—

⚡ ⚡ ⚡

The purpose for this book is to offer insight into the constant suffering schizophrenics experience, as they are tortured by delusions and hallucinations of violence, criticism, prohibition, insult, and condemnation, while dreaming of power, friendship, and success. The comments Trester has made to me when we were driving around or eating, together with the content of the Headline Cards, reveals how much misery plagued his life. My hope is that by reading this book readers will find a better sense of compassion for the mentally ill.

Some readers might find this book repetitive, even boringly so, because many of the entries report the same or very similar comments and events. However, if you really want to get to know someone, to get inside the mind and heart, it's important to spend ordinary time with that person, to learn what his or her ongoing concerns are. My view is that after you read this book, you will feel as if you really know Trester, and you will understand much more deeply what the life of a schizophrenic can be like.

Background

Trester Smith Harris, Jr. was born in Los Angeles, California in 1948, the first child of Trester Harris, MD, and his wife Marie. Trester's childhood was normal and happy.

From the age of about ten Trester became interested in plants. At the house in Inglewood, California, he filled the covered patio with all kinds of plants, some ordinary and some exotic. He had a few orchids, he enjoyed watching leaves grow roots when taped to a curtain, and he preferred the unusual and exotic. His interest began to focus on succulents and later, cacti. By the time we moved to Corona, California, his enthusiasm was such that our father built a lath house just for Trester's plant collection. It was natural for him, then, to take Ornamental Horticulture in high school and to help landscape the barren Corona lot.

The Corona house supplied other opportunities for two youngsters (ages 12 and 10 when we moved). He and I used to play together on our nearly three-acre desert lot, building miniature towns, complete with roads, trees (broken off pieces of bushes), and even a Cinerama drive-in theater (made of cardboard).

We assumed the names of Ed and Jim Carson, and we pretended that we were unstoppably successful businessmen, building , manufacturing, selling, and so on. We had an enemy named Stromagite, who constantly attempted to thwart our plans, but we always beat him.

From fairly early on, say early teens, Trester became an avid photographer. He got a 35mm camera and became the de facto photographer for the family. On every vacation, he would shoot several rolls of 35mm slide film. At home, too, he loved to take pictures of flowers, sunsets, and his plants, many of which, flowering or not, were quite beautiful.

Trester graduated from high school in 1966, and enrolled at California State University, Fullerton, with a major in economics. He immediately became an economic contrarian, falling in love with classical economic theory, especially the Austrian school, and rejecting Keynesian economics. He began to read all the classical economists he could find, including Friedrich Hayek, Ludwig von Mises, Eugen von Boehm-Bawerk, Murray Rothbard, Frederic Bastiat and a host of others. He read voraciously in these economists, underlining and making notes in the margins. He had a way of folding the books backwards to allow them to lie flat, but that stressed the bindings to such an extent that when he was finished with a book, it was obvious from the look, even when closed.

These years saw the beginning of a mild depression. School was challenging and he was not very sociable, staying to himself much of the time.

In 1968 he transferred to the University of California at Santa Barbara, where I was enrolled as a freshman. We ate some meals together, but saw surprisingly little of each other during those two years. We both poured our energies into school work. We talked on the phone from one dorm room to another across the way, and Trester frequently reported being depressed. To entertain each other, we drew comics about an ugly monster bug (that looked like a giant ant, more or less) named Doomper Boompbug. Doomper and his fellow bugs were mortal enemies of Joe Doax, ABL (Anti-Boompbug League).

After graduating with a Bachelor's degree in economics in 1970, Trester enrolled in the Pepperdine Law School and rented an apartment in Garden Grove, California. The law school was at that time in Anaheim, I believe. Trester was a loner in his law school years, and his depression increased. He continued to read economic theory and to rail against the wrong headedness of the Keynesians. He also became fervently interested in Christianity, buying commentaries, listening to Bible teaching radio programs, and of course reading the Bible itself.

Trester graduated from law school in 1973 with a JD degree and sat for the California State Bar exam, which he did not pass. He redoubled his studying for the exam and passed on his second attempt, thus being admitted to the state bar.

Trester moved back home while he waited for job offers to arrive, but none did. His depression continued. After law school, Trester looked around for a job, but finding one was complicated by his depression. He interviewed with the Marines for a job as a military lawyer, but he showed during the interview that he was just not alert or "up" as they say. He worked for a law firm for several months and did a little business, but once again his depression kept him from functioning properly. This was in the early 1970s. His father was adamantly opposed to psychiatrists (which is odd, since Trester's father was a medical doctor). At any rate, it didn't seem to occur to anyone that Trester was clinically depressed. What medicines were available in those days, I don't recall.

Somewhere around this time, Trester convinced our parents to let him start a cactus mail order business, which he named Desert Hill Cactus Growers.

In 1975 our father, Trester Sr., passed away. Trester processed the probate by himself, as executor, and did a good job.

Trester Jr. decided to run for congress (as a Republican in a heavily Democratic district, against a popular and long-time incumbent Democrat). He had no political or social connections and was not known in the community or the district, so not surprisingly, he lost by a substantial margin.

After this experience, Trester decided to move back to Orange County, California, and he used money from his inheritance from our father to make a down payment on a condominium. He continued his interest in photography by painting his downstairs bathroom black and converting it into a darkroom. He bought an enlarger and the supplies to make his own black and white prints.

Trester soon enrolled in an unaccredited school to study psychology, getting a PhD from there in a year or two. He was obviously interested in his own mental condition. At some point he began to see psychotherapists and I believe one or more psychiatrists, because he ended up taking Stelazine for a while (and later Thorazine). One time when he was still willing to see psychiatrists, one doctor said that Trester was "the most mentally ill person I've ever met."

At one point, Trester rented an office and opened up a hypnotherapy business. He rented a small office and put in a few furnishings, but with limited advertising, he had few customers. He did cure one woman of fear of driving, but I think that's about all. He soon abandoned that practice.

Later on, he bought a tobacco business in a strip mall in Anaheim, Gordon's tobacco. He was propelled more by his desire to make money than his interest in pipes and cigars, but he threw himself energetically into the business, until his depression got the better of him and sapped his energy. He hired a sales clerk to help run the business, which ate up pretty much all of the profits he otherwise would have earned. His illness made him too trusting, and the person he bought the business from turned out to be something of a crook, leaving behind a number of debts, having overstated the shop's earnings, and the like. When Trester could no longer support the losses from the business where it was, he moved it to a small office. Once again he was somewhat swindled when he sold the furniture from the business. Lots of people are ready to take advantage of the mentally ill.

Trester's business was essentially invisible on the second floor of an office building, so it soon ceased to earn any money and in 1981, Trester sold his condominium in Anaheim and moved back in with his mother, bringing a surprising inventory of pipes, tobacco, lighters, and other smoking paraphernalia with him. He still seemed more depressed than mentally ill.

By this time, the side effects of those older generation antipsychotics (weight gain, chronic sleepiness) had caused Trester to stop taking medication altogether, and his increasing paranoia prevented him from seeing doctors or dentists. In fact, for several years, he refused to leave the house, saying that assassins were outside waiting to kill him.

Before Trester became mentally ill, he had used some of his inheritance money to build a couple of mountain cabins on speculation. He sold both and made a reasonable profit. By the time the owners of the last cabin got ready to sell it to someone else, Trester had become ill. The problem arose that Trester refused to sign the reconveyance when the trust deed was paid off. No amount of coaxing from his mother had any effect.

Finally, the owner, whom I'll call Perry, came out to the house with a notary public and a witness in hopes of getting Trester to sign. At first Trester was very polite. In fact, he could still act "normal" when he wanted to. If his appearance (his hair and beard, and the look in his eyes) weren't such a giveaway, he could make strangers think he was a normal, sane man. So, at first Trester appeared normal. I happened to be there and even I was surprised at his calm, rational, friendly tone. However, when Mr. Perry introduced himself, with a "Hello, I'm Frank Perry," Trester became instantly enraged. "That's one of my names," he said roughly. "You can't use that name." He may have made some other comments, but I don't remember. His behavior was pretty obviously wild, though, and he had an angry expression. The notary public was scandalized. "I can't notarize a document under these circumstances," he said, as if anyone would now insist that he should. So, Trester didn't sign anything and the men had to leave empty handed.

His family's first indication that something was wrong occurred when Trester was home with them. He got a call from a doctor who apparently asked him how he was doing. After he hung up, Trester said, "He was hypnotizing me over the telephone." What in retrospect were obvious signs of growing mental illness, left my mother and me dumbfounded and confused.

Before he moved home, his mother had begun to understand that something was wrong. Trester called once to say he had bought a large, expensive photocopier. When his mother asked him why, he said, "I wanted you to love me." She assured him that she did, and persuaded him to return the copier to the store (that is, have it picked up, since it was apparently too large for one person to carry).

Back home with his mother, Trester began to complain of electrical bolts shooting at his head. If a light bulb burned out when turned on (making that extra-bright flash and a little "tink" noise), Trester thought "they" were "shooting poisoned light bulbs" at him and sometimes acted as if he had been shot. He began to tape aluminum foil over the electrical outlets and put pipes and boards under his bed to ground out the electrical weapons being used against him.

While talking to himself, Trester would sometimes complain that "they're making me crazy." However, he always refused to admit that he had a mental illness when asked by anyone. It was too stigmatizing. "I don't want to be locked up in a loony bin," was his usual answer.

One of the early signs that his family did not recognize at the time was a personality change. Trester had grown up mildly religious and became increasingly religious during law school (in the 70s). Then in the 80s, he had a change and became anti-religious, mocking God and theology. He became rebellious, angry, and stridently independent. He said he was tired of being constrained, oppressed, and restricted. He wanted to throw off the restraints and have fun. His family suspected at one point that he may have experimented with marijuana, and later he tried dabbling in the occult for a short time (something like a crystal ball or magic or some such engagement — that is, with the spiritual side of this stuff, not the entertainment side). The details are unclear however. Trester became abrasive and impolite, treating his family almost like an enemy, as if they were to blame for whatever was troubling him.

Trester had been studying psychology at the time and began to develop theories about what was happening to him. At one point he said he had multiple personalities, with many — I think he said over a thousand. This may be the seed of his current use of "we" and his talk about "one of us was torn off our head" and the like.

If Trester had developed this rebellious and hostile streak in his early teens, we might think of it as a typical adolescent battle for individuation and adulthood. But Trester was about 30 or so at the time. After this point, he began to study hypnosis and to hypnotize himself. He also began to have hallucinations and delusions, as his illness began to blossom fully. As I mentioned, for a while, he saw a few psychiatrists on his own, taking Stelazine and Thorazine and possibly haloperidol for a while at various times. I still remember how much the Thorazine made him sleep. Those early medications had some nasty side effects. No wonder the patients didn't like them.

Trester's objection to the newer medication, Risperdal, was that it ruined his imagination. His imaginary friends all disappeared and his creative ability was greatly diminished. But you would have been stunned to see what a great difference that medicine made in bringing back his thinking, reasoning, personality, and functioning ability. It's so sad that he won't take it now.

A few years after moving back home, Trester thought the neighbors were "shooting poisoned light bulbs" at him, so he went over and broke all the windows out of their house. He was on the way back to their house with a gasoline soaked rag when the Sheriff arrived and took him down to jail. Trester asked us to "hire a Mexican attorney," which we did. This attorney was evidently not familiar with handling cases involving mental illness—though he professed otherwise—and he thought it would be a good idea to transfer Trester's hearing from municipal to superior court. At the hearing, the attorney simply waited for the prosecutor to declare that Trester must be dangerous because he had been remanded to superior court and asked the judge not to grant bail. As a result Trester ended up in the county jail, where, based on his self-talk later on, he was sexually abused.

Somehow, from a law school friend, he got the name of an attorney familiar with both mental illness and the superior court system. His new attorney knew what was what and, instead of waiting for the next court session to begin, went directly to the judge's chambers and talked to the judge. The result was that Trester was released from jail and moved to a board and care facility. Later, there was a conservatorship hearing, and Trester agreed to let me be his conservator for a year.

Both Trester's mother and I thought that at the psychiatric board and care, he would now be given antipsychotic medicine and taken care of appropriately. I visited him just about every week, but didn't notice much change. We were allowed to go out together on walks and to a meal.

One day during our lunch outing, Trester said, "Don't you know what's going on here? This place is run by the CIA to keep me in prison and torture me." I asked him why the CIA would want to do that to him, and he said, "Because I have secret knowledge." Evidently the CIA didn't want this knowledge to get out. Needless to say, this idea explained why Trester kept begging his mother to let him come home.

When we got back to the board and care facility, I asked the doctor what medication Trester had been taking. (This was after almost nine months of Trester's stay there.) To my enormous surprise, the doctor said, "He's not on any medicine. He's says there's nothing wrong with him." This doctor was a psychiatrist who worked at the facility and whom our mother had been paying weekly to see Trester.

To be a bit briefer, we scheduled a meeting with the psychiatrist, Trester, and two or three staffers (nurses and employees). I asked Trester a few simple questions, like, "Didn't you tell me that this place is a CIA front?" and Trester answered honestly, "Yes." The doctor finally got a clue and put Trester on Prolixin (one of the better then-available medications). Trester's hallucinations (the ghosts choking him) remitted, although his delusions (about the CIA) didn't go away. This is supposed to be common in schizophrenia. The medicine takes care of the hallucinations but the false beliefs take a lot longer to deal with.

Trester continued to beg his mother to let him go home, and she finally relented, sensing that Trester wasn't doing all that great in the board and care place anyway. He promised to keep taking the medicine at home. He took it for about a month and then stopped, saying, "I don't need it anymore." When we mentioned to him that while he was on it, his hallucinations—or rather the flying ghosts attacking him—stopped, he said, "That was something else," meaning that the ghosts stopped attacking him for a reason other than the medicine.

So, Trester's first trip through the system didn't really help much, in the long run. He did, however, become more peaceful because he was afraid of being arrested again.

A few years later, about two or three o'clock in the morning one time, Trester called the Sheriff and told them that someone was murdering babies in the front yard. The Sheriff came out to see what was going on, and in the process—let's use the media euphemism—an incident occurred which left Trester with a broken arm. He was taken to the Riverside County hospital where his arm was put in a cast and then to the mental health lockup where he was put on Risperdal.

After the few days of stabilization, Trester was moved to what the county described as a board and care facility. It was an abandoned motel with an empty swimming pool, dead grass, and gravel parking areas. Even though he agreed to take the medicine, he refused to see a dentist for his rotten teeth. He stayed there for a few months, and Mom and I went to see him once or twice a week, taking him out to lunch regularly.

Then he came home again, promising to continue to take his medicine. While he was on it, he took the driver's test to renew his license and passed it the first try, without studying the booklet at all. (I doubt I could do that.) So he got his license renewed. (Shortly thereafter, he said he didn't need to take medicine anymore and has not taken any since.)

When our mom passed away, he drove her car for a couple of years, traveling around quite a bit and getting traffic tickets from various jurisdictions, such as Los Angeles and Corona. The Corona tickets were for failure to wear a seatbelt and stopping in an intersection. When I found out about these tickets, I tried to get him to go take care of them, but he insisted that he had been "pardoned by the governor." Eventually, as a result, his license was revoked, and as a result of that his insurance was canceled, and as a result of that, he couldn't renew his automobile registration. Then he got a ticket in Los Angeles for driving with an expired registration.

Finally, he got another ticket for driving without a fastened seatbelt (and maybe some other infraction), and apparently the officer found out that his license had been revoked, so they towed his car away. I still couldn't get him to take care of any of these tickets, so we couldn't get his car out of impound. As a result, it was likely sold at auction to pay the hefty daily impound fees.

So, Trester was without a car. All things considered, it's for the best. I didn't want him to drive off and disappear the way he had done several times before, when he still had some of his inheritance money. Many times after that Trester would say, "Can you help me buy a car?" and I would tell him he needed to get his driver's license back first, so he could get insurance and registration. "I need a $300 Lexus," he would say. Occasionally he would point to a car and ask me how much one like that would cost. He didn't like the answers because he thought cars were a lot cheaper than my estimates.

One year he drove from one coast almost to the other. He got a flat tire in some out of the way place, stopped the car, knocked on the door of some poor, unsuspecting person, and yelled at him for "shooting out my tire." We got a call from the local police about that, which is how we know. They sent him on his way.

Another time, a number of years ago, rather late at night, Trester said, "I'm going out to get a taco. Do you want to go?"

His mom and I said, "No." Trester left and didn't come

back. The next day or so, he called from Haiti. He stayed there for about a week or so and finally came back.

He also visited Hawaii several times. He would get some sudden idea, such as that someone in his "group" was waiting to see him, so he would drive to the Los Angeles airport, buy a first-class ticket (I saw one receipt for $1250), and fly away.

One trip was to Molokai, where he spent a month. He arrived at the airport, expecting someone to meet him. When no one did, his behavior was noticed by the police and he was put into a family welfare home, where he stayed for a month or so. He told the authorities that his mother and brother had been killed and that he was all alone. They later called us to let us know he was okay. When they put him on the phone, he was suspicious of us and asked who we were. When he finally did return to the mainland, his first question was, "What do the headlines say?" His mother showed him the paper, with the usual headlines (that is, no mention of Trester) and he said, "I must be really crazy." He started taking Thorazine for a while at that point.

Years later, again unmedicated, Trester took off for Hawaii again, but stayed only a week. Then about two years ago, as his money was winding down, he went once again (flying first class because he could never plan in advance long enough to get a good ticket price). He stayed only about three days this time. The persecutors (ghosts and such) were there in Hawaii as well as here. He couldn't escape them by fleeing the area. He mentioned that one place he stayed charged him $345 for a night's stay. Too bad he likely didn't get anywhere near his money's worth.

One other time, Trester flew to London. However, his behavior was apparently so bizarre that he was not admitted into the country and was put on an immediate return flight.

Back to his Hawaii trip for a minute. As soon as he walked off the plane and met us (without any sign of joy that we really were not dead after all), he asked, "What are the headlines in the newspaper?" We mentioned the usual stories. When Trester realized that the headlines didn't mention him or some earth-shattering events that he expected, he said, "I must be crazy."

And he began to see psychiatrists. Whenever he did, Trester always insisted that I be there with the doctor, since he didn't trust the doctors. (One psychiatrist got really upset when he insisted that I stay, and said hotly, "I don't allow any babysitters." She probably wouldn't have been very good anyway, because her attitude was rather negative and hostile from the outset. She demanded $90 in advance, too. This was in the 1980s, I think.)

Anyway, we took him to a county psychiatrist, who asked Trester if he had any delusions or hallucinations. Trester had done a year or two of study in psychology while he was still sane and had gotten an unaccredited PhD, so he knew what was what. He chuckled and told the doctor, "No, no delusions or hallucinations."

As you might imagine, my eyebrows went up at this and I said, "Yes, you do." Then I described a few to the doctor.

The doctor left the room momentarily, and Trester said fairly loudly under his breath, "Don't say that! They'll think I'm crazy."

Another time we took him to see a psychiatrist connected to University of California at Irvine medical center. The doctor eventually said something like, "You have the symptoms of schizophrenia."

Trester said, "No, no."

So the doctor said, "Well, schizophreniform symptoms, then."

The stigma of mental illness affects the mentally ill themselves. Trester has said more than once, "I'm not crazy. I don't want to be locked up in a loony bin." When he argues with his imaginary enemies, he sometimes accuses them of being psychotic. He sometimes says, "Go away and die, you screwy idiots. Who made you psychotic?"

One day he said, "They pulled a piece of me off and killed a bunch of us and several kids."

I asked, "Do you ever think that some of what you are thinking is not true?"

Trester said, "No, I don't think I'm crazy." One of the multiple times I told Trester that he was mentally ill he said, "Who hypnotized you?"

Here begin the entries from the Weblog that I wrote for several years. Interspersed are texts from his "Headline Cards."

Tuesday, November 9, 2004

The grocery bill was relatively low this week since Trester has quite a supply of soup and stew on hand. I got him his usual favorite TV dinners and some Rocky Road ice cream. Cheetos were on sale, so I got him a bag of those.

We went to lunch at a Mexican buffet, where we've been several times. He always has a Corona beer, too. Then we went to the Smoke Shop where he got some cigarettes. Then to a new One-dollar store. However, when we walked inside, he said, "They don't want me to shop here." That's a pretty common statement when we walk into a store. I told him it was okay, and we got inside and down an aisle or two, but he said a couple of times, "Let's just leave." So we headed out, taking us past the candle aisle. He picked up a few candles and bought them, together with a small calendar.

Outside, he said, "They hit me on the head in there." This is also a common complaint.

Next, we drove to Home Depot to get some eight foot fluorescent light bulbs for the living room. Good old Home Depot nearly always has what I need. We found the right ones and bought them. On the way home, Trester kept making popping noises with his mouth, to explode the ghosts that are attacking him. He kept saying, "Just stop or something." At least he didn't throw up.

At home, I installed the bulbs and they worked. Then I had to climb into the attic to replace a light switch relay so that the kitchen light could be turned on and off. It had stuck in the on position and Trester had to unscrew the light bulbs from the fixture to get them to go off. (My first thought had been that he thought the light fixture was shooting electricity into his head, a hallucination he has had in the past.)

After I left, I went back to Home Depot and ordered a new water heater. The old one was installed in 1991 and is leaking slightly now. Better to take care of it now than wait for the leak to turn into a stream. So I'll be going out to the farm again tomorrow to be present at the installation. I don't want Trester to tell the installers that they have the wrong address.

Trester keeps asking me to get him a ticket to fly to "the main Maui" so that he "can go home." I think by that he means die, since he has said he wants to "go home upstairs."

The sore on his elbow is better.

Sunday, November 14, 2004

Trester called this evening. He says there was a message on the radio telling him that the bank is holding tickets for "Main Maui" and a check for a lot of money. (Earlier he had said the amount was a thousand dollars.) He said he was feeling unwell because helicopters flew over the house last night and sprayed poison gas. Someone else sprayed bugs and worms in the house. He wants to move and wants me to help him get the ticket so he can fly away. He told me he would be joining his other relatives and they all would be called the Sand Cake Family.

He mentioned being cold, so I asked him if the heat was on and he said no. I reminded him about working the furnace and also mentioned the small space heater in the kitchen. He said the space heater "has a spook in it" so he had to put it outside and not use it.

Among other things he mentioned during his rambling talk was that he believes he has a bunch of kids in an apartment somewhere but doesn't know where. He also wanted to know how to call some of his other relatives. I told him he would need their names and phone numbers. He said the phone does not work to connect him to anyone.

I asked him if he had eaten yet, and he said yes, he had some Salisbury steak TV dinners. He had to throw out the corned beef because "it was polluted." I asked him if he was referring to the pepper on it, but he said, no, it had pollution on it.

He said his knee hurts. Once again I offered to take him to a doctor, but he said, "No, I'll be all right." That's always the obstacle. The legal system says that the mentally ill can make their own decisions. But how can you do that when it's your brain that's ill?

Tuesday, November 16, 2004

I went out to the farm early today with the intention of meeting the water heater installers. They had promised to come last Wednesday but got "busy," and then Monday, and then "our first install of the day" today. But when they had not come by 11:30, I called and learned that they could not even find the paperwork. (This after multiple address mix-ups in the days prior.) So I cancelled the order.

Meanwhile, I cleaned up the kitchen counters. They were stained with lime scale from plants Trester had put on the counters and watered. Also cigarette ashes (he just taps his cigarettes haphazardly, usually over something that looks like a container — an ashtray sometimes, but often a bowl, a cup, a flowerpot, whatever). Then there was some renegade rice and quite a few mouse pills. I had put out some more mouse bait about two weeks ago, so cleaning up his counters will tell me if the mouse problem is gone, at least temporarily. A problem here is that Trester is not anti-mouse. In fact, he wants food left out "to feed the little critters." He puts food outside for the same purpose, and everything from cats to rats appreciates it, I'm sure.

In cleaning up the dishes I noticed that Trester has most of two sets of silverware, but only one fork left. In the past I had noticed the forks gradually diminishing, but now he seems to be nearly out. Maybe they get bent or tossed out with the food. I don't know.

I replaced the kitchen faucet today, in what turned out to be a lot more difficult job than it sounds. Sure, when you install a faucet, those little plastic nuts screw on easily finger tight. But a few years later, when it's time to unscrew them, you have to put a wrench on them, way up under there. And each grab of the wrench gives you maybe an eighth of a turn, or a quarter turn if you're lucky.

Had to replace the hot water cutoff valve, too, since it was corroded into uselessness and wouldn't even shut off the water, which is its sole purpose in life.

Trester wanted to go get "a pizza pie" for lunch, so we went to a local pizza place and had their buffet, which consisted of a few slices of pizza and some spaghetti, together with a little salad.

Back at the house, I checked my work for leaks and finished the sink area. I noticed a note on the countertop about flying to "Main Maui," using "Nui" airlines. Trester once said his new name was Petey Nui, so maybe that's an airline he or his relatives started. Currently, Trester says his new name is Auy Axils Poll, and even insisted on having that name put on his bank account and checks (when he still had some money). Of course, that meant that he could no longer write a check to any local merchants (except the cigarette store, whose proprietor knew him already), because his driver's license still had his real name on it. So, no matching ID, no take the check. He has also adopted the name Jumpy in the past, but applies that to someone else now, I think.

I learned today that Trester sometimes uses the Dial-a-Ride service to get around town. He can be competent when he tries.

✵ ✵ ✵

61.95 Headline: Rose Parade in Pasadena Nuked – 300 Bombs Hit Parade
61.96 Headlines: 200 million people killed or Injured – rest riot all over the Place
61.99 Ex Marine Corp sergeants beaten up and attacked all over world —

61.103 8 million Russians dies so far in parade bombing—
61.382 12 Trillion dollar theft per hour now going on—

N N N

Friday, November 19, 2004

Trester called last night, asking me to call the Auto Club to see if two of his friends were in jail in Baja California, where they would each need $100 to bail them out. I told him the Auto Club would not know anything about that. He said he heard on the radio that his friends were in jail. I told him it was probably a false report.

He is always wanting to bail a friend or relative, especially one of his kids, out of jail. He leaves dollar bills around the house in various places, such as a bowl in the family room and a cup in the back bedroom, as bail for friends and relatives. When we go out to eat, he leaves a dollar tip for the waitress and a dollar "for the kids." He puts the second dollar in a different place, often under his glass or beer bottle. He has even put a dollar or two near his stuffed animal platypus, whom he calls "Platty." I'm not sure why, but perhaps it is to bail him out if he gets arrested. Platty has a shirt over him to keep warm. Trester pats Platty on the head occasionally. Platty is a caricatured platypus about two feet long, with yellow and orange skin.

When I was in graduate school, I once saw a man at a fast food restaurant eating across from his stuffed animal alligator, talking to it and moving it around very interactively. A few patrons laughed at him, but even then I thought the scene was tragic, not suspecting that I would later know a mentally ill person first hand. As another friend used to say of Trester, "He's so alone." Don't let the imaginary friends and imaginary enemies fool you.

Trester also said that a car crashed into the garage. I asked him if he went to investigate and he said no. He did open the front door to look out but didn't see anything.

He said his legs hurt. I told him to try a bath and take some aspirin. Once again I suggested getting him checked up, but he always says, "I'll be all right."

Monday, November 22, 2004

I went out to the farm a day early to see Trester since I'll be busy elsewhere tomorrow. I brought in the groceries and showed him the new items I got.

Trester was still concerned about one of his brothers in jail in Baja California. I reminded him that he had told me on the phone over the weekend that some new lawyers were on the case. He said he had heard on the radio that they had failed and that the brother needed $100 to get out of jail. At first he wanted to go to the Auto Club before lunch, but he changed his mind and we went to lunch first.

We ate at an Islands, where the fries (or onion rings) are extra. Trester ordered fish tacos. The waiter asked, "Do you want any fries or onion rings with that?" There are, of course, two tones of voice that waiters ask this question. One implies that the veggie is included and the other implies that it is extra. Our waiter used the appropriate tone to imply that fries or rings would be extra, but Trester is not able to distinguish, and he said, "Fries," in a way that I knew he thought they were included. Life is just too nuanced for those with mental disabilities, especially perhaps for those who have voices in their heads. At any rate, the fries were delicious and we brought the leftovers home.

Next, we went by the bank. Trester has a life insurance dividend check he wanted to cash. I asked him back at the house if he had his driver's license for identification, but he said he had lost it. Later he said, "They kept harassing me and took it." So I wondered how he was going to cash the check. He did have his ATM card, and he thought that would be sufficient. He also expected that the bank would have $1000 for him and a ticket for him to fly to Main Maui. Unfortunately, the bank not only had no money and no ticket for him, but his account had been cancelled, too, since it was below the minimum balance. (Last time I saw a statement, there was about $18 in it, I think.)

So, we drove over to the Auto Club. As we went, I asked him if he had his Auto Club card and he said that he had lost that, too. I told him they probably wouldn't talk to him without it. I waited in the car and he went in. About fifteen minutes later he came back. I asked him what they told him about his brother in jail. He said the place (that is, the Auto Club office) had been taken over by a conspiracy, where everyone was bribed by "the Riverside group" and so they wouldn't help him. One thing I've noticed about paranoid schizophrenia is that its sufferers are often very logical. Irrational, yes, but also logical. That is, they can give a logical reason for any event that conflicts with their beliefs.

Back home, while I was mopping the kitchen floor, I noticed that the linoleum continues to get cuts and gouges in it. Cups and glasses often have a short life at the farm. What I think happens is that Trester goes into a rage at some injustice being perpetrated against him and he hurls a cup or glass down onto the floor. Pretty much every time I sweep or mop, I find little shards of glass or ceramic under the counters. Trester cleans up most of the evidence, but there is always something left behind.

I also noticed a new hole in one of the kitchen walls, made by something being hurled against it, I think. Trester kicked a hole in the living room wall a year or two ago, but this hole was shaped like an angular object, not a foot.

While I did some cleaning in the back bathroom, Trester did a little yelling, which he normally does not do when I'm around. I think he was upset about the Auto Club problem and the persecution he feels he is getting from so many places.

Thursday, November 25, 2004

On this Thanksgiving Day, Trester called to wish me a happy holiday and find out if I was okay. At first he said, "Merry Christmas," but when I told him it was Thanksgiving, he said, "Happy Thanksgiving." He knew it was some kind of holiday.

He asked if I were all right. He worries about me because he is constantly hallucinating major disasters around himself, and he has delusions about my wellbeing. On Monday, he called to see if I had arrived home safely after visiting him. He had heard that people were being blown up by car bombs and thought I might be one of them. Today when he called, he asked if everything was okay.

He said that when he was sitting on the toilet someone blew up the house when he flushed the toilet. I've had to replace the toilet seal in two toilets and tighten the hold-down bolts on one of them repeatedly because he evidently rocks back and forth or sideways when he thinks the explosions are going off. I told him to get up before flushing and maybe that would help. Once he told me that someone kicked the corner of the house into the air when he flushed the toilet. The toilet seat in the bathroom near the laundry room has "Dangerous: Do Not Use" written on it. I think he avoided it for a while, but he has been using it recently.

On Monday I also noticed that one of the light switches in the back bathroom has a sign: "Dangerous: Do Not Use Heat Light" on it (written on an envelope and taped over the switch). A few years ago, when his mother was still alive, he got some pliers and tried to take one of the switches apart in another bathroom. When it arced from the electrical short, he said "they" were trying to electrocute him. Fortunately, he was not hurt.

I cannot express the helpless, tragic feelings I have for Trester. He won't let me help him in getting to a doctor or psychiatrist or dentist, all of which he needs. And as his mother said, "He's so alone."

Saturday, November 27, 2004

Trester called again last night. He said, "I have to leave here right now," in a mildly urgent tone. He said "they" were attacking the house and blowing everything up and trying to get at him. I told him to stay in the house where he would be safe and that I wouldn't let anyone hurt him. I tried using a calm, affectionate, reassuring voice. Either that worked or he gave up on asking for my help to get him out of the house, because he became calmer as we talked.

He said that one of the dollar bills he puts in the bowls had gotten one of his brothers out of jail and that the brother came up on a Petey Nui airlines flight from somewhere near South Africa. The brother was waiting at a bar for Trester, who couldn't get there. (If he still had his car, no doubt he would have driven down there.) So the brother apparently tried to come to Trester, but "a giant spook deal was shooting bombs" and someone bombed the freeway and the bartenders who were traveling with the brother.

Trester again said that there was a ticket and money for him to fly to Little Sand Cake Island. The money was at the bank but it couldn't get to him "because of the war and all the rioting." I told him I would take him to the bank next Tuesday when I go out to see him. He said okay. Later he acted as if he might try to get to the bank today, though I reminded him that this was Saturday and he should check the hours. He said the phone would not call very many people other than me. (He sometimes has trouble getting through to me because he forgets that I am in another area code. His phone bills often show ten or twenty dialings to my number but in his area code.)

Monday, November 29, 2004

Trester called again last night. He said that the restaurant where we ate on Tuesday had been bombed. He asked for the phone number of one of his brothers who is an attorney. I told him I didn't know of any of his brothers. Whenever I ask for the name of one of these people (brother or child in jail somewhere or a business owner or attorney) he always says he doesn't know. If I press him (after all, how can you not know the name of your children?), he says "They stuck a thing in my head and I can't think straight," or some other comment.

The other day when I asked Trester some question or other, he said that "they" had put a sharp poker in his head and that prevented him from thinking straight. He sometimes recognizes his own psychosis by attributing it to an external cause: "They keep playing their pain sounds and making me psychotic."

Trester is still concerned about the brother in jail in Baja California. He thinks the person has been released but is not sure. He's also still talking about getting money and a ticket from the bank to fly to the Main Maui.

Wednesday, December 1, 2004

Trester has six or eight radios, and has bought many more than that, the rest having met with violence or having been simply thrown away. He listens to two or three at most. The rest of them, he complains, do not get the right stations. They either do not get the stations "owned by our group," or they broadcast only two or three bad stations, stations that insult him. Sometimes it appears that the physical radio might be the source of the insult, because when I ask where a particular radio is, he says, "They insulted me so bad that I threw it away."

In the past, Trester has bought radios that receive various bands, including shortwave, TV, and the like. He wants radios that receive stations that will have news of his group—his companies, relatives, and so forth. The radios he owns apparently are not able to get these other stations. When he had a car and money, he would buy a new radio with some regularity, hoping to get a satisfactory one. He was always disappointed. He has a nice stereo receiver that he won't use because it has bad stations on it.

The radios he does listen to broadcast subliminal messages to him, telling him such things as I've mentioned, that he has a brother in jail in Baja who needs to be bailed out. The radio broadcasts used to tell him that he needed to be "tested," which meant that he had to drive down to a local restaurant and order a drink in the bar. I never could get any further details about this testing—what it was for, whether he passed or what.

The radio has also been the source of the information about money and tickets at the bank and his relatives wanting him to join them on Main Maui. When he hears some particularly outrageous thing, and calls me, I often suggest that maybe the message on the radio is lying to him. He will say, for example, that the radio told him that "they are murdering hundreds of my children," so I suggest that the message is just trying to make him feel bad and that it probably isn't true.

When I ask Trester if he watches much TV, he usually says, "No, they keep telling me to turn it off."

Wednesday, December 1, 2004

I went out to see Trester yesterday. He was still excited about going to the Auto Club to see if his brother had gotten out of jail in Baja. On the way down, I asked him if he knew his brother's name, since the folks at the Club would obviously need to know if they were to check. He said his brother's name was Auy Axil Poll the second, or junior (he said both). I asked if he meant his son or his brother and he said his brother.

At the Club he went in and came out after a few minutes. I asked him a couple of times what the folks said, but he didn't answer very clearly. He just said they gave him a bail card (the Auto Club has a $500 bail guarantee card). Since he still could not find his Auto Club card, I'm not sure whether he got to talk to anyone or not. He said once or twice to himself (as he often does when talking to himself), "I don't know *what* to do," emphasis on the word *what.*

I suggested we have lunch at a place I like that serves A&W root beer and fish and chips (one of those two-in-one fast food places), but he said no. This particular place he blames for taking away his car, so he usually won't agree to go there for lunch. Once in a while he will, though. So we ended up at a Chinese takeout place he likes. He brought home the food he didn't eat. When we walked outside, he said, "They hit me in the head." But this time, he didn't seem to be as upset as he sometimes gets when he has that experience.

Next door to the Chinese place is a dollar store, so I suggested we shop there. He likes dollar stores. In the past he wouldn't shop at this particular store because "they don't want me to shop here." But this time he agreed and he bought some hand lotion, bath salts, mouthwash, hand soap, and some potpourri liquid. What he will do with the latter, I don't know. He also bought a bottle of spray cologne.

I took Trester pretty much the same groceries this time, but added some pickle relish. He had asked for Cokes instead of Pepsi this time, too, so I got those. He seems to be letting most of his fresh fruit rot on the kitchen table, even though it is right in front of where he sits most of the time. I did a little house cleaning, including a couple of windows.

If you want an image of Trester, look at the picture of Saddam Hussein after he was captured, with the longish hair and beard. That's a bit more scraggly than Trester, but you will get the idea. Trester trims his own hair (into the bathroom sink, which I have to keep unstopping), and his hair and beard are shorter than the Hussein version. Trester's beard and moustache are also much more yellow, from cigarette smoke.

Since the weather has turned colder, and since Trester's jackets are all either torn or rejected, I offered to buy him a new coat. We went to Target and looked at several, but he didn't like any of them. "We need to have our own store with our own products," he said, to no one I could see. Trester is very particular about brand names. I showed him a nice yellow shirt (the kind he likes, with button down collar) at Target once. It was a Cherokee brand. He said, "I'm not a Cherokee." And he wouldn't take it. Once he refused to wear a coat with a "Gerry" label by saying, "We're not a Gerry." I've debated buying him something and cutting out the label, but haven't so far.

Trester bought some undies, switching from boxers to briefs for the first time in many years. I hope he likes them. Sometimes when he buys something or when I take him some pants or a shirt, he will stop wearing the item or even throw it away, saying, "They switched it." Anyway, no coat on this trip.

Wednesday, December 8, 2004

Trester called the other night and wanted to know if I would help him get his ticket to Maui. I told him that the next day was Sunday and the bank would be closed. (He thinks the ticket is at the bank.) He complained that there had been "17 Sundays in a row," which prevented him from getting to the bank when it was open.

Trester mentioned that "they" were killing his relatives and burying them "under Haiti." Then he said, "I hope they are all right." I asked him if they came back to life after they were killed and he said, "Yes." I asked how. He said, "Doctors and others can put them back together."

Wednesday, December 8, 2004

I went to see Trester again yesterday. I took him the usual groceries and three sets of 100 multicolor Christmas lights. He strung the lights across the kitchen window, the family room windows, and in the living room. Last year he kept the lights plugged in 24 hours a day until they began to burn out. I think I finally took some down a couple or three months after Christmas.

We had lunch at a Chinese buffet that he had introduced me to awhile back. It's really good, but usually each time I suggest that we go there, he refuses. This time he brought it up on his own. After lunch we walked down the strip mall to a One-dollar store where Trester bought some items. He wanted some candles, so he picked up one. The label said, "Novena Candle." (It was a 9-day Novena jar candle.) Trester pointed to the word "Novena" and said, "That means they don't like you." He put it back and went through the candles until he found two without any labels and bought them. He also bought some detergent, some hand soap, some drinking glasses, and a coffee mug. (As I've mentioned, ceramic mugs have a short life at Trester's.)

On the way back to the car someone in the parking lot honked at the car in front. Trester turned toward the car and waved, thinking someone was honking at him. He stood there for a few moments, waiting for a friend to arrive. When no one did, we walked back to the car.

In the car, Trester asked, "What do you do when they pull half of you off?"

I said, "Where did they pull half of you off? You look like you're all there to me."

He said, "They unwrapped me."

Trester wanted to get a newspaper, so he borrowed a

couple of quarters. At one set of newspaper vending boxes, he looked around awhile and then came back. "They don't want me to buy there," he said. We drove to the Smoke Shop and Trester got some cigarettes. Outside he noticed another set of paper vending boxes. He put in a quarter and then started to put in another but hesitated. He looked around awhile. Then he came to the car and said, "Can I have another quarter? I want to keep this quarter. It might be a help deal." So I gave him another quarter and he bought the paper.

Trester is still determined to get his money and ticket to Maui, so we went to the bank next so he could see if they had these things for him. He came back. I asked, "What did you find out?"

Trester said, "The spook guards won't let me in. Let's go over to the Auto Club."

We drove to the Auto Club and Trester went in. After a few minutes he came back. "What's the news?" I asked.

"They never tell me what I want to know," was all I could get out of him.

We went back to the house, where I had to mop the kitchen floor twice. Trester had spilled something on the floor and the whole floor was brown and sticky. My guess is that it was a cola. I asked him what happened and he said, "I don't know."

I asked, "Did you spill something?" And he mumbled something about something liquid, but he was not very clear.

Saturday, December 11, 2004

Trester called yesterday, with a slight eagerness in his voice. "They said you have my ticket and money to fly to

Maui." I asked him who said that, and he said it was a message on the radio, but he didn't know exactly who it was. I reminded him that he had gone into the bank last Tuesday to check on the ticket issue. "One of us went down there and they were being robbed overseas," he said. When he mentioned going to the bank again, he said something about needing a credit card. I asked him what happened to his ATM card. He said, "They harassed us on the radio to turn in the credit card." I had asked him if the bank asked for the card, but after a few questions, he said it was the radio message.

Trester rambled a bit about how "one of us got stranded," and, "They arrested another one of us in Riverside. I hope he's all right." I asked him how he felt, and he said, "They choked me and I almost threw up, and now my chest hurts."

Trester used to throw up most of the time after we ate lunch together, often in the parking lot near the car. When he was still driving our mom's car after she passed away, there were vomit stains on the outside of the driver's door. Thankfully, in the last year or so he hasn't thrown up very often when I'm with him. I do see signs of sickness out at the house, such as a stain on the floor, the porch, or in the shop, so I know he still has some problem with that.

He asked me how to call long distance. I reminded him that I live in a different area code, so that he is calling long distance to talk to me. I said he could do the same thing — dialing 1 and then the area code and so on. He said the phone didn't seem to work on other numbers. He also complained about trying to call the Auto Club (to see about his ticket). He apparently got caught up in an automated system ("If you want insurance, press 2 now" etc.) and couldn't negotiate his way around it or to get what he needed.

✸ ✸ ✸

22.474 Weird killer device here now — dangerous tonight —
22.493 Guru grabber light up in air grabs & krokes people here again —
22.496 House Law Suits: We have 8 million more law suits too on the Glen spas & our palm tree house after already won earlier one!!!
22.499 Local Headlines: Shoot-ins & mass death — over here again today as bodies fly down to southern levels —
22.500 Goods sent back & car blown up — Bob & us beaten up at store —
22.503 One of our little brothers: Knocked out in front of a car in street and hit badly —

✸ ✸ ✸

Tuesday, December 14, 2004

I went to see Trester today and took him some groceries. I added some coffee and tea to his usual fare because he had asked for them. He still had plenty of soup, so it was good that I didn't get any more of that. He seems to eat the TV dinners most readily, so I always get him seven or eight of those.

As I washed my hands, I noticed that there were no towels in the towel drawer. Later at lunch, I noticed his shirt was all ragged and said, "You should throw that shirt away. Don't you have any better ones?" I was thinking of the relatively recent new shirts I had bought for him.

Trester said, "Yes," but, "There were several Christmases and Sundays in a row."

I asked, "So you don't do laundry on those days?" and he said that was right. He started washing a load of laundry when I arrived.

Trester wanted to go to a particular Mexican restaurant for lunch. The last two times we went there, I got sick. I told him that, but said we could go there if he really wanted to. I almost suggested going to one of the other Mexican restaurants in town, like the one with the great buffet, but I didn't. As we drove, he finally suggested that we could go to the Mad Greek instead, so we went there and had a pastrami sandwich.

Both before and after lunch, Trester was still eager about his ticket to Maui. He wanted to check the Auto Club again. I asked him why they didn't just mail him the ticket or bring it to his house. He didn't answer. We did end up going to the Auto Club. After he came back out, I asked my usual, "What did they say?"

And he said, "The lady said she didn't know anything about it."

We went to one of the dollar stores in town and Trester got some candles, three-by-five cards, 3-subject notebooks, and some cologne. He apparently believes that cologne is a disinfectant and sprays it around his head occasionally. Perhaps it wards off ghosts.

As an aside, for at least several months a couple of years ago, Trester thought that talcum powder and later household cleanser, were disinfectants. He sprayed talcum powder everywhere, on the furniture, on the floor, on books and magazines. He really made quite a mess. Recently, he has piled cleanser in a couple of window sills, but that's the extent of the powder for now. One day at a dollar store he asked about Gold Bond powder, but the store didn't carry it. I was relieved.

Trester has apparently stopped throwing away his soda cans. He has a stack of cans in the workshop where he likes to sit and smoke. The stack is about three feet wide by three cans high and perhaps four cans deep. It could be an electrical ground to protect him from electrical zappers, which have troubled him in the past.

After lunch, Trester was angrier than usual, arguing with imaginary people, as he sometimes does. He threatened to sue a number of them for stealing his stores and other property.

I read once of a man who ran down several pedestrians in Westwood, and he later said he did that because others had stolen all the music he had written—which was all the popular music on the radio. Trester has had and may still have a similar delusion, that he has written the songs on the radio and that someone else is stealing all the royalty money.

There seem to be several commonly occurring delusions among schizophrenics. I saw a woman on TV once who had rolls of aluminum foil under her cap to short out the electrical bolts being shot at her brain. Trester has had similar delusions or hallucinations and has tried to short out the electrical bolts all over the house. He no longer seems to think they are hitting his brain so much that he needs direct protection, but even now he has a sheet of aluminum foil over one of the smoke detectors (because it was shooting zappers at him). He has one metal wastebasket under his bed to protect him, and often an electrical outlet will be covered by aluminum foil.

Friday, December 17, 2004

Whenever Trester has a pain, he attributes it to an external cause. For example, his teeth are in very poor condition (he had to have five broken and rotting ones pulled once), and often when he gets a pain in a tooth, he will say,

"They stabbed me in the face." Or he might say, "They shot me in the tooth." When he gets a painful pimple in his ear (which happens every once in a while), he will say, "The stuck a sticker deal in my ear." And when his stomach or other area hurts, he will say, "They stuck something in me. How can I get it out?"

Keeping anything is a problem for Trester, since "they" are always "switching" it. He will often say, "They switched my food." Then he will sometimes stop eating it, since the food in front of him is now polluted, poisoned, or from a group not his own. The same is true of clothing. I have found relatively new shirts and pants in the trash and when I asked about them, he would say, "They switched them for some other group's clothing. We can't wear them."

Other times, he will say that the clothes I bought for him aren't paid for, and even after I reassure him that they are, he won't wear them, at least not right away. He will sometimes ask, "Are these paid for?" And there is always the rejection, "These are not from our group."

When Trester still lived with our mother, he often stared at his food for a minute or two, only to conclude, "This has worms in it," or "Someone spit in my food," and then not eat it. Once he even accused his mother of spitting in his food. Needless to say, this behavior was very hard on a sensitive, elderly woman who loved her son very much.

For a while, Trester was very picky about what he would eat, but in recent times he has become much more flexible, although he still stops eating once in a while when he thinks someone has switched his food. Sometimes he will still eat it, though. I will ask, "How's your food?" and he will say, "Not too good. They switched it." He feels personally offended, of course, to believe that "they" have insulted him by changing some gourmet dish for one that is made from lesser ingredients or even garbage. And, other times, when I ask how he likes the food, he will say, "Real good," so these symptoms are not always present.

Wednesday, December 22, 2004

I went out to see Trester yesterday and took him his Christmas presents. He got some flannel bed sheets, a silverware set (recall that he had only one fork), a space heater, a bath set (bubble bath and bath salts), and some hand towels. As he opened each present, he said, "That's real nice." He seemed happy with what he got.

I took him the usual groceries, together with some celery (that he had asked for). He once again asked to be taken to the airport so he could fly to Maui "for a few months." I told him he needed a ticket.

We went to a nice Chinese buffet (the really good one with the many choices). Trester sometimes doesn't want to eat there, but he does change his mind. We then went to a dollar store (what Trester calls "the one-dollar store") and he bought me some Christmas presents. Outside, he complained that they had torn half of his body off inside the store. As we drove off he said, "We should have waited. Maybe they could put him back together." Up the road a little, he said in a somewhat angry tone, "The place is run by psychos. You just give them a bribe and they can change the president. Then they can steal your stores." Trester apparently thinks he has or had his own stores, and they and their profits are always being stolen from him.

He had to fight off a few ghosts on the way home. He made popping and clicking noises, waved his hand a bit, and told them, "Just go away." He often expresses the incomplete thought, "What is—." I don't know if he's asking, "What is that?" or "What is going on?" or "What is [some event or concept]?" Once in a while, while fighting ghosts, he will say something like, "They're making me so psychotic I can't think straight." He therefore seems to recognize that something is inhibiting his mental processes. Unfortunately, he always attributes it to an external agent and not to a brain dysfunction. His mind fights with his brain, but he just cannot understand that medicine would (and did) help with the brain problem.

I washed his new silverware, did a little clean up outside, and then headed home.

※ ※ ※

50.105 Foods: Sea Food fish restaurant talked about today—
50.106 Ideas again Foods: Meat loaf place in lieu of fast food places ideas: Too put in meat loaf sandwiches & delicious sauces as over [?] kids ealier!
50.122 Houses Attacked: "Tort Wars" around house here now—climbing up & down the walls—
50.139 200 Trillion Police Shots—Huge deaths upstairs in Attack on Main World Areas

※ ※ ※

Wednesday, December 29, 2004

I went out to see Trester yesterday, to take him groceries and have lunch. I brought him two bags of barbeque potato chips, since he told me recently that those are his favorites.

We had lunch at a Mexican buffet. He thought we were going to the one that seems to have made me sick twice, but I had mentioned the name of the other one and he had agreed. So we went there instead. We were going to go to a dollar store afterwards, but he once again wanted to go to the bank to see if his ticket to Maui was there. We stopped by, and he came back out pretty quickly. "They don't want me in the bank," he said in answer to my question about what he found out. On the way home he said we should stop by the Auto Club. I told him, "Why don't you call them when we get home?" and he said okay.

Back home I did a bit of cleaning, pouring some ammonia (lemon scented!) in the toilets and mopping a bit. (In the trade we call this "guy cleaning" as contrasted strongly to "girl cleaning" which girls call "cleaning." Guy cleaning girls call "smearing dirt around." But we won't go there.)

I happened to look in the washing machine and saw the new flannel sheets (that I had given Trester for Christmas). They were still damp, so he must have washed them recently. I put them in the dryer. On top of the dryer was a pile of clean laundry about two feet high. Trester has no system of clothing organization. He has stopped using drawers and closets for his clothes, for some reason. So while the sheets were drying, I started folding his clothes and putting them in piles: rags, socks, washrags, undies, undershirts, and pants. I found all the missing cleaning rags I had wondered about (I thought he had thrown them away). I also discovered that Trester has about five pairs of pants I didn't know about. I put the separated piles on the lower shelf of the laundry room cabinet so he could get to the items more easily.

With the sheets dry, I decided to make his bed for him.

I hadn't looked closely at his bedding for a while, so it was quite a revelation. His pillows and pillow cases need to be thrown out. He had two bedspreads on the bed, one of which had a four or five foot hole in it. I put that one in the trash. He had about four blankets off (not on) the bed, piled in various places (the foot, one side, the other side, etc.). There has been no fitted sheet on his mattress since he took off the previous mattress pad and fitted sheet I bought for him many months ago. At the time he said it was girly stuff or some such comment. However, he seems to like the flannel fitted sheet (no mattress pad this time). I made a note to get him some new pillows and cases and a new bedspread.

I vacuumed a little and had to change the bag. The rule of vacuums is that the bags fill up much faster than you think, especially in a house with so much debris on the floor. Cigarette ash is a real pain in the vacuuming process, since the gray part is so fine.

One new thing I noticed on this visit is that Trester had placed three or four stuffed animals (pandas, teddy bears, and the like) at various places around the family room and had put a five or ten dollar bill under each one. He usually places one-dollar bills in bowls to bail out his friends and relatives in jail. Maybe the price has gone up in some cases. The last two or three weeks he has saved a little money by buying fewer cigarettes than usual, so that may explain where the bills come from.

Saturday, January 1, 2005

Trester called this evening to say that "one of us" has been thrown into jail in Baja again and that Trester needed to put $100 in a bowl to get him out. He said he had put

$20 in the bowl in the past. Trester said that some of his kids and other relatives sometimes contribute to the bail money for his jailed friends and relatives, but he wasn't sure if they were doing so now. "I can't call the other Corona," he said.

I asked him why his relatives keep getting thrown into jail. He said, "That political group got after us, and filed nine million charges against us and has people getting killed and put in jail all over the place." I suggested that if the charges were not true, those arrested would be let off. Trester said he thought that might be possible.

Trester said, "I got klobbered on the head by a spook deal earlier today and got sort of a headache and half dizzy." He added that he felt much better now, though.

I made sure he was warm enough and that the heat was working okay. He thanked me for the new sheets. I told him I had new pillows to bring out on Tuesday. He said okay.

He asked for the area code to Maui. He still wants to call his relatives and get his ticket over there. I once again asked him why they didn't just mail his ticket and he said he didn't know, but that he had to call to get it.

Thursday, January 6, 2005

I went to see Trester Tuesday and took him some groceries and some new items for the bedroom: two pillows, a comforter, two blankets, and another sheet set. I threw away the old pillows and bedspread and may do the same with some of the old blankets later.

Trester was hallucinating more than usual today. We drove to Riverside for a fish lunch. On the way home, Trester said, "I think they left one of us in the other city."

He wondered whether we should go back or not. Sometimes, when he thinks "they" have pulled a piece of him off his body or pulled one of him out, he wants to wait to see if that person is okay or returns. He suggests half an hour to three hours.

When we got to town, we visited one of the dollar stores he likes and he got some index cards (to write his newspaper headlines on) and some candles (to disinfect the air). After we left the dollar store and drove home, Trester made those popping sounds and moving of his head around to deflect the ghosts who were attacking him. He said things such as, "Arrest them all. I don't care if four trillion of them die." He feels persecuted by lawsuits (that take away his money and property and businesses) as well as by those beings who "klonk" him on the head all the time. He said, "They keep hitting me on the head." He will sometimes name someone as the culprit, even though that person has been dead for a while. He remembers those names from the past and brings them up. "That Johnson group is killing everybody," he will say, naming someone I recognize from long ago. He occasionally asks about his aunt and what her telephone number is. I keep reminding him that she died more than ten years ago.

Among the groceries I got Trester was some Entenmann's donuts. When I called them to his attention, he said he couldn't eat those because "that is Jewish food." About five or ten years ago, Trester said that his father was not his real father and that his real father was Jewish. I guess he has changed his mind or something. He often refers to the "spirit world," but doesn't mention any traditional religion.

As usual recently, Trester asked about a ticket to Maui. In fact, when I gave him the bedding and three or four new shirts, he said, "Don't buy me anything more. I plan to leave soon. As soon as I can get a ticket to Maui I can join my group."

Monday, January 10, 2005

    I talked to Trester last night. He was in pretty bad shape. He was desperate to get out of town and go to his relatives in Maui. He said, speaking of his persecutors, "They almost killed me. They shot me with some bullet deal. They made me so angry I threw a mug against the wall. Everybody's psychotic around here." He asked me to help him leave, and that makes me feel especially sorry, since I can't just give him a ticket to fly away where his persecutors will follow (they did in the past when he actually did go to Hawaii—about three times, I think) and where I won't be able to help him with food and other help. I mentioned a ticket and Trester said his relatives in Maui have the thousand dollars in spending money and the ticket is at the airport. When he understood that I was hesitant to drive him to the airport, he said, "I'll just do it myself." At one point he said, "They keep attacking me and I don't know what to do."

    He said they were hurting him in the heart, so that may mean he is having chest pains. I have tried repeatedly to get him to see a doctor about that, but he always says, "I'll be all right." I keep suggesting aspirin as a stop gap idea, but when I ask later, he always says he didn't take any. It is so tragic and frustrating to watch him suffer. But according to the law, he can make his own decisions and no one can force him to get treatment.

    He finally said he had to hang up and would talk to me later because he was too upset to talk at the time. (He didn't use the word "upset" but that was the meaning.)

I told him I would come out and see him on Tuesday, if he was still there. I hope he will be and am pretty sure he will be, but I hesitate to close off his thinking, as in, "Of course you'll still be there. You can't go anywhere." That would be too cruel. I try to sympathize with his pain without reinforcing his wrong beliefs. So when he says they pulled part of his head off, I tell him that's bad and hope he's okay. I don't tell him that didn't happen. When I'm with him, though, I do say something like, "You seem to be in one piece now. I don't see any parts missing."

I plan to call him tonight to see how he's getting along.

Wednesday, January 12, 2005

I visited Trester yesterday and took him some groceries. It was mostly the same stuff, with a little variation to add something different to his diet. I got him some Krispy Kreme glazed donuts. He likes glazed donuts, but as I mentioned in an earlier posting, he wouldn't eat Entenmann's. I asked him this time if he Krispy Kreme was okay, and he said yes. I also got him some oranges. Fruit is a difficult buy, since so often Trester neglects it. I find blackened bananas and shriveled grapes and mealy apples. Yet he does eat some of it sometimes. The pears usually get eaten. When he was younger, he really liked oranges, so I hope he will eat these. He still had several apples, and I had to toss out one for being past its prime. The others still seemed firm enough.

I tossed out a few other outdated food items, too, including three quarters of a bag of corn chips with a June 30 expiration date. Usually I go through his refrigerator every few weeks and toss out the outdated stuff. This time I did a more cursory pass and tossed out some dried-out cheese

(I brought a new pack with the day's groceries). Oh, I also tossed out a bag of Cheetos, unopened, that was a few months past eating date. Trester can do some things well. He can keep clean and do his laundry. Yet he can't toss out a loaf of bread even after it is completely covered with mold.

On the way to lunch, Trester said he had a sore in his mouth. After a couple more questions, I learned it was on his gum. I thought it might be a tooth infection, so I suggested a dentist. He said no, all he needed was a container of lip balm and some VapoRub. I didn't press the issue. I remember when our mother used to keep pressing him to take medicine or see a doctor. Trester would look at her critically and say, "Have they got you hypnotized, too?"

Trester wanted to go to the Mexican restaurant where I don't want to go, since I got sick the last two times. But I thought, I've put him off of this one so many times, maybe I'll just take one more chance. Could have been a coincidence. So we drove down there. As we walked across the parking lot toward the door, Trester stopped and said, "Let's go eat somewhere else."

I asked him, "You don't want to eat here?"

And he said, "They warned us not to eat here." (Trester often speaks about himself using the royal "we.") There was a coffee shop across the street, where we had eaten a few times before without too much incident, so I suggested that and he agreed. We drove across the street. Trester had the meatloaf dinner special (a huge portion of meatloaf and mashed potatoes). He ate nearly all of it and said it was good. That was a relief because he sometimes says that what he is eating is only okay, or has been switched, or tastes putrid.

After lunch we went to one of the dollar stores where Trester got some candles (to burn to disinfect the air), some three-by-five cards (to write newspaper headlines on), and some laundry detergent. Detergent must have a disinfecting characteristic, too, since I noticed a brass bowl with two or three cups of detergent in it, placed on the sink in the half bathroom.

Trester talked as usual about his ticket to Maui. He even asked me if I wanted to go to Maui with him. I told him I couldn't go. He said a travel agency has his ticket. I asked him which travel agency, but he didn't know. He thought there was a travel agency in the mall next to the coffee shop, so after lunch we walked around looking for it. We didn't find one.

So, we drove over to the store where he gets his cigarettes, which is also near the Auto Club. Trester walked over toward the Auto Club while I waited. Next thing I knew he was back with this cigarettes. I asked him what he found out at the Auto Club. "I didn't go in," he said. "We had a warning not to go in."

As we drove home, Trester made a few more popping and clicking sounds to destroy the attackers. However, he was more calm (no arguing with his allies or his enemies) than at other times, and back at home, he seemed generally content—relatively speaking, and keeping in mind his constant feeling of persecution. I mopped the kitchen floor, which once again was rather sticky, and cleaned up a few fallen palm fronds in the yard. As I left, he thanked me for coming. You're welcome, Trester.

Thursday, January 13, 2005

The house Trester lives in was built about 1960. It has had a couple of new roofs, including a recent one just a few years ago, so there have been no leaks during the recent rains. The exterior needs paint, but otherwise the place seems sound enough, though there are occasional signs of termites.

Unfortunately, Trester is helping the house deteriorate. When I noticed that the carpeting was frayed and pulled out along the wall in two or three spots (ideal mouse nesting material) and then saw mouse pellets in the kitchen, I told Trester I would get some mouse traps. He said, "Oh, don't hurt the little critters." So I've had to resort to sleight of hand to put mouse bait in various places Trester can't see. Yesterday I cleaned out a mouse pellet covered drawer where the aluminum foil and plastic wrap are kept. Then I tossed a package of mouse bait behind the boxes of foil and wrap. I had thought I had cured the mouse problem earlier, but I didn't remember seeing these pellets, so I put out more bait. The spilled rice and beans and pistachio nuts provide an ample diet for adventurous mice.

The linoleum floor, especially in the kitchen, continues to gain gouges and cuts from the dishware that Trester slams to the ground when he gets angry. There are some spots of peeled away flooring that are now black, so mopping is a bit of a challenge. I'm not sure which dark spots will clean up as a spill and which are permanent marks in the flooring. The linoleum in the family room is separating at the seams because Trester has several house plants that he over waters, causing an overflow onto the floor. Over time, the overflow has found and lifted the seams.

Several of the windows are difficult to see out of because Trester has sprayed them with the hose so much that mineralization has built up. Water is a kind of disinfectant, I think, and he also uses it to spray the ghosts out of the air. The garage doors are rusting and falling apart from so much hosing, too. But with no cars in the garage now, they don't get used very often. In the summer especially, but whenever the weather is warm enough, Trester will spray water for a long time, washing down the driveway, the windows, the garage doors. The water runs off and waters some of the plants.

I didn't see a new hole in the wall from Trester's thrown mug (that he told me about on the phone). I will try to remember to ask him where he threw it. So far, I know of just the two other holes.

On a positive note, the new digital thermostat I put in to control the central heating and air conditioning works much better than the old mercury bulb thermostat that used to overshoot its target temperature by several degrees.

Sunday, January 16, 2005

I called Trester last night and he sounded good. He said he was feeling better. His voice was clearer and more direct, with less mumbling and no talking to himself. He said he hadn't slept much the night before, so I sympathized with him, not having slept well myself that night.

He said he had walked to the nearby store and bought some cigarettes, even though "I still think they don't want me to shop there."

He told me there were planes flying under the house, and that "they keep bombing the neighborhood." When he went to the bathroom, "They stabbed me in the bottom, and now I have stickers in my butt." These sensations probably explain why the toilet bowl keeps getting loose. I tighten the floor bolts once in a while. I think Trester rocks back and forth somewhat violently when these attacks come on him.

Earlier he said, "They [that is, his friends or relatives]

had two Lexus cars for me, but when they sent them, they [that is, his enemies] blew them up." This makes at least half a dozen cars that were blown up while in the process of being delivered to him. Trester, like many paranoid schizophrenics, is often very logical. Someone was sending him something, but it didn't arrive. Why? Because it wasn't really being sent? No, because it was stolen, blown up, or otherwise misdirected. It's like that ticket to Maui. It exists, but it just can't get to Trester. They want to be logical, so they make sure their delusional structure makes sense.

Sometimes Trester incorporates an experience into his delusional structure. A few years ago we went to see one of the Superman movies, the one where one of the bad guys has something like laser beam fingers. After the movie, Trester said, "I can shoot red out of my fingers." (The laser or whatever beam in the movie was red.) I told him to shoot me with it, but he wouldn't because he didn't want to hurt me. So I told him to shoot a nearby tree. He pointed at it. I don't know whether he hallucinated the beam, but since nothing happened, I guess he changed his mind. He didn't mention that ability again.

※ ※ ※

19.318 News Backwards Lines: News us backwards upstairs & we were blamed for the crimes against us—
19.334 The Watermelon hand soap is real neet!
19:339 To Tomorrow Fly Away go thru to Yevy [?] Corona?
19.451 Adopt all—Sandkik Island ., . . Auy z[?] Poll Axils & Jumpy & Jare...
19.766 Murdered all over place today? Hope ok—Tons of

over & over again attackers etc.
19.1162 Jailss: USA Headlines: Perverted Stuff on Prisonerss Today on Radio [?]

※ ※ ※

Monday, January 17, 2005

Trester called. He was in a pretty calm mood. He asked if I could come over and drive him to the "other" Corona. There seem to be duplicates (or more) of towns, countries, islands, and so forth. He will sometimes say, "One of the Maui islands got blown up." But there are evidently still some left.

Trester asked how he could get some more money, complaining that cigarettes are too expensive and that he had "only two five dollar bills" left. He said he was going to walk to the store but that it started getting dark and besides, they don't want him to shop at any of the stores around his house. He then said, "I had spook problems around here last night. I got klobbered in the head a bunch of times by a spook deal with a klobber deal that almost killed me." I asked him if he was all right now, and he said yes. He was speaking in a bit more mumbling tone, so I had to ask him to repeat himself a few times and missed some of what he was saying. At one point, he said that "a bunch of cousins in Trester's family" escaped to "the peninsula," which he later said was near Baja California.

He asked, "Can we go to the Auto Club to find out if my other brother is dead or alive? They say both things and I don't know which is true. I hope he's okay. He was in jail in Baja. I guess he's okay."

After he asked me to drive to the other Corona once or

twice more, I asked him where it was, naming a road or two we might take. "Let's just go to the mall and I can get my photo on a rubber mat." I don't think I mentioned before that Trester has about eight or nine mouse pads with his photo on them. The rubber mat he refers to is a mouse pad. This time I asked him why he wanted another one. He said, "So they'll know where we are." I asked who "they" were and he said, "My relatives." I reminded him of how much the mouse pad costs (about $17 or $18 I think) and that such an expense would eat into his spending money. He then said we might go to the dollar store. We'll see what happens when I visit him tomorrow.

He repeated the story about the "Lexus car" that got blown up on its way to him and asked if we could drive over to get another one waiting. "Can you get me $100 for a car so we can go get it?" Once when he was talking about cars and when he still had his driver's license, I told him that the cheapest car was probably $12,000. He would point out an SUV or a sedan and say he wanted one of those. When I gave him an estimate ("I think that car is about $30,000"), he said, "Oh, they have cars at every price for you. You can get one for $300." This time when he mentioned the $100 Lexus, I just reminded him that he needs a driver's license to buy a car.

Tuesday, January 18, 2005

I took some groceries to Trester, as usual today. Mostly the same items he likes, including several Salisbury steak TV dinners (and some other kinds). I got him more oranges, since he had mentioned on the phone that he was eating them. It's hard to find fruit he will eat regularly. I had to throw out an apple that was rotting, but the oranges from last week were all gone.

In the living room I noticed a bowl (moved from his bedroom) placed by the fireplace with some money in it. I asked him what that was for. "It's to get our kids out of jail," he said. "They're supposed to pick it up." The cash was still under the two or three stuffed animals.

I asked Trester where he wanted to have lunch, and he said Marie Callender's. So we got in the car. While still in the driveway, he said, "Stop here." I stopped the car and Trester opened the door and looked around a bit. Then he said, "Go on, I guess. It felt like half of me flew out the window." I told him he looked to be all there to me and asked if I would notice if half of him were missing. He said he didn't know. He looked at his left arm rather intently. Then we headed toward the restaurant. Trester said, "After lunch, let's go shopping downtown. One of us has a store there and we can shop at one of our stores."

I asked him if he had slept well last night. The last couple of weeks Trester has been asleep on the living room sofa when I arrived, rather than in his bed. He said he slept some, but "I got zapped. They have a zombie deal over the couch." I asked him if he slept on the couch or in the bed and he said he started in bed but moved to the couch later.

On the way to the restaurant, Trester had a troubled discussion with whomever he has these discussions. He mumbled so softly and so mumblingly that I couldn't make out much of what he said, other than a few occurrences of his interrupted question, "What is—?" and in a dismayed tone, "I forgot about that." At another point he said, "Why don't you use your money more wisely? The least you could do is give ten dollars to your kids."

At Marie Callender's, we each had a chicken pot pie. Trester had the vegetable soup. He later commented that he liked both when I asked him how his lunch was. I reminded him that he had some vegetable soup at home.

On a wrong assumption note, I asked Trester about the bowl of laundry detergent in the bathroom next to the laundry room. He said it was to wash his hands because he didn't have any bar soap in that room. The bar soap was in the back bathroom. I'll add some bar soap to the shopping list. So, the cleanser in the window sill is for disinfecting, but the laundry detergent in the brass bowl on the sink is for hand washing.

This week I noticed that the garden hose was back in the laundry room. For a year or more in the past, Trester has had an old, rather stiff garden hose looped over a cabinet door in the laundry room so that the hose drapes down in front of the washing machine. He had explained that it was for grounding (something electrical, such as a zapper, I guess). A couple of weeks ago I finally persuaded him to get it out of the way when I used the cabinet shelves to put his clean laundry on. But now the hose is back. And there is hardly a scrap of clean laundry on any of the shelves. The dryer has its usual two foot high pile of clean laundry on it instead.

I changed his bed and mopped the kitchen floor, which once again had something brown on it. However, it wasn't sticky. Maybe spilled soy sauce?

When I told him I had to leave, Trester, as he often does, said, "Thanks for helping. And thanks for taking us to lunch." Sometimes he says he will pay me back for the groceries when he gets the money.

Tuesday, January 25, 2005

I drove over to Trester's today and took him some groceries, including eight oranges because he seems to like them so well. As usual, he was still in bed when I arrived a little after noon. While he got up and got dressed, I ran to the back bathroom. I always use this bathroom to keep the sewer line open (that is, I flush the toilet a couple of times to let the water run all the way from the back out to the septic tank at the other end of the house. In the past, the sewer line has gotten plugged by too much toilet paper and sometimes a few paper towels. (Trester uses an enormous amount of toilet paper, about 10 to 12 rolls a week.) This visit I found, as I rather frequently do, a huge pile of toilet paper in the bowl. For some reason, Trester doesn't always flush the toilet. It appeared to me to be too much to flush down, so I grabbed the toilet brush in one hand and the plunger in the other and scooped out most of it into the wastebasket. Then I flushed. Everything worked fine and there was no backup. The bathtub was still half full of water, but that turned out to be a simple matter of opening the drain to resolve it.

When I went back into the living room, Trester looked at me almost fearfully and asked, "Did you get killed?"

I told him, "No, I just went to the bathroom."

Well, Trester once again wanted to eat at the Mexican restaurant where I have twice gotten sick afterwards. I thought I'd give it one more chance. I pray that I don't get sick. As we ate, Trester kept turning around to look over at a couple of the other diners, or at least in their direction. I hoped he wouldn't go over to them and make some comment. I asked him if he wanted to change seats, but he said no. He picked up a tortilla chip and looked at it, and then put it on the table. He took another and ate it. In the course of eating a few chips before our meal, he put down one or two others also. One he dipped in salsa and acted as if he would put it down, but then ate it.

After lunch, Trester wanted to go to a dollar store, so I suggested the one a couple of blocks from the restaurant. At first he said okay, "since we are so close," but then he changed his mind, saying, "They don't want us to shop there." So we headed for another store on the far end of town. On the way, Trester said, "They crunched my head back there with some deal," meaning that he was hurt in the restaurant. After a few more minutes he said again, "They hurt our head back there."

At the dollar store Trester bought four bottles of rubbing alcohol, three jars of Mentholatum, and five or six packages of three-by-five cards. No candles this time.

Outside the store, Trester looked around and asked, "What do you do when they're killing people all around you?" He then answered his own question, "I don't know." Then he began a conversation, but I got only parts of it. "Is he there?" "I don't know." "One of them lives in Little Hill." "Does he know how to get home?" "I don't know." As we left, he said, "We should have waited there four hours to see if they're all right."

We then drove to the smoke shop and Auto Club parking lot. Trester got some cigarettes but didn't go into the Auto Club. He got into the car and said, "Could we wait here half an hour? There are dead people under the parking lot and some of them might be ours." Then he said, "Wait here while I go get a newspaper." He came back in a few minutes with a Spanish language paper. (He took Spanish in high school, but does not read it now.)

As we started to drive away, Trester said, "Could you wait here? They're dumping kids' dead bodies around here in some metal crypt deals." I asked him where and he said they were underground. We made a brief last stop for Trester to get a free telephone book (a small, local listings one). He has about four of those already. Then we headed back to his house. I mopped and vacuumed a bit and put some palm fronds in the trash. Soon it was time for me to leave.

Saturday, January 29, 2005

Trester called yesterday. He was feeling better than he often is, and apparently wanted to see if I was okay. Sometimes he doesn't come out and say it, but he sometimes gets the idea that I've been killed or injured and he calls to find out if that is so. I told him I was doing fine. He asked if it was raining here and I said yes. We talked about the rain a bit.

Trester said, "I was going to go up a couple of levels today, but it was raining." I asked him how he would do that. He said, "I would go to the store near here." I asked him how that would help, and he said, "I don't know." Then he added, "They would tell me how." I asked him why he wanted to go up a couple of levels and he said, "There wouldn't be any wars going on there like there are here."

I think I've mentioned in the past that Trester sometimes says he wants to "go upstairs," by which I have thought he meant heaven. He's definitely discontent down here where all his persecutors are.

I asked him if he had eaten anything and he said he made two ham and cheese sandwiches. He had eaten something earlier but "they switched it." He said, "They are always switching my stuff."

In the process of going through some old receipts, I came across an electric bill that I had paid for him because he had written on it, "This is not the correct bill. Please send me the right one. Thank you. Jump." After the name

Jump he had put his real name in parentheses. He has used the name Jump or Jumpy in the past. Most recently, as I've said, he calls himself Auy Axils Poll (that's pronounced "owie"). Usually when he calls he doesn't identify himself. He just says, "Hi, Robert."

And I say, "Hi, Trester." Only once that I remember has he said, "Hi, this is Auy."

You can't blame the mentally ill for believing in their own sensations. If you felt that someone hit you in the head or kicked you in the rear end, you would not accept the explanation that "no one hit or kicked you." You'd look around for the source of the painful blow. And I suppose if you were seeing flying beings attacking you, you'd attribute the pain to them. Imagine that you say, "I have a headache."

And your friend says, "No, you don't." That's how the mentally ill feel when people deny the reality of their symptoms.

Tuesday, February 8, 2005

I went to see Trester today and take him some groceries. I got him the bread and mustard that he had asked for, together with the usual lunch meat and other items. As I was unloading the groceries in the kitchen, I accidentally dropped one of the plastic grocery bags, thinking it was empty, when it had a small jar of pickles in it. It hit the floor with a bang. Fortunately, the jar didn't break. Unfortunately, Trester was in the kitchen at the time. In a minute or two I heard him ask of no one I could see, "What do you do when they shoot you?" A minute or two later he said to me, "They shot me under the floor." I explained that the sound was only that of a jar hitting the floor and not a gunshot.

I asked Trester where he wanted to eat lunch and he wasn't sure, so I suggested the buffet on the edge of town. He said okay. A few minutes later he said we should eat at the Mexican restaurant that I had been leery of earlier. (Fortunately, I didn't get sick the last time, so I'm willing to go there if he wants.) When I reminded him about the buffet, he said, "Okay."

So I said, "Are you ready to go?"

And he said, "Can we wait here a few minutes? I just got shot."

So, while he sat at the breakfast table holding his hand to his face, I looked in the fridge and tossed out a long expired salad dressing and a box of old lard. Why he ever bought lard, I don't know. I didn't get it for him. I also tossed some corn chips with a Sept. 21 expiration date. The bag was open to the air (that is, not closed up at all), so I figured the chips were plenty stale by now. I also tossed a moldy orange and apple.

Once again, Trester said, "They shot me in the head." I explained once more about the jar of pickles. In a minute or two, Trester said, "I've been killed or some deal." He was fairly distressed, as his words indicate. He then said to those he talks to, "Have Robert take us over to get our ticket." He's still trying to fly away.

In the car, as we drove toward the buffet, Trester said, "Let's go over to the mall and eat somewhere there, and I can get my photo on a mat." I've mentioned before that he has six or eight or more mouse pads with his photo on them, all nailed to the wall in his bedroom. As we approached the mall, Trester said to his listeners, "They'll kill us or something. What should I do or some deal?" and then after a pause, a heartfelt, "Oh dear." Then in a minute, "They kill us all the time." You can imagine how bad

I felt about dropping that jar of pickles. Sometimes a backfire on the freeway or other noise sets him to thinking he's been shot, but this is the most extended grief over a noise that he's expressed.

At the mall Trester looked at the listing of restaurants in the food court and picked out the Udo Japan and we ate there. He liked his chicken and shrimp dish. As we walked along the stores after lunch, we came upon an Abercrombie and Fitch store. Trester stopped and looked around, then leaned inside a bit. He said, "That's the law firm they hired." I asked a few questions but couldn't get any intelligible details out of him. Earlier he said something that makes me think now that he believes Barnes and Noble is a law firm, too.

Trester bought a couple more glass paperweights (the kind with the laser-etched image inside). Then we headed toward home, stopping at the smoke shop and then to get a couple of newspapers. I mopped quickly because we had spent quite a bit of time driving (he wanted to take the side road home and skip the freeway) and my time was about up. At one point Trester asked me what kind of gift I wanted for helping him with groceries and taking me to lunch. I told him I didn't want a gift. He offered me a cigarette as a gift. I said no thanks. Maybe I should have thought of something around the house that he could give me to make him feel better. If he asks in the future, I'll be more astute.

✦ ✦ ✦

18.182 All the ones who attacked us killed & soon to be gotten rid of!!! hope so!
18.285 Call & go to Maui – pots blown up here –

assassination tomorrow again —

18.635 10 million pharmacists arrested — eye glass men did it last night —

18.660 Big mob attack underway at El Cerrito stores and "Big K" down town too

18.672 Vicious bomb attack on houses here again & one of ours in car & another at gas station in El Cerrito.

18.676 10 local residents' cars blow up as they try to leave —

N N N

Wednesday, February 16, 2005

 I visited Trester yesterday, as I usually do, taking him his groceries. He had objected to the pickles I bought him last week (the jar I dropped with a bang), so he hadn't eaten any. He told me on the phone that they said "Kosher" which meant, apparently, only Jews could eat them. So yesterday I got him some regular dill pickles. Trester said, "Make sure they don't say Kosher." And he looked at the label closely. He seemed to like the other items I got him, including some chocolate frosted donut miniatures, more oranges, and the usual Rocky Road ice cream.

 I asked him where he wanted to eat. After he hesitated, I suggested the root beer and fish place and then the buffet at the edge of town. He said, "Why don't we just eat at the local Mexican place?" There's a really great Mexican restaurant just about a mile from Trester's house, and we eat there every once in a while. Driving down the road, you probably wouldn't stop there, because it looks like a rundown bar. But it's very good. We got in the car and started to drive and Trester said, "Let's go to the Chinese place over on Lincoln street." He switched back and forth a couple of times, but we eventually decided on the Chinese (which is a buffet). As we headed down the freeway, Trester said, "It's farther out than I thought."

I said, "What is, the restaurant? Farther away than you thought?"

He said, "No." So I asked two more times what he was referring to, but got no answer.

In the restaurant, while we ate, Trester looked to one side and later on to the other, as if he were looking at someone (though not the other diners). As he often does, he gave a little wave of the hand to signal "Hello."

After lunch, Trester bought some cigarettes. He came back to the car and got in. Then he said, "I should have got two more." Then he started to get out of the car, then didn't. Then he got out and started to close the door. Then he started to get back in, then out, then in, then almost all the way in, then out. Finally he got back in and said, "Let's just go home."

On the way home, I took the back roads instead of the freeway. Each time I got in the left turn lane to merge onto another street, Trester said, "Go straight," or "You should've gone straight." One time I did go straight and we took some other roads, but of course had to turn eventually. I told him the road we were on took us home.

When I left, Trester said, as he often does now, "Thank you for helping us."

Tuesday, February 22, 2005

I went to see Trester again today, taking him his usual groceries. It was raining, so I suggested we eat near his house at the little Mexican cafe we both like (the one you'd never stop at if you drove by and took a look). I had the special and he had fish enchiladas. As is not unusual, halfway through, Trester stopped eating and said, "They switched my food." Ultimately, he took home one of the enchiladas, so he might eat that later on. My chili Colorado burrito was great as usual, and once again that little place has the best tortilla chips of any Mexican restaurant I've been to.

We then drove to the cigarette store, accompanied by Trester's usual banter about someone pulling his friends or parts of himself off his head, mention of tickets to Maui, and wanting to check the bank to see if they have a credit card for him. A few days ago on the phone, Trester said, "One of us is freezing to death on a mountain and another is in jail in Baja." I report these incidents not to be amusing. Trester truly suffers because of these beliefs because they cause him worry and stress. Wouldn't you be stressed if you thought one of your children was freezing to death on a mountain? Trester is only half sure that these events are occurring, and he said, "I get two different stories," indicating that some of the voices say the relative is in jail, for example, while other voices say it's not true. So, his suffering is not quite as intense as that of a real parent would be, but it is similar to the worry a parent has when not sure what has happened to a child.

We went to one of the nearby dollar stores. Trester got some note cards (400 cards) to write headlines on, some potpourri (both liquid and bagged), some candles (which I later had to put in metal bowls so the wax wouldn't run down the window sills), some pens, and a notebook. He has something of a limp when he walks now, and complains of back pains occasionally.

As I've mentioned, Trester doesn't do laundry when he thinks it is Sunday, so he had apparently built up quite a bit of washing. I wanted to change the sheets on his bed, so I put them in the washer. Next thing I knew they were in the dryer, with a huge amount of other laundry. There were so many items that the clothes just rolled around in the dryer in a ball. They couldn't get tumbled the way they are supposed to. As a result, some of the items didn't get quite dry.

I defrosted Trester's freezer (a 1960 model top freezer refrigerator) and then made his bed. I reminded him of the cooked, fried chicken I left in the fridge for his dinner. He probably won't remember, but he may find it when he looks for something to eat.

Thursday, March 3, 2005

I visited Trester Tuesday. When I had talked to him a couple of days before, he had said he wanted to eat at Marie Callender's, so I reminded him of that and he remembered, with some enthusiasm. On the way downtown, Trester asked me, "Can you get a car for $100?" I told him that you couldn't get one that would run for that price. Later, after lunch, he would ask me again, only this time it was, "Can you get a car for $300?"

As we drove down the offramp past a CalTrans carpool lot full of cars, Trester pointed to the lot and said, "We were going to buy this for a restaurant, but it didn't work out." After a minute or so, he added, "It was going to be Jumpy's Stay and Shop. Two buildings in one." I think he meant a combination hotel and restaurant or shopping mall. When we neared the restaurant, he pointed at another coffee shop and said, "We were going to buy these," meaning the chain of restaurants, I think. Then he continued the conversation with himself: "How much did they want for it?" "I don't know."

We had an uneventful lunch with a couple of turkey pot pies. Trester continued his conversation with himself and his hallucinated audience, but as is often the case, he spoke so softly and indistinctly and the background noise in the restaurant was so high, that I could not make out what he was saying. As we left the parking lot, Trester wanted to stop at a furniture store across the street because he thought it was owned by "one of us." He got out of the car and acted as if he would head toward the door two or three times, but then got back into the car. Apparently, he expected someone to come out and meet him or at least to see someone that he didn't see. So we headed home. About halfway home he suddenly said, "They put a snake in our head."

When I had first arrived, Trester was all intent on going to a travel agency to get his ticket to Maui, and to what I have been calling Sand Cake Island. I noted on a piece of paper that he spells is "Sandkik," so that's what I'll call it from now on. He said Sandkik was an island under this continent. Other times he says it is next to Maui. At any rate, when we were finished with lunch, I asked him if he wanted to go to the Auto Club or to the dollar store, but he declined both and just wanted to go home (after he got his cigarettes).

If you've seen the movie *A Beautiful Mind*, you'll recall that the mentally ill character posts papers all over the walls, with apparent secret codes and so forth. In the kitchen, Trester has some things taped to the walls also. There are the cut out cardboard sides of an Xtra detergent box and a Surf detergent box, the cardboard side from a 12-pack of Pepsi, the side of a carton from Basic cigarettes, two fast-food receipts with the order number in very large type, and one of his mouse pad photos (the latter nailed into a wood cabinet). While I'm visualizing that wall, I might also mention that nearby is an office refrigerator up on a table. The fridge is covered on one side with refrigerator magnets (fruit, bottles, cars, anything you can make into a little magnet).

I did some weeding and got ready to leave. Trester showed me a photograph of Stephen Spielberg that he had cut out from a *People*-type magazine and pasted into a notebook. He had written Spielberg's name underneath. "This is one of our brothers," he told me. He said that next week he wanted us to drive to the "other Corona" by taking the high road. So I said okay.

Wednesday, March 9, 2005

I visited Trester yesterday, taking him his usual food supply. He was, as usual, eager to leave and fly to Main Maui, since Sandkik Island is right next door, apparently. He was rather confused about first flying to "the other Corona." At any rate, he wanted to go to the airport to pick up his ticket (the one his group has waiting for him, with some money). I told him we could go to the Auto Club instead, since I didn't want the nearly one hour drive to the nearest airport. He agreed.

We ate at a Mexican buffet. Trester had a Margarita, too. Then we walked down the strip mall to the Auto Club. This time I went inside with him. Here is approximately how the conversation went.

"I want to fly to Main Maui on a ticket from my group."

"You want to go to Maui?"

"Yes."

"When do you want to fly there?"

"I'm not sure."

"Well, we have to have a departure date to know what the fare will be."

"I'm supposed to have a ticket already."

"You already have a reservation? What is the name? Is it under Trester?"

"I'm not sure. Try Auy Axils Poll."

"I don't see any reservation in the Auto Club system under that name."

"It's at the airport at the airline."

"Which airline?"

"I'm not sure."

"You'll have to call the airline to check for a reservation. We don't have that information here."

"Okay."

"Here's a map of Hawaii."

"Thanks."

I haven't mentioned yet that Trester used to buy two or three magazines every time he went to the store (when he was still driving). He never throws any of these away. As a result, there are half a dozen shelves (some built into the wall in the family room and bedroom and some on those metal shelving units) that must hold over 500 magazines of every type, ranging from *Architectural Digest* to the *National Enquirer*. Included are issues of *People, Maxim, Time,* and other typical grocery-store offerings. There are also a few dozen paperback books, also picked up from the grocery store.

In the 1970s and 1980s, Trester collected many nonfiction books, especially on economics, but on many other topics, too. He had probably a few hundred. Then, as his illness got worse, he began to believe that he had written all those books but that the publishers had changed what he wrote so that the books were wrong or false. As a result, he began to tear out pages, scribble Xs on other pages, make angry comments in the margins, and so on. Eventually, he tore up and threw away virtually all of his books. Only a few family-owned books remain at the house now, such as a Time-Life World War II picture book and the like.

Before I left, I vacuumed (cigarette ash on the carpet is horrible) and pulled a few weeds.

Tuesday, March 15, 2005

As usual for a Tuesday, I drove out to see Trester and take him some groceries, mostly the same stuff, though I added some berry horns for his breakfast and some mini chocolate cupcakes with green frosting to commemorate St. Patrick's day in a couple of days.

Trester had several notes near the phone about flying to Main Maui, this time on Nui Airlines. Recall that Petey Nui is one of the names he is interested in—a relative or member of his group. Trester asked me, "Can you help me get a $300 used car?" and I reminded him, "You need to have a driver's license to get a car." He said, "Oh? Okay," as if recalling the fact that I had told him that before.

We had lunch at the Hometown Buffet, a place I like to take Trester since he can have all kinds of choices in both food and beverage. In the past, we went there regularly until he got it into his head that he was not welcome there. "They don't want us there," was his comment. I finally persuaded him to try the place once more. After we had started eating, I got up to get my second helping. The busgirl knew us pretty well from our past visits, so I went over to her and told her that Trester was mentally ill and thought that he was not welcome at the buffet. I asked her to stop by the table in a few minutes and tell him he was welcome. She did this brilliantly, telling Trester she hoped he would come back again soon. I left her a nice tip that day.

Today, we happened to sit in the same busgirl's section. I said, "Hi, stranger," to her. She came over eventually to clean off the empty plates. She asked me where we'd been. I told her we had been eating around the universe, but I had finally persuaded Trester to come back here. She looked Trester directly in the eyes and said rather winningly, "It's nice to see you again." Trester looked at her and nodded with a pleasant expression. That girl needs a reward better than just a lunch tip.

While I was finishing my coffee, Trester said, "They keep shooting darts at us." I looked at him quizzically, so he added, "Hear that clanking noise?" I said, "You mean the plates clattering together?" (We were near a dish station where the dirty dishes are collected, with the usual clatter.) Trester said, "Yes. I can hardly stand it." So I took a last quick sip and we left.

As we drove away, Trester asked, "Do you know where a Lexus dealer is? They are supposed to have a car for us." I told him that he needed to have a driver's license to get a car. He said, "Oh. Okay."

There is a cigarette store across the parking lot from the buffet, so we drove over there. Trester got out of the car but didn't close the door. He made a couple of feints into the car and then out and finally got back in. "They don't want us," he said. "Let's go to the one in the old Ralph's center." So we drove over there. I waited for several minutes, seemingly longer than necessary for Trester to buy a few smokes. Then he came back empty handed. "They won't sell to us and I half pooped in my pants," he said. "I need some new pants and some underwear."

I said, "What do you mean they won't sell to you?"

He said, "The lady wouldn't sell to us."

I said, "She's always sold to you before."

Trester said, "Let's go to Vons."

I said, "How about if I go in to this store with you?"

He said, "No. Let's go to Vons."

I said, "Why don't I buy the cigarettes for you?" But no, Trester still wanted to leave.

So we drove up the road to Vons. This time Trester was much briefer, but the story was the same. "They didn't want us," he told me.

Driving around was getting a bit old by now, so I said, "Maybe they don't want you to have any cigarettes this week." Trester agreed. So we headed toward home.

A mile or so down the road, Trester said, "Go to the tea shop." I asked what that was and he said it was a neighborhood store near his house. So, since it was on the way home, I agreed. We got to this store, which seemed to be similar to a Seven-Eleven type store. Trester got out of the car and walked over toward the door. He soon came back, once again empty handed. "They're being robbed," he said. "Let's just go home." So we continued toward home. As I turned right on the trip home, Trester pointed to a Circle K across the street and said, "Go there." I pretended not to hear. Then he said, "They're being robbed, too."

We got home and I did a little mopping, finding a spot of dried cola on the floor (the spot was about a foot square, so there was a lot to mop up). Trester came into the kitchen and said, "Before you leave, would you take me to Mike's?" I asked where it was and he said it was in the center near his house. So I said okay.

While I was still mopping, Trester said to whoever usually listens to him, "My body's damaged, and I'm all half dead. It's these demon things. Can't you get the thing out of my head or some deal?" His tone was one of frustrated anger.

We drove to the center in a few minutes and looked for Mike's. There was no such store. Trester said, "Let's go into Target."

I said, "Target doesn't sell cigarettes."

Trester said, with a tone of surprise, "They don't?"

But after we looked over all the other stores in the shopping mall, he still wanted to go to Target, so we parked and I waited for him. He came out in a few minutes with some candles. I don't think he bought any underwear. He did buy two large candy bars. He offered me one, but I said, "I'm stuffed." We finished the buffet at about 1:30 and it was now 2:30.

Trester said, "I'm sort of hungry," so he ate one of the candy bars on the way back.

We stopped by Stater Brothers grocery store on the way home and he finally bought some cigarettes. He had to smoke half a one before he got into the car.

I had a chance today to do a quick count of the empty soda cans in the workshop where Trester likes to sit and smoke and listen to the radio. The cans are about 60 cans side by side, three cans high, and from three to seven cans deep. He doesn't have a complete wall yet (a few spots are only two cans high and some spots are only three or four deep), but he's got quite a collection. Maybe that's the twenty first century version of aluminum foil under the cap, grounding out the electrical zappers that attack.

Wednesday, March 23, 2005

Out to see Trester yesterday. In addition to his regular stuff, I took him a chocolate Easter rabbit and some of those new cheddar and sour cream potato chips.

While he was getting ready to go to lunch with me, I noticed that he had three new bottles (of the vinegar and oil storage type) that he had bought from the World Market, about a mile from the house. He said he walked down there and back. I was impressed.

I also noticed that the four stuffed animals in the family room had some additional accompaniments. The large panda bear had a ten dollar bill next to it and about half a dozen pieces of popcorn. The small panda had a five dollar bill and popcorn; the moose a ten dollar bill and popcorn; and the rabbit about a dollar or two in assorted change and some popcorn. The rabbit was sitting on the sofa, so I wasn't sure at first if the change belonged to it or if the coins had just fallen out of Trester's pocket. So, as we were about to leave, I asked, "Do you want to take some of that change with you?"

Trester said, "No, that's the rabbit's." He picked up a coin or two from the coffee table and was about to take that when he put them back down and reached into his pocket. "I already have some change," he said. So we left.

We had lunch at a little Chinese restaurant with an inexpensive buffet. It's fairly close and always good. Just before we left, Trester said he had to use the bathroom. The wall of the restaurant near the bathroom is covered with a large mirror and Trester in the past has waved at himself in the mirror and even said he wants to go over to the other side. I think he believes that he is seeing another reality in the mirror and wants to join it. So he will sometimes test to see if he can go over. At any rate, I thought he might want to do that.

As we left the restaurant, Trester closed his eyes tightly, grimaced, and covered his face. "Someone is hurting me," he said. A minute or two later he added, "They had a ghost hold me in the bathroom and made me barf." I asked him if he felt better now, and he said he did. These comments were unusual in that he actually said "me" instead of "us." A few minutes later, he said, "I barfed up a bunch of stuff, but I don't think it was what I just ate."

As we got near the car, Trester looked across the parking lot and said, "They're killing someone over there." Then he added, "Yes, you can see it."

Instead of getting in the car, Trester wanted some cigarettes. I suggested the Smoke Shop, but he said, "They didn't want to sell to us." So we walked across the parking lot to Sav-On. Just inside, we waited near the cigarette counter for a minute or two when Trester said, "They don't want us here. Let's go to the Smoke Shop." So we drove over there and he got some cigarettes. He had to smoke one before we left, so I waited for him to finish one before he got in the car.

I now asked Trester where he wanted to go. Before lunch he had mentioned the Auto Club and the local airport (still thinking about going to Maui), but now he just wanted to go home. I asked him about a dollar store, but he said he didn't need anything.

I cleaned up the kitchen and tossed out some very stale food. The microwave was overdue for a cleaning, but cleaned up quite well. As I left, Trester thanked me profusely for my help. I told him I was glad to be able to do it.

Wednesday, April 6, 2005

I visited Trester last week as usual. I suggested going to the fish and chicken place I like, but as he almost always does, Trester said no because that place has wronged him. He used to say they took away his car, but now he said they did something else against him. I couldn't make out what, since he mumbled too low.

Trester suggested the IHOP, but that's at the far end of town and I didn't want to drive there because that would eat into my time working around the house. So he agreed to go to the buffet. As we drove over, we passed a Claim Jumper restaurant. Trester said (to his friends, not to me), "I forgot about Claim Jumper. Jumpy owns that, I think. Can you check on that?"

We ate at the buffet. When we were ready to leave, Trester said, "Let's go out the back door." I told him there was no back door. He said, "We should go out the back door. They got blown up out there." Apparently, he meant that people out front got blown up.

Trester wanted to go by his former bank again, to see if they had issued him a credit card. He continues to think that someone has a card and some cash for him, and some airline tickets to Maui. So we stopped by the bank. He came out with a credit card application. "What did you find out?" I asked.

"They don't know anything about it," he said.

We stopped by the Smoke Shop where Trester got some cigarettes. On the way home, he said, "They tore somebody off our head in that store." Then he added, "We need to get our own stores so we can buy something." I think he meant that if he and his group owned the store, he could shop without being attacked.

After a little cleaning and weeding, I left.

Wednesday, April 6, 2005

I visited Trester yesterday. Once again he wanted to eat at IHOP, so I relented and we went. I should mention that the reason he wants to eat at a particular restaurant is not because he likes the food but because he has gotten an idea that it is important somehow. The reason may be any of the following:

1. Someone is going to meet him there and help him, rescue him, or give him a message.

2. He has been told (on the radio) to go to that restaurant to be "tested."

3. One of his people (friends, relatives, pieces of himself, children) needs help and is at the restaurant waiting for him.

4. The restaurant is far enough away from the ghosts and zombies that he can eat there without being attacked.

5. There is some kind of gate at the restaurant that Trester wants to go through, evidently to another city or reality.

As we drove to the restaurant, Trester again asked me to take him to the airport so he could fly to Maui. Once again I told him he needed a ticket. He said one was waiting. I told him to call the airline to be sure so we wouldn't make a useless trip. He said, "Another Bob is waiting for us in Maui, and he will help us." I guess he's rather disappointed in this Bob for not helping him get there.

As we continued our drive, Trester said, "Can you help me find where I used to live?" I asked where that was. He said, "It was in Yibi Corona." I told him I didn't know how to get there.

We had lunch at the IHOP. Trester kept his hand over his chest. I asked him if his heart hurt and he said yes. I offered to take him to a doctor, but as usual he said, "No. I'm all right." I asked him if he was taking aspirin and he said no. I can't get him even to take a pain pill. We finished lunch and then drove over to one of the dollar stores he likes. As we neared the store, Trester said, "They're writing on my forehead again. It's some zombie deal."

We entered the dollar store, and Trester bought some candles, some coffee mugs (they keep getting slammed onto the floor, so he always needs more), 1250 note cards (3-by-5), some notebooks, some liquid hand soap, and some underwear.

As we left, Trester said to me, "Our little friend called for us at the restaurant back there. He got arrested and they put him in a box." Then he continued with himself: "What should I do? Should I have waited? I don't know."

Back at the house I had only enough time to spray a few weeds.

Wednesday, April 6, 2005

Trester called this afternoon. First he asked, "Are you okay?" I said I was fine. He said, "Are you nearby? I'm supposed to go to the bank to see about my credit card, but they set a bomb off." I told him I was at home, which is not nearby. He said, "The house is being zombied." I asked him what that meant. He said, "The candle holders got too hot. They choked us and half our body flew out the window."

When he asked again about the bank, I said, "I took you to the bank last week to see about your credit card."

Trester said, "That wasn't us. It was different." I told him I would take him again next Tuesday. He said okay.

Then he said, "I just called to see if you were blown up by a car bomb." I get the impression that many times when he calls he has had a message that I have been killed and he wants to confirm that or at least find out whether the message is true. He often begins a call with, "Are you okay?" In the past when I would call him, he would answer eagerly until he found out I was the caller and then sound disappointed, almost as if to say, "Oh, it's just you." Then he would imply that my call cut off another, more important call trying to get through to him. He was expecting one of his friends or group to call, I guess. So now it's nice that he is concerned about my possible death. But, of course, it's also very sad knowing the suffering he is going through.

Oh, and it's not just the radio that tells him to call me. One time he said, "The man who speaks from the refrigerator told me to call you. He said you have a message for me."

Wednesday, April 13, 2005

When I arrived at Trester's house yesterday, he greeted me with an urgent plea to take him to the airport. "I have to leave here," he said, as he often does. We went through the same dialog we often do:

"Take me to the airport."

"Do you have a ticket?"

"It's a the airport."

"Which airline?"

"I don't know, any of them." And so forth. A bit later he asked how much a taxi costs to go to the airport, so he was clearly trying to make other plans than relying on me. In the course of his requests over time, Trester mentions different airports, including small ones that do not have any airline service. This day he did mention a larger one, Ontario I believe.

I asked him where he wanted to eat lunch and he said, "Some restaurant over near the IHOP," which, as I have said, is on the far end of town. So we drove over to a Chinese buffet in that direction. We've eaten there a few times. I had suggested Islands, but Trester said, "We almost got blown up there the last time."

On the way to lunch, Trester said, "We're being followed by 200 killers, who are hurting us." A few minutes later he said, "One of us just got tortured and cut into pieces." Then he added, "I hope he got put back together."

I asked him how his heart was doing and he said the pain was less. "They don't have that sticker deal in there anymore," he said.

Again thinking about the airport, Trester said, "See how I can get a $100 car." (Recall that Trester usually talks to his friends or his group, and not to me.)

We had a really good lunch (Trester liked his, too) and decided to go to the dollar store in the same shopping center. "They didn't want us there the last time," Trester said.

"Maybe it's under new ownership," I suggested. So we headed for it.

Outside, Trester said, "They don't want us to shop here."

I said, "Sure they do. Come on." So he reluctantly went in with me.

When we got inside, Trester said, "We're not supposed to shop here." Then he said to his friends, "They don't want us. Can we go down one level to Jumpy's?" And then Trester jumped up and down two or three times.

A minute later, Trester came over to me and said, "Do you know how to go down half a level where the kids are?" I said no. He then said, "They don't want us to shop in this store. Let's go." So we left.

In the car I asked him where he wanted to get some cigarettes. There is a store at the other end of the center where he has shopped in the past, so I suggested that. "We shouldn't shop there, either," he said. Then he added,

"Just go there anyway." So we drove over. On the way, Trester asked, "Can you fix the car like a homing pigeon, to take us home?" I asked what he meant. He said, "Did you fix the car before, to go down a level?" I said no. By now we were at the cigarette store.

He got out, went to the store, hesitated, then looked at the newspaper rack outside. Finally, he came back to the car. "Let's go to the drive through dairy to get some cigarettes," he said. I didn't know where that was, so he directed me through town. On the way, Trester said, "A bunch of us are trapped underground back there."

I should mention that my accounts of Trester's comments are only a small part of what he actually says when we are together. He mumbles most of the time, since he isn't talking to me anyway, usually. And he says so many things that I can't remember more than a few of them. Much of his commentary revolves around persecutorial delusions (such as the 200 killers), harming him or his kids or friends, or around political and economic battles (people stealing his money, invading his island or national property, suing him or being sued by him for some kind of theft of ideas or goods). The mentally ill do not all have a happy fantasy life as some people think, where they imagine they are a famous and important person and that boosts their ego. In Trester's case, at least, the fantasy includes slights, insults, persecution, injustice, theft, cheating, killing, torture, robbery, car bombs, nuclear war, attacks, "zombie rays," "klonker deals," and the like. By his account, he should be both rich and famous, but his enemies continue to steal his products and money and sabotage his work and kill his relatives, friends, and group members.

But to return.

We found the drive through and Trester bought some

cigarettes. A matronly woman employee stood in front of the car while we took the cigarettes and handed over the money to the salesgirl, probably the woman's daughter. Clever way to prevent grab and dash theft, I thought.

Back home I sprayed some weeds and defrosted Trester's small refrigerator (where he keeps his soda). As I left, he again thanked me for my help. I wish it were more.

※ ※ ※

40.532 Ideas: Tropical plants that have rare blooms & mimic vines & other types of plants made thicker and tropical —

40.547 Personal Purchases: Get our group's new world radio —- a 49.00 one at Circuit City
40.592 Judges Attacked here— & gunmen come in—

※ ※ ※

Wednesday, April 20, 2005

Trester was already up when I arrived at the house yesterday. He was, as usual, anxious for me to take him to the airport, this time not to go to Maui but to the "other Corona," which he sometimes refers to as Yibi Corona. He said that all his relatives live in that town and that's where he used to live. He added, "I've got to leave this place. They don't want us to live here anymore."

We headed toward the small Mexican buffet that he regularly wants to go to. As we drove, he asked, "Can you drive to the long distance gate bounce around deal, or do you have to fly there?" I asked him what he meant, and he said he wanted to get to Yibi-Corona. I told him I didn't know how to get there.

After lunch I suggested the dollar store near the restaurant (his town has at least four dollar stores), but he wanted to go to the one on the west end of town, so we drove there. When we got inside, he said, "They don't want us to shop here." I told him it was okay. Trester picked up some three-by-five cards and some notebooks, and then said, "That's all. They don't want us here." I told him I needed to look for something in the store, so I went over to the cleaning supplies. As Trester slowly followed, he picked up some pens, some all-purpose cleaner (two bottles) and some other items, totaling twelve in all. He kept insisting that we should leave. We soon did.

As we walked back to the car, Trester said, "I broke a leg or some deal." He shook his right leg and wiggled his foot. Back in the car, he repeated the comment and wiggled his foot again. He must have concluded that someone did this to him, because he became somewhat upset and in a minute or two said angrily (but softly), "Oh great. There are eight million Russians in town now."

Trester wanted to go to a new cigarette store he had spotted because he thought none of the others wanted him, so we found it along the street. He got out of the car, walked up to the door, and then came back. "It's not open," he said. "There's a motorcycle parked in front of the door." There was also a huge delivery truck blocking the parking lot, so I couldn't see just what the situation was. So we left.

We drove to another of the dollar stores, but as soon as Trester walked inside, he said, "The loudspeaker told us they don't want us to shop here." He wouldn't stay inside. I looked for the cleaner I was trying to find while he waited outside.

Finally, we went to one of the cigarette stores where

Trester bought some cigarettes. Then we went home.

The only thing different I got Trester grocery-wise this week was a can of that aerosol cheese spread and some crackers. Oh, and a bag of pretzels. Otherwise, the same stuff. I did get him a Chinese TV dinner in addition to his favorite Salisbury steak ones. The weed killer I used on the weeds in the driveway has worked quite well, in spite of Trester's propensity to water the driveways regularly. He loves to spray water with the garden hoses. In the air, on the ground, sometimes on the plants.

Wednesday, April 27, 2005

Trester was already up when I arrived yesterday, though I was actually almost half an hour earlier than usual. He helped me unload the groceries. He even put away a few of the TV dinners. His helping is unusual.

As I was unloading things, I noticed that there were several oranges left, a couple of which were growing mold. "Your oranges are getting moldy," I said.

"Somebody put disease on them," Trester said. So I washed out the fruit bowl with soap and water and put in the fresh oranges. Even though a couple of the old oranges looked okay, I tossed them along with the moldy ones just to be safe.

As we were getting ready to leave, Trester couldn't decide whether or not to change his pants. He put his wallet into a clean pair and then took it out again. He seemed undecided about how dirty his current pants were. I told him to go ahead and change. He said, "We need to get some new pants and shoes. These aren't ours. They are just on loan." I told him that they were his pants and that I had bought them just for him. He put on the clean pair.

Trester changed his mind a few times about where to eat lunch, but decided we should eat on the west end of town (far from the house, which is beyond the east end of town). The big Chinese buffet is out there and that's what he suggested. We sat next to a very noisy table with loud talking women, and I hoped Trester would not react in a negative way. There was also a TV hanging about ten feet away, and Trester turned and looked at it a few times, but he didn't react. So we ate in peace.

As we got back in the car, I said, "There are at least four dollar stores in town. Which do you want to go to?"

Trester replied, "The trouble is, none of them want us to shop there." So I suggested we go to the Smoke Shop for his cigarettes. As we headed through town and I passed the street where one of the dollar stores is, Trester said, "You should have turned there. Go to that dollar store." I told him we had passed it and could go to the dollar store in the center with the Smoke Shop. He said okay.

We went to the dollar store first. As we walked across the parking lot, a truck was just pulling up to the curb outside the store. Just as we walked behind it, the truck let out the air blast from the air bakes being set. We went on inside the store. In a minute or two, Trester said, "Let's get out of here before they blow the place up." I reminded him he had said he wanted some candles, so we went to the candle aisle. I pointed out the Novena candles he usually buys, but all the ones here had pictures of the robed, long-haired Jesus on them. (He usually buys the ones without pictures.)

"Here are some jar candles," I said.

"Those are for some guru group," Trester said. He picked up some other candles, some potpourri leaves, some liquid potpourri, some hand lotion, two boxes of toothpicks, and some other items. Sometimes I think he is shopping almost randomly, because he picks up several items from whatever aisle we happen to walk down. But I think he sometimes sees a meaning in what he buys. Either the product is good to ward off disease or it is made by a member of his group or some such idea.

We went by the bank to see if there was a credit card and tickets and money for Trester. When he came back and I asked what he found out, he just said, "Their computers are down for a few days."

On the way home, Trester said, "I need to get a used car so I can drive to the other world." Then he turned to me and said, "Can you help me? It feels like they keep pulling part of my head off." I told him his head looked normal to me.

At home, Trester said, "Did you hear that blast at the store?"

I asked, "From the truck?"

He said, "Yes."

I asked, "What about it?"

Trester said, "The truck blew up, I think."

At one point, I asked Trester if his heart was still hurting, and he said, "They pulled something out of me, so it doesn't stab anymore." He said his heart felt better. However, he thought his left arm was broken at the elbow and held it some as if in pain. I asked him if he had been taking aspirin for the pain, but he didn't respond.

I did some mopping and a little weeding and then had to leave. Trester thanked me again for my help. Bless him.

Thursday, May 12, 2005

Trester was already up and dressed when I arrived on Tuesday. He helped unload a bag of groceries, and then got distracted by his voices. I finished the groceries and also unloaded a new vacuum cleaner, a new mop, and three new toilet seats.

I asked him where he wanted to eat and he said City Mall Number Two, in San Bernardino, about 35 miles away. I told him I didn't know how to get to that mall (there isn't one by that name) and that the city was too far away. He then asked if there was another restaurant on the far end of town, near the IHOP we have been to. Apparently he wants to get away from where he is by as much distance as possible. A few days earlier he called me to say, "I tried to go up to the main world but there was a helicopter chopping people up and their body parts were falling through the roof." The battles and bloodshed he imagines at the house seem to be his reason for wanting to eat far away, and for going to Maui — to get away from the horror.

Trester finally named another, closer mall, where we eat occasionally. He said, "Let's go to the Tyler Mall so I can get my picture on a mat." As I've mentioned, he has eight or ten pictures of himself on mouse pads. I asked him why he wanted another, and he said, "I don't know." (Once he said it was so his kids or relatives would know where he is.) We drove over to the mall and ate some Mahi Mahi at the food court. It was very good.

During lunch, he again said, "Do you know how to get through the gate? I need to get back to Yibi-Corona." I asked where that was. He said it was where his relatives lived.

Trester said, "My shoes are terrible. Let's go to a shoe place." So we looked at the directory and I named off a few shoe stores. He decided that Payless Shoe Source was the place. He has bought belts there in the past. When we got outside the store, Trester stopped and said, "Let's go somewhere else." I reminded him that he had said his shoes were in bad shape, but he wouldn't go into the store. He then wanted to go to Robinson's May, but when we took a few steps in that direction, he changed his mind about that, too.

So, we walked to a store somewhat like Cost Plus Imports called the Alley. He has bought glass paper weights there in the past and mentioned those as we walked. However, after walking inside for less than a minute, he said, "Let's go back to Corona and get some cigarettes." So we walked back down the mall and drove off. As we left the parking lot, he said, "Where around here can we get some cigarettes?" I said I didn't know.

We drove back to Corona and into the parking lot of another mall where there is a dollar store and a smoke shop. We were going to the dollar store but as we neared it, Trester said, "Go to the grocery store so I can get some cigarettes." So we headed down to that end of the parking lot. I parked and Trester was about to get out of the car but stopped. "Let's go get some cigarettes at the gas station," he said. I parked nearby and he walked over. When he got near the door (he may have looked in), he stopped and came back to the car. "They don't want to sell to us, either," he said, "and besides, they are getting robbed or some deal." I suggested the smoke shop. He said okay.

At the smoke shop, Trester got out and walked inside. But he was soon outside again and got into the car. "They don't want to sell to us."

I reminded him that the woman had sold to him many times. I also said, "Why don't you give me the money and I'll buy the cigarettes for you?"

He said, "Let's just go."

I said, "This is the last stop for cigarettes. We are going home after this if you don't buy any." Then I added, "If no one will sell to you, maybe you should just give up smoking."

He said, "Maybe I should."

As we drove away, Trester said, "Go to the grocery store down the street." I told him that they would just tell him they wouldn't sell to him, either, so I wasn't going to go there. I guess I had a bit of a stern tone—though it was pretty mild—because Trester said in a vulnerable tone, "Don't be mad at us."

So we got home for the first time without any cigarettes. That's just as well, since they are not good for the poor guy. I've read that many schizophrenics smoke in what is believed to be an unconscious attempt at self-medication, the nicotine offering a calming effect.

That may explain the fact that back home, while I was vacuuming, Trester started shouting angrily at his persecutors and those cheating him. He went outside and sprayed water in the air at them while he yelled at them. When he came back in and kept shouting angrily, I said, "If you keep shouting, the neighbors might call the police." He knows the consequences of his anger in the past.

As a side note, the vacuum was miraculous. It is one of those bagless models. I had to empty it every one or two minutes, since it filled with dust and fuzz and so forth that fast. What a cleaning job it did. That means the old vacuum was not doing its job at all. I got only a couple of rooms done, it took so much time emptying. Didn't have time to install the new toilet seats this trip. I mopped a little and cleaned up a little.

Trester had the sprinklers running as I left.

Tuesday, May 17, 2005

When I arrived at Trester's today, he was still in bed. I asked him how he was doing and he said that he hurt all over. Later he said his back was hurting. He seemed to feel better after lunch, though.

When we were getting ready to leave for lunch, I asked him where he wanted to go, and, just as in the previous week, he said he wanted to go to a mall in San Bernardino that's 35 miles away. Before I could say, "That's too far," he said we should drive out to the west end of town and look for a restaurant near the IHOP. I mentioned that the Chinese buffet was in that direction (not quite as far) and he soon suggested that. (Sometimes he acts as if he doesn't hear me and then suggests the same thing, as if he imagines he just thought of it.)

I noticed that the yellow shirt he put on was pretty dirty in the front so I asked him if he didn't have a clean shirt. He reached for one that looked torn, so I mentioned that it was damaged. Then I saw one on top of the dryer where he keeps his clean laundry in a pile. He pulled that one out and acted as if he was going to put it on. I took the opportunity to use the bathroom. When I got back, he was just buttoning up his dirty yellow shirt again. "I'll change shirts when we get back," he said. "This one is okay." So we headed out the door and got into the car. I said, "Buckle your seat belt." (Forgetting this task cost Trester two tickets when he was still driving.) Trester said, "Do you want me to change my shirt? I can change it if you want." I told him it was okay. Then, talking to someone other than me, he asked, "Should I change my shirt?"

We drove to the Chinese buffet. We got our food and sat down and began to eat. Trester looked at me and said, "It feels like half of us went up into the air back there. Do you know how to get us back down?" Then he said, "They attacked me outside there when I opened the door, with their shredder deal." I told him he looked okay and intact to me.

After lunch we drove to one of the dollar stores in town, where Trester got some 3-by-5 cards (another 1000), some notebooks, pens, and photo albums. Back in the parking lot, he said, "It feels like the outside of my head floated away." We got into the car and Trester said, "Wait a minute. One of our kids got lost." He opened the door and looked toward the back of the car. He repeated this a couple of times. Finally, as he looked toward the back of the car, he said, "Come back over here," to whoever was lost, apparently.

I asked Trester where he wanted to get some cigarettes and he said, "I wonder who will sell to us." I said they all would. He then said we should go to the drive through dairy store, so we did that. The store had only six packs of cigarettes of the kind he likes, so he bought those instead of a whole carton.

We then drove to another dollar store near the dairy store, where Trester bought some candles and two bags of potting soil.

At some point during our drive, I heard him debating with himself about wanting to fly to Maui versus just staying where he was. I mentioned that if he stays where he is, I could help him and bring him groceries.

Back home Trester headed for the workshop to smoke a cigarette and start writing on his note cards. I vacuumed two of the back bedrooms (empty of furniture now) that had not been vacuumed in, shall we say, quite a while. Okay, I admit it. The carpet changed color as I vacuumed, if that gives you an idea. Once again, with the miracle bagless vacuum, I had to empty the chamber about once every two minutes. There was a lot of dust. I also had time to install one new toilet seat and tighten the floor bolts a bit. The toilet in the half bath has been moved off square. Trester apparently sits on it and experiences attacks or explosions that cause him to rock back and forth or move around violently. It's tough keeping the toilet in place. In fact, I may need to replace the seal again soon, even though I reset the bowl less than a year ago. I did a little trimming outside to fill up the green waste bin and then headed home. Trester was for some reason particularly expressive in his appreciation for my help today. He thanked me about three times.

Tuesday, May 24, 2005

Trester was resting on the sofa when I arrived. He was already dressed. I told him, as I usually do, that I brought him some groceries and would unload them. "I hope you brought toilet paper," he said. I told him I had, so he went out to the car and picked up the package. He distributed it to the three bathrooms while I unloaded the rest of the groceries.

He again asked about a mall in San Bernardino, but he wasn't clear on which one he wanted to go to. I asked him why he wanted to go so far away to eat. He said, "Is that far away? Then let's go to the mall in Riverside," about 13 miles away. Then he asked, "Where should we eat?" I named a Mexican buffet just downtown. He said okay. Then he spotted a roll of film that he had taken with his one-dollar camera and said we should go get it developed. Rather than wait an hour for the film, I suggested we eat near the photo place or else leave the film until next week. "That's right," he said, "I think I left a roll somewhere to be developed."

As we started driving, Trester asked, "Do you think I should buy a camera that takes pictures of me?" I told him that any camera would take a picture of him, including the cameras he had. (He has two or three of those one-dollar plastic cameras, purchased from one of the dollar stores.)

At any rate, he said we should go to the photo shop near Vons. So we drove over there only to discover that the shop had gone out of business and been replaced by a real estate office. As we drove in, though, Trester spotted a Wendy's, and he said we should eat there. So we drove across the parking lot and parked.

Just inside the door, Trester said, "They don't want us to eat here."

I said, "Yes, they do."

He said, "Let's go over to the steak house in Norco."

I said, "What if they don't want you to eat there, either? You'd go hungry." I then coaxed him inside and we got in line. He protested once or twice more, but we finally ordered. I had chili and a hamburger, while Trester had chili and a malt (which I think they call a frosty) and some fries.

When I asked him how his food was, he first said it was okay in a somewhat displeased tone, and then added, "It tastes icky." I told him that mine tasted good.

After lunch, Trester suggested we go to the green store, by which he meant the Dollar Tree store, since it uses green letters. Then he changed his mind and said we should go to the dollar store "in Baja, over on the far end." He meant the dollar store on the west end of town. I think he wanted to go there because he remembered another photo store there. We arrived and I told him we could leave the film but that I couldn't wait an hour for it to be developed. He said, "Let's skip it, then." So we went into the dollar store. Soon he said, "They don't want us to shop here." Just inside the entrance of this store there is a radio playing rather loudly and I think that whatever is said or sung on the radio makes Trester think he is being told to stay out. He did buy a bottle of dishwashing detergent but then left without getting his usual supply of note cards and candles.

Outside, Trester said, "They hurt me with that music as I came in." Later in the car he said to himself, "I'm about to die."

As we drove across the parking lot, Trester said, "Go over to that grocery store. They have smokes." So I pulled in to the store. Instead of getting out of the car, he said, "Go to the smoke shop on the other street." So we drove over there and Trester got some cigarettes.

On the way home, Trester began arguing with his friends about the injustices happening in his life. I heard him say, "Can you find out how we can get out of here and fly to the island? We keep getting killed here." Then he added, "The prostitute ring is over on the islands, too. Everybody over there is a spy for some killer group." He turned to me and asked, "When they pop you and disappear, do you know where they go?" I said I didn't.

Back home I vacuumed some, using both the new vacuum and the old, trash vacuum for places where I might accidentally pick up shards of broken coffee cups or coins. There are a surprising number of coins everywhere on the floor and I sometimes vacuum one up by accident. It makes quite a noise.

I also had to mop the workshop where Trester sits and smokes. He had spilled one or more cans of soda on the floor. (He may have slammed it or them down during one of his rages.) The floor was sticky. This made me realize that I'm not really able to do all the work there that needs to be done. I wished for a helper. In fact, I took the Penny-Saver home to look for a gardener to help with the outside.

I forgot to mention that a couple of weeks ago Trester dumped all his empty soda cans in the recycling bin and the trash can, filling both. So his wall of cans in the shop is gone now.

He said we was feeling pretty good today, so that was encouraging, since he was doing better than last week.

Tuesday, May 31, 2005

Trester was dressed but lying on the sofa and covered up when I arrived today. I asked him how he was feeling and he said, as he often does, "Not too well. I feel old." I unloaded the groceries. On my visit to the back bathroom I noticed that Trester had not drained the bathtub from his last bath, so I opened the drain. I've done this several times. I don't know whether he forgets or if there is another reason, such as a tricky drain lever.

After Trester got up, he said, "Robert, they took one of us and hit him and then burned him. I think he's dead." As is often the case, I didn't say anything because I never know quite what to say and whatever I do say has no effect that I can discern. So about ten minutes later, Trester repeated the statement. He added some comments similar to "They're always killing everybody around here." Then he asked me, "Do you know how to drive through the main gate so we can get to Yibi-Corona?" I said I didn't know where the gate was.

Trester remembered that he wanted to get his roll of film developed so we took it by a 30-minute processing place and went to a nearby Chinese buffet. This buffet is a pale imitation of the one on the far end of town, but it's close. After we got our food and sat down, Trester put his hand on his face and grimaced as if in pain. He mumbled some things but I couldn't understand what he said. I asked him if he was okay, but he didn't respond understandably. He started eating and eventually said the food was good when I asked him. The clank of some dishes across the room made him look up and say, "Don't let him get hurt."

It is so sad that Trester, who is a compassionate and generous person, feels so much pain for all the people he imagines are being tortured and killed. And it seems to be the pain of a parent often, since he regularly says that the persons being hurt are his children.

The interior of the restaurant has mirrors on all the walls. Trester waved at himself in the mirror as he usually does.

When we left the restaurant, a car alarm went off, honking the horn for a minute or so. Trester waved in the direction of the sound and said, cheerfully, "Hello!" Two other times today, one driver honked at another in a parking lot, and each time Trester waved and said, "Hello!" (The path to sanity really does lie in realizing that "it's not about you.")

When we got back to the photo processing store, only 10 of the 24 photos could be printed at all, and the rest were dark and shadowy, as if taken by slow film on a dark day or evening. I think the one-dollar camera Trester used was a piece of junk. At the photo store he bought a one-use camera with some 800 ISO speed film in it and a built in flash. That should brighten things up. Back home he had me take about 10 or 12 pictures of him, sitting and standing in various places: by a house plant, at the kitchen table, in the workshop, at the picnic table, and so on. He even took a couple of pictures of me.

Before we went home, however, Trester again mentioned that he needed new shoes, saying that his current ones had holes in them that let stickers through. When he showed me his soles, though, I didn't see any holes. Anyway, we went to a Payless Shoe Source store and he bought two pairs of athletic shoes just like the ones he was wearing. One was a size 9W and the other a 9 1/2 regular. I could barely convince him to try them on and he had the second pair on one foot for only two seconds. I hope they fit.

Trester bought some cigarettes at the photo store. I showed him that the carton was on sale for $7 less than the individual pack price, but he bought five individual packs instead, saying, "These are the good ones."

After we got home, Trester got what was apparently a junk phone call. After he hung up I asked who had called. He said, "One of the stores we went to called. They didn't say which one, but they have one of us down there. Can we go back and see?" I pointed out that none of the stores we went to knew who he was or had his number.

I mopped the usual places and vacuumed the living room (much cleaner now and had to empty the tank only a few times). Last week I called three gardeners but haven't heard back, so I need to call them again.

Tuesday, June 7, 2005

Trester called a couple of days ago to tell me, "We just bought Glen Ivy Hot Springs," naming a nearby hot springs spa and resort. I told him we could go out there next time I saw him and look it over. Meanwhile I got on the Web and looked up the resort. It was still in business and had a "cafe" page. So when I got to Trester's today, I suggested we go there for lunch. He agreed with some eagerness.

On the way over, Trester said, "We need to get on a plane and fly to the other world." He said he didn't feel particularly good today, but had some pains in his lower abdomen.

The resort has been recently remodeled. It seems to be a health spa now, charging $35 weekdays and $50 weekends. We waited in line and then asked if we could just eat at the cafe. Since the answer was yes, we walked around to it. Turns out the cafe is a small room with counter service and a few sandwiches. The clientele is the same as the customers of the spa: mostly young—and mostly tattooed—women. Their tattoos were visible because most were wearing bathing suits. It was something of a fish-out-of-water experience for me.

On the drive away, I asked Trester how he liked it. He said the place was "real nice," but that "they should have better food cheaper." Then he asked himself, "Did they leave half of us there?" We headed downtown toward the Smoke Shop. Trester said, "I ought to fly home someday, on another planet."

As we pulled into the parking lot, he said, "Let me try to buy some cigarettes at the gas station." He went in and soon returned empty handed. "They don't carry the right brand," he said.

We went to the Smoke Shop and got some cigarettes. Back in the car, Trester asked, "Do you know how to find the gate to drive to the other world?" I said I didn't. A minute later, he had a short conversation with himself: "This is where we live."

"It is? Okay." The "it is" had a slight tone of surprise to it.

Back home I mopped and gave the fridge a blast with

my heat gun to reduce the ice buildup. It's a 1959 model, made before frost free was common. I asked Trester if I could get him a new refrigerator. He said he didn't have enough money. I said I'd pay for it. He said he didn't want to spend that much. Instead, I could pay the plumbing bill.

I should explain that Trester called Saturday to say that the drains had all backed up and the toilets had almost all overflowed. I called a plumber who knows the situation with Trester and who is willing to go out and fix the problem and be paid later. He went out the next day and opened the line back up. Trester sometimes flushes paper towels down the drain, in addition to the vast quantities of TP he uses. But we've been fortunate not to have a stop up for a long while.

I noticed that Trester needs some new pillows, even though a couple of them are not that old. I guess he uses them robustly. So I put that on my list for him. I put his bed sheets in the washer and made his bed with clean sheets. By then it was time to go.

Tuesday, June 14, 2005

Trester was still asleep when I arrived with his groceries about 12:15 today. When he was awake enough, I asked him how he was doing. He said, "I feel old." He's 56 now. He added, "I think I'm about to have heart failure. I have to lie in bed a long time to rest." I asked him if I could take him to a doctor to get a checkup and he said no.

When I asked him where he wanted to eat, he said, "Could we eat at Glen Ivy?" naming the same hot springs that he said he or his group bought last week, and where we ate last week. I asked him if he liked the food there. (It was rather perfunctory.) He said, "I think they stranded one of our kids there. What happened to the car they blew up? Do you know?" I said I didn't. I suggested we wait a week or so before returning to the spa. He said okay. I suggested the dinky Mexican place near Trester's house. I did this partly because there was a traffic jam on the freeway that I wanted to avoid. He said okay, so we headed there.

At the restaurant, Trester ordered a fish enchilada and a beer (he always orders "Corona cerveza"). I had the special, which was a huge carnitas burrito. Couldn't finish it. Before our food arrived, Trester dipped a tortilla chip in the salsa and was about to take a bite when he stopped. He first shook off the salsa, then wiped it off with his finger, then broke off the part of the chip with the salsa on it, and finally dropped the rest of the chip into the salsa dish and got another chip and ate it plain. He must have thought there was something wrong with the salsa. However, later, when I asked Trester how he liked his food, he said, "It's real good." As you know, he sometimes says his food tastes bad, so I was happy that he enjoyed it today. He ate most of his plate of enchilada, rice, and beans. Last week he threw up a bit after lunch, but this week he was fine.

Near the end of the meal, Trester took out a dollar bill and put it next to his plate. I thought he was leaving a tip. Then he put the bill away and took out a five-dollar bill and put it first next to his plate and then on top of the salsa dish. Soon we had the bill on a tray, so I asked him if he wanted to put the five dollars on the tray. "No, no, that's not a tip," he said. "Here, want me to leave a dollar for a tip?" He got out a dollar bill and put it on the tray. I asked him what the five dollar bill was for, if it was not a tip. He said, "That's to get five kids out down south." I asked him if they were in jail (because that's what he often says—they need bail). "No," he said, "they are being held down south." At any rate, the waitress got a six-dollar tip on a nineteen-dollar meal. I'm always touched by Trester's generosity and compassion, as "crazy" as it may seem on the surface. He cares about those he imagines are in trouble.

We drove to one of the dollar stores. As usual, they all seem to play their background music in the foreground — that is, too loud. Trester picked up some batteries, but then said, "Let's go. They don't want us to shop here."

I said, "Sure they do."

He said, "That man just said they don't want us," referring to the pop song playing too loudly in the store. I suggested we get him some 3-by-5 cards so he agreed and grabbed a candle on the way up to the register. He got out of the store with just four items, a record low.

There was an auto parts store next to the dollar store, so I went in for a minute while Trester smoked a cigarette near the car. When I returned, he said, "I got shot at." I asked if they hit him and he said, "I'm not sure. It's right there." He pointed to the right side of his chest. My guess is there was a loud noise, like a backfire or something, that he was responding to.

Back home (after a stop by the Smoke Shop), we got out of the car and Trester again said, "We're about to die. They shot us at that store." He went into the house and covered his face with a wet cloth.

I mopped, vacuumed, and swept a little and put one of the batteries in the clock that had stopped. I cleaned the clock with some detergent. It was both dusty and smoky. (Remember that old expression, "I'll clean his clock"? Well, I can say I did, literally.) I also put the three new pillows on his bed and on the sofa, with one of the new pillow cases. I tossed out the three old pillows and one old pillow case. I gave him the new yellow shirt and the three pairs of boxer undies I bought for him and he seemed very pleased by all the new stuff.

By the time I left, Trester was smoking a cigarette and drinking a Pepsi somewhat cheerfully, feeling much better.

※ ※ ※

8.26 Hitler takes over in England --- Shoots queen & one of us there too –
8.27 One of ours moderates won the election with Ronevy [?] as VP. Both killed – his kid in our family killed too –
8.28 Neighbors of kidnapped kids were killed or hanged for it already –
8.30 Viscious attack on us over here – again just now.... Chopped the guard up into pieces - -- --
8.31 Old Gold "Cigarettes" smokes remembered . . . just called Smokes - --
8.37 Salt store idea for each district – make sure is world wide – to wholesale there too & rain maker items etc.
8.41 Commercial Clothes CO. where can't buy pants etc Watermelon shirts & undies & shalls for ladies, etc – lots of items-- & a cosmetics shelf – for men, women, teens, & kids etc

※ ※ ※

Wednesday, June 22, 2005

Trester was still asleep when I arrived at ten minutes to twelve yesterday. He got up soon while I was unloading groceries. I added some French cream puffs and snack size candy bars to his regular food of bologna, salami, ham, cheese, TV dinners, rocky road ice cream, frozen burritos, and so forth. He still had a few oranges, so I didn't get him any more. Got him some TP and Pepsis, together with some 7 UP Plus (last week the variety drink was pink lemonade).

Not long after he got up, he asked me, "Did they shoot at you?" I said no. I hadn't heard any bangs or other noises that he could interpret as a gunshot, so he may have thought this happened earlier. I suggested the Hometown Buffet for lunch, since we hadn't been there in a while. Trester acquiesced, but then suggested the Chinese buffet on the west end of town. He looked at his pictures that I brought (developed from the disposable camera he bought earlier). These pictures came out amazingly better than the ones taken with the dollar camera. Big surprise. He liked them and said we should buy another camera like it. I said okay.

Just before we left the house, Trester said, "We can go to the buffet you wanted to," meaning the Hometown Buffet. So we got in the car and started out.

As we drove on the way to lunch, Trester said, "Can you take us to the airport so we can fly over there? We need to get to the island." Later he added, "Can you help me fly over to where I live?" As usual, I told him he needed a ticket. Just as we were about to turn toward the road to the buffet, Trester said, "Let's stay in town and go to the Chinese buffet." He acted as if he had gotten a message that it was dangerous to leave town right then. So we changed direction and headed to the Chinese buffet.

Lunch was great as usual, and uneventful. I asked Trester about his food and he said it was very good. He went back for a small plate of seconds and a couple of slices of watermelon.

After lunch, I asked him if he wanted to go to a dollar

store and he said, "Let's see, who will sell to us?" I told him they all would. We had just left the parking lot when he said we should go to the dollar store in the same strip mall as the buffet, so I turned back in and we went there.

Just after we walked in the door, Trester asked out into the store, "Will you sell to us?"

I was behind him, and I said, "Yes, please shop here. We will be glad to sell to you."

I don't think he was fooled, since in a minute or so he said, "They don't want us here. Let's just get some detergent and leave." He bought some laundry detergent and a couple of candles and checked out.

Driving down the street, we passed an Auto Zone auto parts store. Trester saw it and said, "We're supposed to go to the Auto Zone and go up ten levels." Then he got into one of those conversations that I'm never sure if I'm the audience or if someone else is. He said, "Can't we just fly away?" Then he added, "We have to go upstairs sometime."

He said the tobacco store in the mall we passed wouldn't sell to him, so he suggested the dairy drive through, where we had gotten cigarettes before. Of course, the price is much higher there. He asked for two cartons of Basic, which came to $76 there, pretty much emptying his wallet. As we drove off, he said, "That's too expensive. I shouldn't have bought them. I should have saved some money for the kids."

As we neared home, he said, "We should go back to that center and see if they left one of us."

Back at his house, I discovered a water leak in the service entrance pipe, so I had to call a plumber, who promised to come out the next day.

I started to take out the big trash can and Trester started to roll the recycling can. I asked, "Is this week recycle week?" The service picks up recycling every other week. I went inside and checked the list. "Recycling isn't until next week," I told him.

"That's okay. Let's put it out anyway." So he put out the recycling can.

Trester saw the green waste can near the front door (I was trimming weeds when I discovered the water leak) and he said in a tone of disgust, "Where did that come from? That's Parkers." He named his former next door neighbors. I told him, for about the 50th time, that that green waste can was his and for his weeds. Then I put it out by the street to be emptied. I can't seem to get that idea through to him.

I mopped and cleaned a bit. His kitchen sink had rings of shaving cream sprayed in it. He bought the shaving cream last week at the dollar store. Since he has a beard that he trims with scissors, I wondered what he wanted it for. Apparently it is a "disinfectant," like many of the things he buys. He spreads Comet and Ajax cleanser all over the place, and used to spread baby powder everywhere as disinfectants. He does less of the powder than he used to, though.

I said goodbye and we waved. Overall he seemed to be feeling somewhat better than last week, and didn't complain about any pain in particular. I still worry about him. I seldom get through when I call in the evening, since he apparently is in the workshop with a radio turned up. I wonder every time I go out if I will find him still alive or not.

Wednesday, June 29, 2005

I arrived at Trester's yesterday to find an enormous

swarm of ants on the kitchen countertops. Trester had left out a small amount of uneaten corned beef hash and the ants had found it. They were also finding or looking for other tidbits, and as a result were all over the counters. I sprayed them with some all-purpose cleaner (which works just as well as ant spray) and then wiped the countertops off. I put out some ant bait traps near where the ants were entering the kitchen.

While Trester got up and got dressed, I unloaded the groceries. This week I got him mostly his usual food of bologna, ham, TV dinners, and ice cream, with the addition of some peaches instead of oranges, together with some pastry.

I inspected the area by the front door where the water leak had been repaired by the plumbers and it seemed to be drying out. The plumbers left the planter area dug up (too hard to do much with supersaturated clay mud, I guess) and a few pieces of water pipe left behind. When I had talked to Trester earlier in the week, he said, "They want to charge me a million dollars. Next time, don't have them fix it. Just leave it as it is." Whenever I suggest a repair, he always says, "I don't have any money. Don't do it." Trester said he signed the plumbing bill for $702. I'll see when it arrives, but that's probably an accurate number, because the repair took two days, the second with two men, apparently. The leak had doubled the water bill.

We decided on the Hometown Buffet for lunch (Trester forgot a couple of times that we agreed to go there and asked again and again where we were going), so we headed on over. I have a tin of Altoids on the console between the seats of the car, and when I turned a corner, the tin slid over to one side and made a slight clink. "Ouch," Trester said instantly. "I'm being shot at."

Before and during our drive, Trester brought up the

usual topics of driving through the gate to get to the "other Corona" where his family lives, of flying to Main Maui, either to live or for a vacation, and of going to Auto Zone in Riverside (as a means of leaving the area, apparently).

Lunch at the buffet went pretty well. When I asked him how his soup was, Trester said it was good. However, he was making faces and complaining about something in his mumbling way, so I could not understand what he was saying. I went back for another helping and when I returned, he said, "They klonked the deal or something." I asked if he heard clanking dishes, and he said, "It almost killed me." Then he began mumbling about his food and said something that sounded like, "This tasted like barf with pee in it." Not a very high compliment to the buffet. Those weren't his exact words, but that's what I got from whatever he said. Then he said, "That guy switched your plate," speaking of his own food. Then he asked, "Can we leave now? Let's go out through the window." He pointed toward the back of the buffet where the walls are mirrored and you can see the reflection of the windows in front (we were sitting at a window, in fact). I told him there was no rear exit.

We left through the usual exit at the front. In the car, Trester held his hands on each side of his head and said, "They hurt me with a klonker deal. My head hurts." I tried to inquire about the nature of the pain, but couldn't get a clear answer.

I asked him about buying cigarettes or going to a dollar store, and he gave the usual, "Nobody wants to sell to us." I gave a little speech saying that whoever is telling him that is lying because every one of the cigarette stores and dollar stores are eager to sell to him and welcome him as a customer. I don't think he was persuaded. In a few minutes he said, "Maybe we can get some cigarettes and fly home."

As we got on the freeway, a pickup truck cut off another car on the ramp and got a honk from the other car. Trester turned and waved and said, "Hello!" in a friendly way.

At the Smoke Shop I offered to go in and buy the cigarettes but Trester said he would, and he did. Then I offered to go into the dollar store for him (this after he said they didn't want him to shop there), and he agreed. So I went in and bought him some 4-by-6 cards (they were out of 3-by-5 cards), some notebooks, and two jar candles.

At home I noticed that the workshop had once again had what I think was laundry detergent and water poured on the floor, so I did some sweeping of cigarette butts and then mopped the workshop floor (it's concrete) with some pine cleaner. Trester always comes around to see what I'm doing, and when he did, he said, "That smells real good." I said I was mopping because he had said last week that there was a poison smell in the shop. He said, "They said 80% of the diseases in the world were in the shop." I used an unwrung mop and really slathered the pine cleaner all over the place. The mop water became so disgusting that I poured it out on the ground instead of down the drain and into the septic tank.

When I left, Trester again thanked me for taking him out to eat, so I guess the food wasn't as bad as his comment would otherwise seem to suggest. Except for his head hurting, he had fewer complaints of pain than he sometimes does.

Tuesday, July 5, 2005

Last night Trester called to see how I was doing. He

complained about the usual noises in the house that keep him from sleeping at night. At one point he said, "When I sprayed water on the driveway, it looked like it has blood in it."

I arrived this morning with his usual groceries, plus some cherries that are now in season. When I started to unload, I noticed another ten thousand ants on the kitchen counter tops. I guess my ant traps didn't work very well. (The manufacturer does recommend removing other food from the area, something I can't do during the week.) I hit them with kitchen cleaner and then wiped thousands of them up with warm, soapy water.

When Trester got up, he said, "Let's go to the IHOP to go up ten levels." I reminded him that last night he had said he wanted to go back to the Glen Ivy Spa. He said we should go there. We were getting ready to leave when Trester said, "I have the wrong person's belt on." I looked at it and discovered he had it wrong side out. I told him to remove it and replace it the right way. He took it out and then began to examine the printing on the inside (several lines of information about content, care, and the like). Finally, he replaced it, but was not satisfied. "Can't we get a belt that we own?" he asked. He hunted in several rooms for another belt. While he did, he complained that the belt he had on was not his. "Somebody switched it," he said. We eventually located another leather one in the laundry room.

"Here you are," I said.

"That's not mine, either," Trester said, after a cursory glance. I pointed to the fabric belt nearby. "No, that's somebody else's," he said.

Trester entered into a prolonged debate with himself about where to have lunch. He really wanted me to take him to the airport to fly to Maui, but after the usual "no ticket and no money" talk, he debated between the IHOP and the spa. Finally, he decided we should go to Glen Ivy. "This place [referring to his house] has been renamed to Glen Ivy," he said. I asked him what the other Glen Ivy was now called. "It's still the same, only in a different area," he answered.

While we drove out to the spa, Trester said, "We should have gone to the IHOP. I hope they don't leave some of us here." We got to the spa and noticed that the line to the small eating area was pretty long. Trester and I decided that the wait would be too long. As we left, one of the employees said it would be at least half an hour. So Trester said, "Let's go to the IHOP." It is in the opposite direction about 15 miles, but I agreed anyway. So we got back in the car and left. A few miles down the road, Trester said, "We should have eaten there anyway." and later, "We were told to wait there half an hour." I kept on going.

In a couple of more minutes, Trester began to complain: "They're grabbing me on the testicles." I asked if he had pain there and he said yes. "They're squeezing me."

Generally speaking, Trester was in more pain than usual and was hallucinating much more than usual. He got into one of his angry arguments with whoever was attacking him. Once he turned his head angrily toward the back of the car and yelled, "What's the deal here, anyway?" A little while later, he told me, "I'm getting zombied here through the floor of the car, just like in the house."

We finally got to the IHOP and went in. The outside double doors didn't fit well and they banged shut behind us. When we got through the inside doors, Trester said, "They're killing me with those doors." He repeated this after we sat down. Every bang or klank seems to be a bullet shot at him.

Lunch was uneventful. When I asked Trester how he liked his patty melt, he said, "It's real good." He ate almost all of his lunch. And he didn't throw up afterwards, either. He throws up after lunch much less now than he used to.

At the end of the meal, I asked, "So, did you go up ten levels?"

Trester said, "Yes, we should. Should I ask them?" Apparently he needed to ask someone to help him go up. But when I told him I didn't know what to do, he dropped the subject.

Since we were on the far end of town, I suggested we go to the dollar store at that end of town. Trester said, "We'll have to see if they let us shop there. The last store there didn't like us very much."

When we drove into the parking lot, I said, "I think this is a new store and they want you to shop here."

Trester is pretty on the ball when it comes to my fabrications, so he said, "We'll have to find out." Unfortunately, the store had that same bad music and those same weird pictures with silly sound effects right near the entrance. I thought sure we were doomed. But to my surprise, as we walked in, Trester asked the checker, "Is it okay to shop here?" The clerk was a native Chinese who didn't speak much English, so he didn't quite get the question.

After I made a few more tries, ("He wants to know if he is welcome to shop here" — didn't work, "Can he shop here?" seemed better), the checker smiled and nodded and said, "Yes." That was good enough for Trester.

Trester bought some cards for his headlines, some notebooks, and a plant. I found a pack of 30 AA batteries for a dollar (doesn't that seem cheap?) and got some dishwashing liquid and two bottles of all-purpose cleaner for

Trester's house.

As we drove from the dollar store, there began a debate about where to buy cigarettes. Trester at one point suggested the drive-through dairy, but I reminded him how expensive that place was. We were headed back toward one of his usual places, somewhat grudgingly, when Trester spotted a new place. We stopped there and he bought a few packs. When he came out, he said, "They switched them as we drove up."

Back at Trester's, I discovered that one of the bottles of cleaner had a defective cap and had leaked a quart of pine cleaner into my trunk. In the house, I discovered another ten thousand ants. Needless to say, the day didn't end on a particularly high note. I wiped up the ants and sprayed the spot where they were entering with some real ant spray (the kind that kills for six weeks) to keep them out, if possible.

I left almost an hour late because of our long drives around town. But Trester was happy and grateful.

Wednesday, July 13, 2005

I took a helper out to Trester's with me yesterday, to see if we could make a dent in the jungle that the grounds around the house have turned into. So we left early and arrived with groceries about 10:00. We unloaded quietly and then began the weeding. Trester slept through everything, even when I thoughtlessly banged a plastic flower pot against the wall to knock the dirt out of it. (He was sleeping just on the other side of the wall.)

At noon, I woke Trester and told him we would leave for lunch in about twenty or thirty minutes. He got up and got dressed. When we were ready to leave, he suggested we eat at Del Taco, a fast-food Mexican chain. We drove downtown. On the way, Trester made his usual requests to be taken to the airport, first to fly to Maui and then to fly to the "other Corona." My friend asked him how long he had lived in this house, and Trester said, "I'm not sure. Three or four years, I think." Then he added that he had lived in a house similar to it for many years, since 1960 (which is correct). Apparently he believes that he now lives in a kind of parallel universe, where the current house and town are not the same as "Yibi-Corona," the original place he lived for so long. (You may have had the sensation after coming home from a long vacation to feel that your own house seems strange and foreign, even though familiar. Imagine that to a stronger degree in a mentally ill person.)

I asked Trester how he slept the night before and he said pretty well, but he had trouble getting to sleep. He often complains of being awake most of the night and sleeping most of the day. I asked him how he felt, and he said, "Pretty good," then edited that to, "Okay, I guess." He said he didn't have any pains today, and he seemed to be in a better mood than he often is. He clearly felt much better than he did last week, when he has hallucinating quite a bit.

We ate at Del Taco and all three of us liked the food. I usually ask Trester how he likes what he's eating, and get varied results. This time he seemed quite pleased with his milkshake, burrito, and taco. While we were eating, he asked, "Can we wait here an hour? Someone might come from the other group and come get me." Earlier he had pointed out a Penske repair place and said, "Another Robert owns that name." So he thinks there are several of me and maybe another one will be more helpful in taking him to the airport. I'm sorry to have to disappoint him all the time.

After lunch, we drove to a dollar store, but Trester wouldn't go in, saying that they didn't want him to shop there. I told him to ask the checker (as he did at another store the previous week), but he wasn't interested. He asked me to get him some 3-by-5 cards and some mentholated rub. So I went in while he smoked a cigarette outside.

When we got back in the car, Trester said, "We should have waited at the restaurant."

I said, "I'll drive by it on the way home and you can see if anyone is waiting for you." He liked that idea. As we drove by, he looked intently at the restaurant and parking lot, but he didn't say anything.

At the Smoke Shop, he went in himself and got his cigarettes. On the way home, he again asked about flying to the other Corona, and when I brought up the ticket issue, he said, "It shouldn't cost too much to fly to the other Corona." Later he asked if I knew how to go through the gate and fly to the other Corona. I asked him how I could find that out for him, but he didn't know.

My helper and I worked on the weeding until we conked out about 4:00 and then had to head home. I was glad to see Trester feeling more perky and relatively content this time. He again thanked us for coming and when I pointed out the cleared patches, he said, "It looks much better." I was happy he approved, because sometimes he doesn't want any plants (that is, weeds and volunteer trees and palms) removed. I told him we might be back soon, and he said okay.

Tuesday, July 19, 2005

My weed-whacking friend and I went out to Trester's yesterday and wore ourselves out weeding. Our voices must have awakened Trester, because he came to the back door to see what was going on. After he saw us, he got dressed, but he stayed in the house most of the time. At noon we broke to have lunch at the nearby shopping center. I asked Trester if he wanted to go with us, but he said to bring him a hamburger and a malt. So we did. The areas we have cleared of overgrowth look enormously better. Trester hasn't said anything against our cutting out the palm trees and other volunteer plants.

Today I went out to take Trester his groceries and see him. I added some deli ham and some salami to his usual list. (Yesterday, we noticed he was out of bottled water, so we took him two cases.)

I was in the mood for Chinese food, so I suggested that to Trester and he liked the idea. I asked him which place he wanted to go to, and he named the place in a shopping center nearby, where the buffet is modest but inexpensive. On the way there, we passed some construction about half a mile from Trester's house, where workers were excavating a large pit and piling up the dirt. I remarked on the high dirt pile and Trester said, "That's a bomb crater. They've been dropping bombs all over the place."

As we neared the restaurant, Trester renewed his request to fly to another place or another city. He also mentioned "the island."

I asked, "What city are you talking about?"

He said, "Maybe the other Robert will help me fly there."

I asked, "Do you have another brother named Robert, too?"

He said, "Yes."

I asked, "Does he come to visit you also?"

Trester said, "Yes. He comes on Tuesday." I told him today was Tuesday.

He said, "I have to leave because I keep getting killed here."

At the restaurant we filled our plates and sat down to eat. Trester had ordered a Chinese beer with his lunch. After he drank a few sips, he indicated that he didn't like it. I asked him if the beer was not good. He said, "It tastes like skunk beer." While he continued eating, he said, "We should have gone to the other place." Then he added, "Next time let's get some different food." After a while, he said, "They're hurting my teeth." He kept eating and later reported that the pain had passed. When I asked him how his food was, he said it was okay. Just the beer was not good, apparently.

This restaurant has mirrored walls. Trester looked at one of the mirrors, reflecting the front windows. "Can we go through the window?" he asked. I'm not sure whom he was asking. I told him he was looking at a mirror. When we got up to leave, Trester turned toward the mirror, gave a little jump, and waved. Recall that he jumped in one of the stores once, trying to "go up half a level." He waited a moment but nothing happened. As we got near the door, he turned to one of the employees and asked, "Is there another way out?" They didn't understand the question. He then asked, "Can we go up the stairs and go out?" The fact that there were no stairs in this one-story restaurant, coupled with the fact that the employees appeared to be Chinese nationals with limited English, caused a communication gap. The employees just smiled. I told Trester there were no stairs and he told the employees, "Never mind," and we left.

Trester got some cigarettes and some 4-by-6 cards and hand lotion at one of the dollar stores and we went home. The fact that the temperature was in the high nineties encouraged us not to shop around too much. Summer is hot at Trester's.

At his house, I mopped and cleaned a few countertops. I noticed on one of the bedroom doors (his old bedroom that he no longer sleeps in) a sign written on a 3-by-5 card: "Warning! Don't use this bedroom. There is a killer disease in the walls that klonks people."

On the way home and at home, Trester hummed a little bit and seemed to be in reasonable spirits. He had a fresh supply of Kleenex, toilet paper, cigarettes, and Pepsi. Those are his comfort supplies. I also got him some pink lemonade. He waved goodbye as I left.

Thursday, July 28, 2005

Monday, the 25th, my weeder friend and I went to Trester's to attack yet another overgrown patch near the house. Just before we started, I went inside and discovered ants everywhere, much worse than even the horde before. Now I know why people use words like "trillion." They were carpeted across the counters and a four-inch wide stream ran from the kitchen out the back door. I hit them with surface cleaner. I left their bodies for later since we needed to get started. (Meanwhile, my helper unloaded a truck load of mulch.) I wiped the counters and mopped the floor before we left.

Tuesday, the 26th, I was greeted with about a quarter as many ants, so I quickly knocked them down before unloading the groceries. They especially seemed to like the cheese popcorn Trester had left. Trester has a tendency not to close bags when he is through eating, so the potato chips, corn chips, popcorn, and the like stand open to all comers and get stale if they aren't eaten by the ants. He also leaves lunch meat and cheese in the refrigerator lying open, where it gets dried out fairly quickly.

Trester was up by the time I unloaded the groceries. I brought him more toilet paper and some paper towels in addition to his regular fare. I asked him where he wanted to eat, and when he hesitated a moment, suggested the root beer place (the one he always rejects). He said, "Let's see. . . ." Then I suggested the Hometown Buffet and Mexican and Chinese to give him some choices. He considered a few moments and then said we should go to the pizza place at a nearby center.

We got in the car and Trester made his usual flying request, this time to fly to the "other Corona." I told him I didn't know how to do that. He asked of some other audience, "Can I leave? I can't take the war going on here."

As we continued down the road, he asked, "Where are we going? I forgot where I said I wanted to go." I told him the pizza place and he acknowledged it. He said he had slept okay, somewhat better than usual.

We ordered the buffet lunch at the pizza place, though when we lined up for the buffet, there was not a slice of pizza left, the salad was gone, and the whole line had been cleaned out. There was a small amount of lasagna left. Fortunately, more food soon arrived and we got some pretty good food.

After lunch, Trester seemed to be having some pain in his lower abdomen, as he seems to get occasionally. "They're squishing me in the gut," he said, pressing in the area of his bladder. "I have to go poop all the time." What I fear is that he has a tumor or worse. But I can't get him to a doctor.

I asked him about getting his cigarettes and he asked, "Where will they sell to us?" Then he said, "Let's go to the drive-through place." I reminded him that the drive through charged $78 for two cartons, which is quite high. I suggested the Smoke Shop, so we went there. Outside, Trester was uncertain about going in, so I told him I would go. We finally agreed to go in together. He used a couple of coupons and got two cartons for about $54 if I remember right. I pointed out to him how much cheaper that was than the drive through.

Trester next wanted some more cards to write headlines on, so we went across the parking lot and I went in to get some cards while he stood in the shade. (It's in the 90s now in Corona.) I should have mentioned that Trester's card collection numbers in the thousands now. He buys about 500 to 1000 each week and has done this for some time. So this week I brought him four boxes to store his cards. He has them organized by some method (I don't know exactly what), so he put some in one of the boxes before we left for lunch. The workbench in the workshop where he sits and smokes much of the time is covered with his headline cards, in some places a foot deep or more. I got him another 500 cards.

As we headed home, Trester said, "Could you take me to the Auto Zone? We're supposed to go there and go up three levels." I told him it was on the other side of town and we could go there next week. He said okay. Not long after we got home, he said again, "Can you take me down to the Auto Zone so I can go up ten levels? We're supposed to go there." I again told him I'd do that next week. A few minutes later I heard him ask his imaginary audience, rather roughly, "Who's keeping us here?"

I did some more work on the ant bodies and the new ants who had arrived to replace their fallen comrades. I also vacuumed the living room with the miracle vacuum and got another load of dust. I need to get one of those for myself. Trester was alert and as happy as he gets by the time I left. He waited on the breezeway as I drove around back and down the driveway, waving to me as I passed.

Tuesday, August 2, 2005

Trester called last night to see how I was doing. He sometimes calls to see if I am still alive, having gotten the idea that I've been injured or killed in whatever war is going on at his house. Last night he said, "I just called to see if you are all right. There is a huge attack going on here, with nuclear bombs all over. Two trillion guards are outside, in military trucks, blowing up the place."

I assured him that I was okay and working on my usual projects. He then said, "They said on the radio that the Auto Club has my car. Can we go down and get it?" I reminded him that I would be out today and that made him happy. I guess we are in for a trip to the Auto Club today. I did remind him that he needed a driver's license and insurance and he said, "Oh, I forgot about that."

I asked him if he needed any special groceries and he said, "Bring lots of Pepsi and some Coke, too. I'm about to die of thirst here." I asked him if he drank tap water, and he said he thought it was bad. So I told him I'd bring him some water and pink lemonade, too. He said the lemonade was "real good."

I asked a couple of other questions, but he was talking to his hallucinations. Soon he came back and said he had better go, so we hung up.

※ ※ ※

38.246 One of ours "killed" in huge Attack up north -- apparently – hope ok & Love you!
38.250 USA Headline: Buckly Elected President & Blow to pieces – chopped up by Big Tutles etc—"I vote for 210 frogs" Mr Big Tutle says!
38.256 Fam: 10 of our new little friends hurt too – hope ok! put back in house if cant leave! home if possible please!
38.257 World Disaster Headline: Billion Planes hit tall Buildings
38.261 Radio Tips Overlap! Kids we went to school with are horrable as adults!!!
38.262 Upcoming: Tons of Water Dirt & Snow Bombs too! Real World Disaster to Destroy the Place if they don't give up soon & quit!!!

※ ※ ※

Thursday, August 4, 2005

I took Trester extra beverages this week, since during his phone conversation Monday evening he had said he was "about to die of thirst." I brought him his usual Pepsi (though not two 24-packs as he had hinted), some pink lemonade, root beer, water, and Sunny Delight.

I asked Trester how he was doing and he said, "I've been worried about everyone. They're putting our kids in jail and killing some of us." He added that he had put ten dollars in a bowl to bail out one of his people or relatives.

When I asked him where he wanted to eat, instead of his usual deliberation and hesitation, he said, "Let's go to the Mad Greek." I asked if he had the pastrami combo lunch in mind and he said yes. So we headed down there and ordered the pastrami meal (sandwich, French fries, fried zucchini, fried onion rings, and a salad). During the meal, the busboys clattered a few plates and some silverware during cleanup and Trester looked in that direction with a pained expression. Later, in the car, he said, "They attacked me in the Mad Greek." After a while, he said, "They pulled half of us off our head."

Since we were near one of the dollar stores, I suggested going there. This store has the 3-by-5 cards he likes. Trester said, "They don't want us to shop there."

I said, "Yes they do. Remember last time you asked the clerk and he said you were welcome."

Trester said, "Oh yeah. I forgot." On the way to the store and even after we got out of the car, Trester raised the same objection, and each time I reminded him that the clerk had said he was welcome. He didn't appear to remember or else his voices were still telling him he wasn't welcome.

Inside Trester bought about 1000 cards, two or three jar candles, and some dishwashing detergent and some rubbing alcohol. As we were heading toward the checkout, he began to talk to someone in the air in a directive tone. I couldn't understand what he was saying, but it apparently had something to do with helping him go up a few levels. After our purchase, outside, he looked up into the air and made a few more comments, but again I couldn't make them out.

As he left, he wanted to check a former tobacco store again that had become a lottery outlet or something. We drove by and it was still the same. Trester had thought it had been converted back again. So we stopped by another tobacco store on the way to the freeway ramp and he got six packs of cigarettes (remarkable for being so few). I asked him why he didn't get a carton, and he said, "I got separate packs this time."

As I mentioned in an earlier post, Trester thought the Auto Club had his car for him. So he kept reminding me to go by there. That was our next stop. He pulled out his keys and was humming a little tune in happy anticipation. When we pulled into the parking lot, we saw that the office (a strip mall spot) was gone and "For Lease" signs were in place. This surprised me and no doubt Trester, too.

Back at his house, I took care of more ants. Trester has been battling them, too, for a change, since I noticed some cleanser and some dead bodies on the countertops. I used kitchen cleaner to kill a few thousand more and then wiped up both the living and the dead with warm soapy water.

Other than his complaint about being attacked at the restaurant, Trester didn't mention any physical pains this time, and he seemed to be maintaining as well as he does. Fortunately, the day was cooler. Earlier, he had told me, "It's been too warm here." He sometimes complains that the air conditioner does not work right, but he leaves all the windows open when he runs it, so it can't cool the house the way it should.

With his usual gratitude, Trester thanked me (for about the third time) for helping him and taking him to lunch. He was always generous when he was well. His main fault was a short temper. Now that he is ill, he still shows his humanity when he can overcome his brain chemistry.

Tuesday, August 9, 2005

I took Trester extra water and juice today on my grocery visit, because the weather has been mid-nineties every day there. Trester was already dressed but snoozing on the living room sofa when I arrived shortly after noon. I was delayed a bit by the need to stop at two hardware stores to get some parts for Trester's washing machine connection.

The ant traffic was moving smoothly on at least eight lanes across the kitchen countertops, so I put the brakes on with some household cleaner and later wiped up as many bodies as I could.

When I asked Trester where he would like to eat, he said Marie Callender's. So we headed down there. On the way down, he had one of those constant conversations with his friends (or whomever). I couldn't understand much of his talk, because he mumbles a lot, but two things I could make out were, "We ought to start our own political party, " and later, "They moved me to the wrong world again." This last comment soon began the usual requests for a ticket to fly to "the other country" and then to "Yibi-Corona," the other town just like the one he lives in except that it is far away and his relatives live there.

At the restaurant, just as we were seated, Trester asked the hostess, "Is this where the candidates are that I can meet?" She just smiled and left, apparently noting by his appearance that Trester is not normal. I asked him what he had asked her and he said that he was going to meet "the Republican candidates" and go live with them. It seems that he sometimes (often?) gets an idea into his head like this which determines where he wants to eat. It's not the food, but someone he's going to meet.

When the waitress came over to ask about drinks, Trester saw a picture of the "Ultimate Margarita" on the menu and pointed to it and ordered it. I asked for a lemonade. We both ordered turkey pot pies for lunch. His margarita came with a shot glass of some brownish liquid.

He started by sipping that down fairly quickly. I asked him if that was tequila or whisky. He said something I couldn't make out. When I asked him again later what it was, he said, "It's heroin." No doubt upper management at Marie Callender's would be interested in knowing that. There happened to be a drink menu on the table, so I took a peek and learned that the ultimate margarita comes with a shot glass of Grand Marnier.

While we waited for our incredibly too hot pot pies to cool (I burned my *finger* twice while stirring it), Trester asked, "Do you know where Marie lives? Did she move?" Marie, by the way, is not only in the restaurant name, but was our mother's name, too. I think he believes there is a connection.

After lunch, I asked Trester if he needed to do any shopping and he said he needed some underwear, so we went over to a nearby Mervyn's and he bought two pair. We then went to a Big Lots nearby (having seen it from the parking lot) and he bought a cloth decoration. Seeing a Radio Shack in the same strip mall, he said, "Let's go to Radio Shack so I can get another radio." He has half a dozen radios, but they (1) don't get "the right frequencies" and (2) often suffer calamitous events that render them inoperable. As we were about to enter the store, a couple came out and the doorbell chimed. Trester thought that was important and that we should not shop there. (We almost didn't get into Marie Callender's because there was music playing in a speaker right over the door and the singer's words made Trester think we were not welcome there. But I reassured him and we did make lunch.)

So we drove to the Smoke Shop for some cigarettes. On the way Trester again said, "Can you buy me a ticket to fly to the other world?" I told him I didn't know where that was or how he could fly there.

Back at his house, I changed the water valves and the fill hoses on the washer. I should explain that last week Trester started the washer when we left for lunch. When we got back an hour and a half or so later, the washer was still running. Filling the tub for wash and rinse was taking forever. My repair solved the problem and now the machine fills normally. There were mouse pellets under the washer, so I mopped those up before shoving the machine back in place.

I told Trester to keep cool as I left. (I had closed all the windows and turned the air conditioner on.) He waved goodbye as usual.

Tuesday, August 16, 2005

I called Trester last night to see if he needed anything special. He asked for a large package of toilet paper and some vanilla ice cream. He said, "A lot of toilet paper gets used around here." I asked him why that was. He said, "I don't know." He was, as usual, encumbered by his hallucinations. He said, "They're trying to drive us out of the house."

I asked, "Who is?"

He said, "They have attack guns and are shooting up the place."

I asked, "Who is 'they'?"

He said, "They have bombs going off outside, too. The whole place is wrecked. Maybe I can move to the mountains."

When I arrived today, Trester was still asleep, so I said hello and he awoke. I unloaded the groceries while he got dressed. The ants must not watch much TV at night because they seem to spend all their time making more ants.

The countertops were streaming with commuter traffic as usual, though perhaps a bit lighter than previously — especially lighter than the first couple of times. I sprayed pine cleaner on them and that pretty much rained on their parade.

I asked Trester where he wanted to eat and he said the mall in Riverside. I thought he wanted some of the grilled fish we get at one of the food court places. We got into the car and started out. As we headed down the street, I said, "You said you wanted to go to the mall, right?"

Trester said, "No, let's go to the Panda Bear." There is a strip mall Chinese takeout (or eat in) place just a couple of miles away, and that's where he wanted to go. As we pulled into the parking lot, Trester asked, "Where are you going?"

I told him, "The Panda Bear. That's where you said you wanted to go." He said okay.

The cashier recognized us and greeted us warmly and said she hadn't seen us in so long that she thought we had moved away. We each had the usual enormous amount of food (I had a one item combo and Trester had a two item so he could take part of it home for another meal).

After we finished, Trester told me to leave a dollar on the table, which I thought he meant for a tip. I put a dollar down and he put a quarter on top of it. After we left the restaurant, he said, "Let's wait outside here for a while to see if one of our brothers got bailed out."

We stood around a bit and I then said, "Do you want to go into the dollar store?" There is a dollar store next to the Chinese place.

At first Trester said he did but then said, "They don't want me to shop there." I told him I would go in for him, so he asked for some note cards, some "balm" (by which he means mentholated rub), and some notebooks. I also picked up some toilet bowl cleaner (active ingredient: hydrochloric acid) to see if I could make Trester's toilet bowls look a little less like a toxic hazard. When I got outside, Trester asked, "What happened to the guy who got out for a dollar?" Evidently the dollar on the table was bail money and not a tip.

On the way home, Trester kind of grunted and breathed with a bit of a groan, and then said, "Something is squishing me day and night."

Back at Trester's, I used the bowl cleaner on two of the toilets and it was really worth the dollar. It got off the rust and encrusted whatever and left the bowls looking quite nice. I had been using cleanser and other stuff to no avail. I also treated the new ants to another strafing run from the cleaner and fixed their wagons.

Outside I heard Trester say, "Can you help us? They shot the guy who got out at the store deal." He came in the house and gave me a dollar bill, saying that it was in repayment for the dollar at the restaurant.

I started to vacuum, but part of the dust holder got clogged with dust and I had to stop and take apart the holder and wash all the parts and the filters. That's one of the "features" of a bagless machine working on tobacco ashes all over the place.

As I left, I noticed a plate of rice on the breezeway, covered with ants. I pointed it out to Trester and told him that didn't help the ant problem in the kitchen. He said he would get rid of it. I once more admired the great job my weeder helper and I did on the front planter (cleaned it off and covered it with decorative bark). It looks tremendously better. Trester waved as usual and seemed to be cheerful.

Tuesday, August 23, 2005

In accord with my new schedule, I visited Trester on Saturday. I included some pink lemonade with his usual groceries.

He was dressed but lying on the sofa when I arrived. I noticed that his pants didn't have a belt and asked him about it. "I need to get a belt," he said. I asked him where the other belts were that he had. "Those weren't mine," he said. "They switched them for someone else's. It was some mob deal." Later, I noticed one of his belts in the trash.

"Did you throw all your belts away?" I asked.

"Yes," he said. "Where can I get one of my own?"

After a short uncertainty about where to eat, we settled on a Mexican restaurant near the house. Lunch was very good and relatively uneventful. The only distraction was that a busboy clattered some dishes behind Trester at one point and as a result Trester kept turning around every minute or so to see what was going on. Or perhaps who was shooting at him. After lunch Trester put a dollar at the back edge of the table and said, "This is for the bartender." I told him we didn't have a bartender since he had iced tea and I had water. I took the dollar bill and put it in the payment folder as part of the waitress' tip. As we got up, Trester (acting as if he was being surreptitious) put another dollar bill at the back edge of the table and then watched me to be sure I didn't take it.

The restaurant is in a shopping center, so after lunch we went to look for a belt. We started at Ross where we found a rack of belts. Calvin Klein, Perry Ellis, Ralph Lauren, Chaps. We found several the right length, but there was always an objection to buying any given one. "That's not our brand" was one. "They won't sell to us" was another. "We're not a Perry" was a third. So we went to the next store. As we walked, Trester said, "We need our own distribution place."

For some reason he wouldn't go into Kohl's and wouldn't say why. After we walked past Marshalls and I tried two or three times to coax him inside, he said, "That store is only for cops." He wanted to go to the next store, which was SportsMart. He asked, "Will they sell to anyone?" I said they would, but that it was a sporting goods store and probably wouldn't have belts. We were about to enter when Trester said, "Let's go home. I don't feel good." I asked him if he wanted to wait while I brought over the car, but then he said, "Let's go on in." So we went in and discovered there were no belts for sale. As we left, Trester saw Best Buy across the parking lot. "Is that a department store?" he asked. I said they sold TVs and stereos. "Let's go there. Would they have a twenty dollar radio?" I said they might.

We went into Best Buy and found a remarkably nice looking table radio for $15, but Trester didn't want to buy it. It must have been the wrong brand, since that seems to turn him off of products. It was some brand I had never heard of.

Two or three times when we got in the car, Trester complained that they had put a sticker in his testicles and he couldn't pull it out. He seemed to have some discomfort there.

As we were about to leave the shopping center, Trester said that we should wait because one of his kids got left behind. Then he said across the lot, "Don't hurt him." It was fairly hot that day, so we headed home and didn't do any other shopping. When we had been home a while, Trester said he would take the dollar ride down to the supermarket to get some cigarettes later on.

I did some mopping and a little ant cleanup and then

headed home.

Sunday, September 4, 2005

I visited Trester a week ago as usual. He was already up at 9:30 when I arrived with my weeding partner to work on the landscape. Trester said he was feeling better than usual and wasn't so tired. He also said he was not having the pain he often complains of.

We went to lunch at a Carl's Junior for a hamburger, mostly because my weeder and I were a bit too dirty to go to a regular restaurant. Trester had a hamburger, fries, and a vanilla malt (his favorite fast food beverage). He said his food was good.

We then drove over to the Smoke Shop where Trester got some cigarettes. When he got back in the car, I asked him if he wanted to go to the dollar store across the parking lot. He said no, and added that they didn't want to sell to him. As I was backing the car out to leave, he said, "Can we wait here a while? I think one of our kids is calling to me." I told him we needed to get back to weeding. As we drove across the parking lot, Trester said, "Do you want to go to the dollar store right here? Let's stop here." So we parked again. We were about to get out when Trester said they didn't want him to shop there, so I offered to shop for him. He said okay.

When I returned with his cards (that was all he wanted this time), he was standing outside with an unlit cigarette in his mouth, looking around. It occurred to me that his asking to shop at the store was a ploy to get me to stay in the lot so he could wait for the kid or kids he had imagined. Trester can actually be quite devious when it suits him.

We went home to more work. Trester sat in the workshop smoking and filling out cards. He came around to see what we were doing every ten or twenty minutes. He is definitely one to check up on what's going on.

Sunday, September 4, 2005

Trester was dressed but snoozing in the sofa when I arrived yesterday. He asked me where I wanted to eat, so I suggested the big Chinese buffet at the far end of town. He said that was a good idea. I decided to take the side roads because of the heavy freeway traffic this Labor Day weekend.

As we passed a large church, Trester said, "We were supposed to live there, but they turned it into a church."

As we drove down the road and reached a straight stretch where we could see some distance, Trester said, "Can you keep on going down that road until we get to the gates where we can drive through to the other Corona?" He added, "It looks like you can do that from here."

We turned on down the road toward the buffet and passed another church. Trester said again, "We were supposed to live there, but they turned it into an illegal church."

At the buffet, we had the usual feast, for a higher price than the weekday price. Trester said he liked his food when I asked him.

After lunch, as we walked back to the car, Trester said, "There's a spook deal pressing on my gut, making me have to throw up." He proceeded to throw up several times in several places. Then he appeared to feel better. In the past, a year or two ago, Trester used to throw up almost every time we went out to eat. This was the first time in a long time that he has done that.

After my usual "need tickets" response to his request to be taken to the airport, he said, "We've got to get somebody to help us."

Trester didn't want to stop at either of the dollar stores I mentioned, because he said they didn't want him to shop there. We went to a cigarette store near the buffet, but Trester soon came back empty handed. I asked him where his cigarettes were. He said, "They had a bonker deal that almost killed us." Then he added, "They only sell to Democrats." I later asked him for clarification and he said, "They had a sound bonker deal that went 'Bong, Bong, Bong' that almost killed us." I think he was referring to the doorbell.

As we drove toward another store, Trester said, "What should we do? They try to kill us everywhere we go. They don't want us to shop in the whole town, and now they have right wingers who try to kill you when you try to shop anywhere."

We got some cigarettes at another tobacco shop. Back in the car, Trester asked, "Do you know of a store where we can get some miner clothes?" Before I could answer or ask for clarification, Trester said, "Let's just go home. I have to go to the bathroom."

I was so tired from my new work schedule that I didn't get the cleaning done I had intended. I did spray the ants on the countertops three times and wipe them up. Trester had left a plate of melted ice cream and two or three rings of something sweet that the ants were attacking in huge numbers. It's hard to keep them under control when they are encouraged so well.

Sunday, September 11, 2005

I took Trester his groceries yesterday, including a 24-pack of water and some Gatorade so he can keep hydrated. I also included some pink lemonade.

I shot the ants with a 20 percent solution of pine cleaner (that works amazingly well) and we headed off for lunch. Trester wanted to eat at the South of the Border Mexican place we had tried a couple of weeks ago so that he could go to the nearby Target also. He said, "I need to go to the Target store. I need shirts." So we ate a filling lunch and headed to Target.

In the shirts department, I pointed out some of the short sleeve, collared shirts that he likes. He looked at the label, which was Cherokee, one of Target's house brands. "I'm not an Indian," Trester said, turning away from the rack. We found a different brand, but he was choosy about pattern or had some other objection, and he finally said, "Let's go look at pants." They had a great sale on Khaki pants (I ended up getting three pair for myself), but he didn't seem very interested. He said, "Let's go look at underwear." He went over to the undies department while I went to try on some pants. When I got back, he had nothing in hand, but said, "I need to leave now. They don't want me here." So he went outside to smoke while I finished my shopping.

When we got back in the car, Trester asked, "What do you do when your head blows away?" It was a little breezy outside, so the wind may have bothered him. He soon added, "They tore one of us off back there." And then, "They are hurting one of the kids who got separated."

I asked him if he wanted me to take him to a smoke shop and he said he did. He said, "I wonder where I can get some cigarettes." I suggested the shop we often go to, and he said okay.

Back home Trester helped me install four new fluorescent bulbs in the workshop where he spends so much time. One bulb was completely out and one fixture didn't light very reliably. After we installed the new bulbs, both fixtures worked perfectly. Trester made a little gleeful noise and said something about how good the lights were. So he was happy about the improvement.

I sprayed and wiped up ten or twenty thousand more ants and threw away some of their temptation. They had overwhelmed a sugar box, some Cheetos, an open honey bottle (which by now had a layer of drowned ants floating on top of the honey a quarter inch deep), and some other food, all in open containers. And these things were on the kitchen table. The countertop ants were eating at entirely different restaurants.

Trester was in good spirits when I left. He didn't throw up after lunch this week and said his stomach felt okay.

He said he has trouble getting to sleep but that once he does, he sleeps soundly. He didn't complain of any tooth or heart pains this week, either.

Sunday, September 18, 2005

When I arrived at Trester's house on Saturday, I noticed the garden hose running full blast down the breezeway steps. When I parked, I saw that the backdoor was open, so I knew Trester was already up. He came outside as I walked toward the door. I told him the hose was running and he said, "It is?" Then I asked him to turn it off. He acted as if he didn't know it was running, but in the past I know he has let the hose run for considerable lengths of time to wash the poison out of the water lines.

When I brought in the first load of groceries, I noticed that there were virtually no ants this week, only about half a dozen scouts wandering around. I was quite surprised. Maybe my previous work set them back a bit.

When I asked Trester where he wanted to eat, he asked if we could drive to the other Corona, which he now said is 300 miles away up by a lake. I told him I didn't know of another town like that.

I suggested we have a pastrami sandwich at the Mad Greek downtown because Trester had said he needed to shop and that place is near one of the dollar stores. He said okay. As we walked toward the door, Trester had two quarters in his hand. He said, "Let me get some other quarters. These just showed up under the deal, and I don't know if they were messages or if somebody needed help or not."

As we drove toward the restaurant, Trester said, "Will you take me to get my Lexus car? They have one waiting for me." Last week and a few times previously, he had said, "They had a Lexus car waiting for me, but I couldn't get to it. Then they tried to deliver it, but they blew it up."

A bit later he said, "I need some moisturizer for my body. I'm drying up."

I asked, "Do you have some lotion?"

Trester said, "Yeah, but they switched it for poison."

When we were nearly there, he acted as if his stomach hurt. I asked him if he felt okay and he said, "They stuck a sticker in me." I asked if he were nauseated, but he said no.

We had a very good pastrami sandwich, with fried zucchini and onion rings and French fries. I asked Trester how he liked his food and he said it was "real good." When we got in the car, Trester said, "They're hitting me in the head."

I asked him if he wanted to go home, but he said to go to the dollar store. (I had reminded him that the clerk at this store had said he could shop there.) We drove over and Trester bought some candles, some mentholated rub (which he calls "balm") and 1500 3-by-5 cards. He also got some aftershave (which for a non-shaving bearded guy might seem odd, but he seldom uses products for their intended function). He also got some rubbing alcohol, which he later put on his head instead of taking aspirin for his head pains.

When we left the store, he asked me to wait five minutes. Then he asked, "Can I get out and smoke one cigarette?" and I said okay.

I asked him where he wanted to go to get cigarettes and he said, "The store with the Spanish lady." I didn't know which store that was but we finally clarified it and I took him to the Smoke Shop he often patronizes.

At home I mopped the kitchen area. Even though my sense of smell is very poor, there seemed to be a bad smell in the kitchen. I hope the mopping with pine cleaner took care of it. I also sprayed a few weeds.

Trester thanked me as usual when I told him goodbye.

Monday, September 26, 2005

I took my weeding friend to Trester's Saturday, so we arrived with the groceries earlier than I usually do. Trester was already up, though, and greeted us. As I unloaded the groceries, I was relieved to see that the ants were gone, at least temporarily. My friend and I worked in the front, chopping down small tree shoots that had volunteered and turned the front area into a brushy mess.

At noon, we three went out for a hamburger and fries (the two of us being not presentable enough for a real restaurant). The shake machine at the fast food place was broken, so Trester had a slurpee. He liked it.

Unfortunately, Trester complained of tooth pain several times, saying that someone had stabbed him in the teeth. He held his hand to his face much of the time we were in the car.

After lunch, Trester said, "Let's go to the Target store. I need some pants." We had been there last week, I think, but I said okay.

Trester pointed to the left, which was the opposite direction, so I asked, "Do you want to go to the Target near your house?"

He said, "No, go to the one in the next town. I want to go there so I can bounce up ten levels and get to the other Corona." When we got to the store, Trester looked around outside for a few moments, then walked inside and stopped by the shopping carts. He looked up at the security monitor two or three times, for a minute or so each time. Eventually, we walked toward the men's department a little ways, but soon Trester said, "Let's go home."

On the way home, Trester said, "Can you get me a ticket to fly to the other Corona? I tried to get there at Target, but it didn't work."

At one point, Trester mentioned that he has been walking to the mailbox (about a quarter of a mile away — it's a rural area), so he is getting a little physical activity. We said goodbye. This time he wasn't in the breezeway to wave.

Sunday, October 2, 2005

I went to see Trester as usual yesterday, this time without my weeding helper. I got the usual groceries, plus TP and paper towels. Trester didn't have a suggestion for lunch, so I mentioned the big Chinese buffet on the far side of town. He agreed.

In the kitchen I noticed the two blankets from his bed on the floor. I asked him what they were doing there. He said, "They have little stickers in them. Maybe I should get rid of them." I suggested he wash them.

On the way to lunch, I tried to have a conversation, which is what I usually do. It went like this:

"How have you been sleeping this week?"

"I sleep pretty soundly. But they keep attacking me with zombie deals."

"See that haze? That's smoke from some brush fires."

"They're killing people and throwing them out of airplanes."

Once again, as we drove down the street, Trester said, "I'm supposed to go through a gate to the other Corona. Can you take me?" I asked him how and where, but he didn't say anything.

I asked him how his teeth were doing, and he said they were better, though one still had a sore spot. (His mouth would give a dentist a stroke. I wish I could get him to get some help with what's left of his teeth.)

Just before we got to the buffet, Trester said, "They hit me in the head. They attack me everywhere I go." I asked him if his head hurt now, and he said no.

We had the usual great lunch (it's fancier on Saturday than it was on Tuesdays) and when I asked Trester how his lunch was, he said it was very good. He went back for some soft serve ice cream. And I was again grateful that he didn't throw up this time.

We drove to the dollar store nearest the buffet. They were out of 3-by-5 cards, so Trester got some 4-by-6 cards, some candles, notebooks, and some aftershave (since he doesn't shave, it must have some other value to him). As we drove out of the parking lot, he said, "Let's go back to the buffet and wait a while. One of our kids may be waiting for us." Then he said, "Never mind."

So I asked, "Do you want me to stop?"

He said no. Then he added, "They hit me in the head at the buffet."

We stopped at a smoke shop on a street near the freeway (where he has shopped once or twice before). He got out of the car, walked to the door, hesitated, came back almost all the way to the car, stopped and stood, as if contemplating or listening, then finally went in and bought some cigarettes.

As we drove, he said, "I need all kinds of things. A wristwatch, a ring, and a new car." I looked over and noticed that he wasn't wearing his watch or the ring he used to wear. I should have asked him what happened to them. I'll try to remember to ask next time. I asked him if he wanted to go to Wal-Mart to get a watch and at first he said yes, but later said, "Let's just go to Circuit City. They're supposed to have a $49 radio for me." He is on an endless quest to get a radio that "gets the right frequencies." None of his current radios do. Then he said, "Let's just go home. I don't have enough money left. I need more spending money." (I'm trying to keep his smoking down a bit by limiting his spending money.)

I did a little weeding on my own. As I left, Trester said, "Thanks for helping and have a nice trip home."

Saturday, October 8, 2005

Trester was already up when I arrived with his groceries today. I unloaded the groceries and sprayed some ants, which were back in the low thousands. At least they weren't quite as bad as before.

Trester told me, "I need some new clothes." I saw two or three shirts and asked about a fairly new looking yellow one. He said he didn't know about that one. I found another that was practically ripped to shreds, so I told him he couldn't wear it and tossed it in the trash. He said, "I don't have any pants." I found what looked like pants in a two-foot pile of laundry on the floor. They turned out to be shorts with a broken zipper. I tossed them in the trash, too. I found a pair of over-washed cords and before I could say anything, he said, "I can't wear those." I asked what happened to all the pants I bought him. He said, "I don't know." I asked about any other pants, and he led me into the living room. There were two pair on the sofa.

"What about these?" I asked, holding up a pair.

"Those are banker's pants," Trester said. "And besides, the button is missing." The fastening button at the top of the zipper was gone. Then I asked about the other pants. "I can't wear those or Fred will attack me." I asked him if he had any jeans. "The LAPD [Los Angeles Police Department] won't let me wear denim. There was a warning on the radio." I told Trester we would find him some new pants.

I asked where he wanted to go to lunch and he said, "Let's go to Del Taco." So we drove downtown. On the way, Trester held his hand on his heart and complained of constant pain. I asked him if he had taken any aspirin and he said no. At Del Taco we ate some tacos and burritos. He had a vanilla shake, which he particularly likes.

I asked Trester where he wanted to go next, and he said, "Let's go to the electronics store near the house. They have a radio." So we drove over to Best Buy. We got out of the car, but right at the door, Trester said, "They don't want me to shop here." He wouldn't listen to my insistence that he was welcome to shop anywhere. So we went over to Ross to look for pants.

I found some Haggar pants in his size, but Trester said, "Those pants are for various families, with family names on them. We need to find some for our group. What is our group?" He didn't like any of the brand names. He said, "Let's go to the sports store and get some sports pants." So we went to SportsMart. He looked around for about five minutes but didn't find anything he liked. He said, "I just want some normal pants." Outside the store, he said, "Let's go to Jumpy's store." Then he jumped up and down a couple of times and waited for something to happen.

Back in the car, Trester said, "I just want some normal, old man pants. They cost five or ten dollars each." A little further down the road he said, "Can you help me find the kids they pulled off my head back there?" Later, he said, "I can't shop anywhere. There are ten stores in town that won't let me shop there." I gave him a little speech about never having seen him rejected by any merchant and that he was welcome anywhere. I doubt it had any effect.

We went to the cigarette store. Before he got out of the car he said, "They don't want me to shop here, either." But then he got out and said, "Maybe I'll go find out why." He came back with his cigarettes and a few cigars. I asked him if he needed anything at the dollar store across the parking lot, and he said he needed some rubbing alcohol and some headline cards. But he wanted me to shop for him. So I went in while he stood near the car and smoked a cigar. When I got back to the car, Trester said, "They're shooting people out here."

On the way back to the house, we picked up Trester's mail, which was all junk mail. When we got inside, Trester looked at the "Have you seen us?" missing persons card that came with a mailer. He looked for two or three minutes. Then he said, "She worked for the Reagan administration," referring to the woman in the photo on the card.

To my dismay, the ants had found the powdered sugar donuts I had just bought. The donuts were on the kitchen table to keep them safe from the countertop ants, but my simple expedient didn't work.

The blankets from his bedroom were still piled in the corner on the floor of the kitchen, so I asked Trester, "What are you going to do with these blankets? Are you going to wash them or throw them away?"

He said, "I don't know. They looked like they had pieces of people in them."

I mopped the kitchen and wiped up the ants. As I was walking out the back door, I noticed a 3-by-5 card taped to it that said, "Warning: Do not shop at the center down below. Stater attacked us real bad then."

When I left, I asked Trester if he wanted me to get him some pants, and he said okay. He said, "Get 41s. These are too tight." He wears a 38 right now. I told him I'd see what I could find.

We waved to each other as I drove down the driveway.

Monday, October 17, 2005

I visited Trester Saturday as usual and took him some groceries and a 24 pack of TP, which as I have said, he uses up quickly. I also took him two pair of pants just like the ones I got for myself a week or so earlier, in a size 40 as he had asked. He tried on a pair and to my surprise they fit well and he liked them. He wore them to lunch.

We ate at a Mexican restaurant downtown. No buffet on weekends, but the menu order was very good. Trester, however, didn't like his food. He said it was "not very good." Back at the car, he gagged some and spit up a bit. I asked him if he was okay and he said, "There's a ghost stuck on my throat."

As we drove to the smoke shop, he mentioned wanting to fly away on Aloha Airlines, to go to the other Corona or an island. I didn't comment. At the smoke shop I noticed that generic cigarettes were ten dollars a carton cheaper than the ones he usually buys. I pointed this out and asked him if he wanted to try them. I asked if they would be okay. He said cigarettes were all about the same. So as he got out of the car I reminded him to try the generics. He got back to the car in a couple of minutes. I asked him if he had bought the generics and he said no, he forgot. I reminded him that he could save ten dollars a carton and he said, "Maybe I'll just give up smoking." I told him that was a great idea.

Back home he brought me a piece of junk mail that said "Urgent Letter" and the like on it. It was an ad for a car dealership. Trester said, "There's an urgent letter waiting for me at the post office. We were supposed to go down and get it." I told him it was not a notice of a letter but an ad. He was not convinced. He pointed to some print on the back that said something like "time sensitive" or some of the other usual advertising baloney. I showed him the pictures of cars inside but he was his usual stubborn self.

As I cleaned up a bit, I found a dead mouse in the kitchen. Very few ants this week. I vacuumed the living room and Trester's bedroom and the family room.

Trester was not complaining of pain this week, so he must have been feeling somewhat better. He did mention that he had been throwing up some, though.

This week he mumbled quite a bit, so I didn't catch much of what he said.

Sunday, October 30, 2005

Trester was sound asleep on the sofa when I arrived. The back door was unlocked and he was dressed, so he had been up, but I had some challenge awakening him. I let him sleep while I unloaded the groceries and did a bit of cleaning in the kitchen, but eventually I woke him by running the garbage disposer. (He hadn't awakened when I repeated his name loudly several times.) As I cleaned up the sink, I washed his rice cooker bowl and noticed that it was quite dented. It's a thick aluminum, so it must have been hit pretty hard against something. I also noticed that Trester still had the "Urgent Letter" (a car ad) on the kitchen table, evidently still believing it was a claim for a letter at the post office.

I suggested a pastrami sandwich for lunch and Trester agreed, so we started off. Down the road, he asked me, "Do you know when the war will be over so we can leave?" It's a question he has asked many times in the past. I told him I didn't know. (A few days ago, he called and said, "I need to fly to another world, but they keep blowing up the house by throwing bombs.")

He also asked me, "What do you do when your heart hurts all the time?" I asked him if he had been taking aspirin, and he said no. I asked if he wanted me to take him to a doctor for a checkup, but got no response.

We ate our sandwich at the restaurant and Trester then

used the restroom. When he returned, he said, "When I came out the door of the bathroom, it felt like half of us floated up and away." Later in the car, he said, "They tore off half our head back there."

We went to one of the dollar stores, where Trester bought rubbing alcohol, 1,000 3-by-5 cards, some hand lotion, some cleanser, laundry detergent, dish washing liquid, mentholated rub, and some Scotch tape. After he put in each item or two, he said, "That's all I need. Let's go."

After we left the store and headed for the smoke shop, he said, "Do you know where there's a Jumpy store? They're supposed to be all around." I said I didn't. Those are apparently stores owned by his group so that it's okay for him to shop there. If only they really existed. He continues to complain that "they" don't want him to shop at pretty much any store I name or that we visit.

Trester vomited a little bit after lunch ("Ghosts are choking me") but seemed to feel pretty well and was almost cheerful by the time I left.

Monday, November 14, 2005

When I arrived at Trester's this week, I noticed that he had put out a plate of left over corned beef hash for "the critters" to eat. The ants had found it, near the back door. Last week he had left a plate with popcorn on it and a plate containing some rice and meat on the floor of the kitchen. I saw a mouse scamper from near the plates down the hall, so Trester is definitely feeding the wild animals. I made a note to get some mouse bait.

I unloaded the groceries and then asked Trester where he wanted to eat. He suggested a Mexican restaurant where we've been a few times. But then he began looking over his shirts and said, "They switched my shirt." Later he added, "They keep stealing my shirts." He reluctantly put on a blue one, after asking, "Do I have another yellow shirt?" He seemed to be indicating that he couldn't eat at the restaurant in a changed shirt, so I suggested that we go for Chinese. He said, "Okay, but I'll have to change shirts." I'm not sure if he needs to wear a particular shirt or color of shirt to eat at a certain type of restaurant, but I thought he might be indicating that.

We soon went down to a Chinese takeout and had a nice lunch. I usually ask Trester how he likes his food and today he said it was "real good."

The rest of the day's events are the same as usual. When we left the restaurant, Trester said he had been hit on the head inside. When we went to the dollar store, he picked up a few items and then said, "That's all. They don't want us here. Let's leave now." Then he wondered who would sell him cigarettes, and we ended up at the usual smoke shop.

Back at his house, I mopped the kitchen floor and did a bit of dusting (I had to soak the dust rags before they were clean enough to put in the washing machine, if that gives you an idea). Poor Trester. He used to take care of his plant collection, growing cactus from seeds and carefully repotting succulents and other plants. He never did get the hang of housekeeping, though. Fortunately, he does laundry frequently, but he just doesn't vacuum, mop, or dust. But he doesn't feel well, either. If I were being attacked by ghosts every waking minute, I doubt I'd do any dusting, either.

He waved goodbye as I left.

Sunday, November 27, 2005

Last week when I visited Trester, he still had the car advertisement that said, "Urgent Letter" on it and was still saying that it meant he had an important letter at the post office. However, he had written on one side, "Warning! Kill at Post Office. Don't Get murdered." I told him that he would be arrested if he presented that at the post office, because they would interpret it as a threat. He said it was a warning to him that they wanted to kill him at the post office. At any rate, we didn't go.

This week, he still had the letter and was insistent that we go to the post office. I told him about the message again, so he scribbled it out and wrote, "Be careful." He also scribbled out a message on the other side, but I couldn't read it. Trester's handwriting is getting nearly illegible in places and at times.

I asked him where he wanted to eat and he named a local coffee shop. Then he said, "They don't want us. Let's go to the Mexican place down here." He meant a restaurant we have been to a few times. So we went. The food was good, though Trester added a pricey Margarita to the bill. After lunch, he threw up a little bit, claiming that ghosts were choking him. "They came up from under the ground there and choked me," he said, pointing to the planter outside the restaurant.

He still wanted to go to the post office, so we went. There must have been a long line, for it took a while. I noticed that Trester was limping and walking like an old man who ought to have a cane. When he returned I asked, "Did they tell you it was a car ad?"

He said, "I don't know. They took it and didn't give me anything."

At the cigarette store, Trester hesitated to go in. He

would start in and then stop and look around. Then start again, then stop. After four or five times, he finally went in and bought his cigarettes. Back outside, he looked down the sidewalk as if he saw someone. He walked down the sidewalk about fifty feet and waved in that direction, then came back.

We went to a drugstore so he could get some bandages for a sore finger and he also bought a copy of the Spanish paper he buys occasionally. (Again, he doesn't read Spanish.)

Back at his house, I fixed a leaky toilet with some parts that turned out to be a poor solution. I also gave Trester another box to put his headline cards in, and I gave him a new wristwatch, since he had said he wanted one. He liked it and wore it all day.

Saturday, December 10, 2005

Trester called Thursday and said, "Hi, this is Auy." He must have written his new name on something (maybe his old checking account) because I have seen junk mail at his house addressed to Auy Axils Poll. But I digress. Trester called to tell me that he might be moving. "We're supposed to move to the other house in town," he said. I asked him where it was and he was rather vague. I asked him who told him he was supposed to move to another house, and he said, "Platty told me." Platty is his stuffed animal platypus, who sits on an armchair and is covered with a sports jersey. He also has five or ten dollars in dollar bills next to him.

Trester asked, "Do you know what level we're at? Or how to get to the group level where everyone else is?" I told him I didn't know the answer to either question. He then said, "They popped me a couple of times and the other half comes off like a spook." At the end of the call, he said, "I'll call you if we move to the other house."

Today I went to see Trester and take him some groceries. I took him some extra goodies, such as a jar of peanut-butter-filled pretzels, and guessed pretty well what he was low on. Sometimes he eats most of his TV dinners and sometimes he eats only a few. It's difficult to know what to get, but today I guessed well.

We decided on the big Chinese buffet on the west end of town. As we drove, Trester said, "When I go to bed at night, half of me gets up and walks out the window. Do you know how I can stop that?" Then he added, "It's real. It's not a delusion."

I might have mentioned earlier that Trester has an unaccredited PhD in psychology, and he has studied mental illness and is aware of it. On the way home from lunch, he was mumbling something about "they're making everybody psychotic." He knows what psychosis and delusions are, but he won't ascribe them to himself—unless he says something like, "They're hitting me in the head and making me psychotic."

We had a great lunch. Trester was very pleased with his. We stopped at a dollar store where he got five packs of 250 3-by-5 cards, some rubbing alcohol, hand lotion, spray cleaner, soap, detergent, note pads and a few other items, about 20 in all. He got some cigarettes at one of the usual places.

On the way home, Trester said, "We're going to have a rare plant business and have plants like miniature palm trees." I asked where he was going to get these plants. He said, "We're going to make them out of different plant materials."

A bit later, he asked, "Is this Sand Cake [or Sandkik] Island?" I told him I didn't think we were on an island. He said, "I have an idea. They need a commercial supply house with 3200 items."

Near home, he said, "Maybe a doctor could put all our brothers together and we could see them again. They're keeping them apart."

Back at the house I mopped the kitchen. I swept up more insulation from the dishwasher that the mouse or mice had torn off. I noticed that Trester had thrown away the mouse bait I bought. He has said more than once, "Don't hurt the little critters."

When I left, Trester was quite emphatic in his thanks, saying something like, "Thank you very much for helping me." He seemed closer to rationality today than he sometimes is. He said he didn't sleep well, but otherwise didn't complain of pain.

※ ※ ※

45.15 People News: Phony Mr Magoo died again — are millions of Rockefeller ones pouring money to everyone for their side of war — "not our family —"

45.16 Magoo Cartoons: Are stealing real one's cartoons on law claim & used them already — long term perhaps —

45.17 Brothers Arrival!!! Our 2 brothers arrived over here — 8 billion miles from correct Island — but near us Love and hope are ok —

45.18 Headline: World Wide Swipe [?] British Spys occupy almost all the Hotels and Rentals of the world today (Now) etc. — real problem here —

45.19 Headlines: Today (Tonight here) British Killers here too — war declared on Briton again —

45.20 Land moves Headlines: England moved over

here near Australia —

※ ※ ※

The rain limited itself to mostly mist when I drove out to visit Trester on Saturday. I got the usual groceries for him and added some Goldfish crackers and cinnamon rolls and red licorice candy just to vary his enjoyment. I also "got a clue" and bought him a carton of cigarettes so we wouldn't have the usual debate and driving issues about where to get them.

Trester was still asleep when I arrived, but soon got up and dressed while I unloaded the groceries. When I asked how he was doing, he said he had some pain in his heart. I once again recommended that he take some aspirin and he said he might do it after lunch.

He suggested the big Chinese buffet on the west end of town, so we headed that way. On the way, he shifted uncomfortably in the seat and said, "Ow" several times. Then he said, "What do you do when a ghost is stabbing you in the back?" Then he added, "They're stabbing me in the heart and the back. Oh, dear." I asked him if he took aspirin when he had pain and he said no. I asked him if he wanted me to get him some, and he said he had just found his bottle at home. He seems unwilling to get any kind of medical or pharmaceutical help. Once when I asked him how he felt during the week, he said, "Yesterday I wasn't feeling well, so I drank some extra Pepsi."

We arrived at the buffet and enjoyed a good lunch. When I asked Trester how his food was, he said it was very good. After lunch he debated which dollar store to go to and finally determined on the one on Main Street. We drove over, but when we arrived, Trester wanted me to go in and shop for him while he stood outside and smoked. So I went in and got his list: 3-by-5 cards, birdseed, band aids, laundry detergent, and some cheese.

Trester next wanted to go to Best Buy. I reminded him that the last time we went there he wouldn't go in and asked if he would go in this time if we went there. He said, "Oh, yes." So we drove over. We went inside and he looked for a radio "that gets local frequencies." The table radio they had before was gone and only a few boom boxes were available now. So he didn't buy anything.

On the way to Best Buy he saw a store called Beach Bum and thought they "might have something for me." He chuckled as if the idea were comical. We stopped on the way home and he walked to the store but soon came back and said they wouldn't let him shop there.

Back home, I cleaned off the kitchen table and washed it. (Believe me, it was way past due.) I noticed a sign (written on a 3-by-5 card) taped to his old bedroom door, "Warning: Don't use bedroom here. Killer device in wall klonks people." There was also a new sign on the back door (in addition to the one warning about not shopping in the shopping center nearby) that said, "Don't get mail anymore. It's too dangerous."

I also noticed evidence that Trester has been burning pine needles in a couple of brass pots in the house. When I stopped by last week to give him some groceries, there was a sort of smokiness in the house that must have been from such burning.

When I was ready to leave, on a whim I asked, "Would you like me to store your headline cards at home?" and Trester said okay. He helped me load ten or eleven boxes of cards into the car. My tentative plan now is to transcribe some of these cards so that you can see how and what Trester is thinking.

※ ※ ※

45.21 Tons of Lunitics Invade our Islands & riot Kill peoplle & take over the Rentals & houses too —

45.22 Is Daytime now on Island & real nice — -

45.23 Headlines: Another Bill of Attainder passed — we Broke relations with England — again — (?)

45.24 Headlines tonight: More Rioting than we can stand over here! Zillions of people go way down South to Ireland test [?] 2 — tonight

45.25 Another Car bomb on Bob's car — just now — hope ok — [this may explain why Trester calls me sometimes to see if I got home safely]

45.26 Other's Ideas: Horse [?] to guard the newspapers against take over that could cause problems like this riot & attack!!!

45.27 Inglewood Headline: Adoby House Kids Shot up again this evening over here — [Trester lived in Inglewood in an adobe house as a child]

45.28 Local Headlines: Everybody on Island Killed each other again just now — -10 million shot by Police & Island cleaned off 10 times so far — today & yesterday many [?]!

45.29 Island Headlines: Police shoot off whole Island 10 times today — Ton of Invaders, many take over Rentals — taken out! Lunitic attackers won't end for some reason —

45.30 Ideas Earlier: Get $10.00 boxes of Records & round ones from our group as Gifts —

45.31 Nuked target [?]: All — — - [?] — — — [?] blew up all the White Houses & Killed all the USA Presidents & other Leaders of the wor[l]d & bragged about it —

45.32 Other Countries & USA Blew up All the — —-[?] — —-[?] in Retaliation

45.33 Headline: Tonight [?]: 8am where occurred harm Kissinger family & — —-[?] Assinate Nixon — in main area

USA— Car runs one of kids over here—

45.34 Headline: Tonight: Spys go up north of here & Krokes world—blow up just now—

45.35 Headlines: $89.00 for Assembly Candidate this time. Unconstitutional [?] law—only Assemblymen [?] were murdered [?] or jailed over it—GOP quit country over there as majority party too— [Trester ran for a state assembly seat in the 70's before he became ill]

45.36 Headlines: Attack went too far! Both Networks pay Trillion & half dollar fines (ea) for attack on — —-[?] & Jimbo [?]

45.37 Sales Ideas seeds herbs & — —-[?] etc: Specialty natural & local flavors for foods here! Make sauces and seeds on Steaks, Stews Tacos & most of the local foods—

45.38 $14.95 / day for Drink rep & or smokes too— Cigs Idea too—

45.39 1000 Products Trillion gals per day type for a superior store! Top grade products all over the world—

45.40 Headlines: Today: — —-[?] shoot everybody in other valley district today over —[?] —-

N N N

Last week when I visited Trester, he asked me, "Do you know where our group's store is so we can shop there?" He said none of the stores in town would let him shop there, but he could at the one his group owned.

This week, he asked the same question, so I asked him if he knew the name of the store. He said no. Later in the car, he asked again, "Do you know how to get to our group's store?" I asked, "Do you know its name?" and he said no. I asked, "If you don't know its name, how will you know when you see it?" He said he didn't know.

I asked him how he was feeling and he said, "Okay, I guess." Then after a pause, "Actually, I'm half sick." He said he hadn't been sleeping well but that he slept till 3 p.m. the day before.

I asked where he wanted to go to lunch and he said the Sizzler in Norco (even though there is one in Corona, too). So we drove over and ate there. On the way home, Trester said, "Let's drive up this street and see if we can find our group's store. It's a general supply store." We drove up the street and Trester said, "Turn in here." We drove into a strip mall and looked at all the stores but didn't find his group's. Then he said to drive the other way down the street, where we drove into another strip mall and looked in vain for his store. He seemed frustrated, saying to himself, "I don't know where it is."

We headed down another street where Trester saw a gas station. "Do you need gas?" he asked. "You could pull in there and I could get some cigarettes." I pulled into the mini mart section of the station and waited as Trester went inside. After enough time for him to buy some cigarettes had passed, Trester returned, but empty handed. "I couldn't get in," he said. "They're attacking me all over the place. Let's go to the one-dollar store."

We went to one of the dollar stores in town. When we walked up to the entrance, Trester suddenly said, "They won't let me in here." I reminded him that he had specifically asked to come to this store. He just said, "Get me some bird seed, some cheese, and some black ballpoint pens." So I went in for him while he stayed outside and smoked.

After the dollar store, Trester wanted to buy his cigarettes at the drive though dairy (in spite of my frequent reminders that they are much more expensive there). So we went there and he got a carton.

On the way home, he suddenly said, somewhat angrily, "They grab you and murder you as you drive along. What should I do? I don't know."

When we got home, Trester complained that they had switched his cigarettes not long after he bought them.

I cleaned up his living room coffee table, scraping off the ashes and candle wax and tossing out some trash. Last week I cleaned the furnace filter to be sure he was ready for the winter heating. The heater was working well, in spite of the fact that Trester leaves several windows partly open.

It was starting to rain when I left.

※ ※ ※

45.42 News Headlines & followup—"Baja Riot Shot Dead!"

45.43 Another head klomped off one of ours over here—need to stop them!

45.44 Ideas: Cook or Salad— Food House & Neighborhood 40,000 to a million plant vines [?] etc of one main food for us & Critter groups, birds Etc to grow— like vege meat or special liquored [?] dope "squash" on vines etc—

45.45 City Headlines: Machinegun attack on City Restaurant—tonight—eve—

45.46 City Headlines: 3 of Customers Shot at Pizza hut—hope ok [crossed out:] "Mad Greek did it"

45.47 Gift and Food Ideas: Get a string of gifts like vine fruits & tomatoes for one at a time gifts for new kids— String of veges too from family or group ok too. Pick ours out later!

45.48 City Headlines: Buckler [?] car bomb at library, blow one of our older kids — —-[?] — —-[?] up—

45.49 Airport Headlines: Murdered at Airport Again just now — protested —

45.50 Law Headlines: Russians Hanged for stealling another Bosses Airplane — Stole 10,200 of them — from — — -[?] 10 & family & group here!

45.51 New Plane Purchase: 1800 were crashed & burned —-

45.52 Island Headlines: Absolute prohibited entry died off — Island no go! Ton of people (one critter) went there —

45.53 Security Prob Headlines: 2 Million Airplanes were swiped by the Ex kings [?] (of — —-[?]) failure [?] & Russian Leaders all over world — half ruined in flyin to buildings crashes etc —

45.54 Info Lines: Headlines & Facts: 800 Trillion people die of black text [?] on voodue stunt on people — like "Harry Potter" things — — & "Blair Witch Project" —-in City etc —- is going too far —

45.55 Secret Ideas: Spleno popper around house needed! for Instant results —-

45.56 Put Ideas: Atheist out flower rather than red popy agent [?] — — —-[?]

45.57 Put Ideas: Luciferites [?] out Island — like a powder garden — fun — —-[?] from trees & plants & grasses any sin [?] get 'em double!

45.58 Put Ideas: Poppy & Plant for "Tudalls" [?] & male prostitutes & eye poker outers etc — Pee in Booze too!

45.59 Ideas: Family Protect Plants around house (have already) adopt the house & famile etc —

45.60 Put Protests: One of people had eyes put out & fed to someone here — said was one of ours on Radio — ask for Instructions [?] & help for him —

※ ※ ※

I went to visit Trester yesterday. He was asleep when I arrived but soon got up as I unloaded the groceries. I picked up his telephone bill to take it home and pay it as I usually do. I got him some vanilla ice cream for a change (from his usual Rocky Road), some grapes, and some frozen corn dogs as a change from his other frozen food. I also got his usual TV dinners, burritos, lunch meat, and so on. I also got him a carton of his favorite cigarettes (once again, to preclude running all over town to find a suitable cigarette store). He was opening the carton to get a cigarette, so I asked him if those were the ones he wanted. "They switched them," he said, in a tone of mild disgust. However, he proceeded to smoke.

I asked him where he wanted to eat today and he said, "Let's go downtown to the taco stand so that afterwards we can drive down Main Street and find our store." So we drove to the taco place. We each had a burrito and a taco. Trester ordered a vanilla shake, as he often does. When I asked him how his food was, he said, "I don't know. They switched it." I tried to ask who switched what, or whether he didn't get what he had ordered, but couldn't get anywhere. Finally, he said, "It's okay, I guess."

After lunch, Trester wanted to drive down Main Street to find his store, so we did. After a couple of blocks, he said, "Turn right here onto Main Street." I told him we were already on Main Street. He wanted me to turn right anyway, so we did. In a couple of blocks, he said, "Turn in here. This is it." We pulled into a small parking lot in front of a cigarette store (that I hadn't seen before). Trester went in. In five minutes he returned with a pack of cigarettes. "This isn't the right store," he said. So we drove out of the lot and continued down the street. In half a block, he said, "There it is." We stopped in front of a tiny little independent income tax service store. The sign said, "Closed."

Trester said, "They're being attacked so much, they can't even stay open." Then he said, "Let's just go to the dollar store down the street."

As we headed toward the dollar store, Trester said, "Let's go down this other street and see if our store is there."

I told him that I thought he had said that the other place was his store. Then I asked, "Was that your store or not?"

And he said, "I don't know."

We soon arrived at the dollar store, where Trester bought some headline cards, some underwear, some bar soap, and some toothbrushes (ten for a dollar).

On the way home, Trester kept looking out the back window every few minutes. I couldn't quite understand his mumbling, but I think he was having his usual idea that part of himself or one of his kids was being left behind.

Back home, I installed the new garbage disposal without very much trouble. I noticed that Trester's pink rocking chair was in the shop, so I asked him why. "They don't want me to sit in it anymore," he said. "So I had to put it out here."

There was a new note taped on the back door (joining the warnings about not getting the mail and not shopping at the local center near his house). This warning was written in red ink: "Be careful! Guru attack out behind shop at nut tree. Avoid place. Please. Love, Auy."

I showed Trester the new disposer and he tried it out and said it was good. Then I headed on home.

Saturday, January 28, 2006

As I was buying groceries for Trester today, I reflected on the fact that his grocery bills are higher than mine. It turns out that he throws out some food and lets other food spoil. When I arrived today, I discovered an unopened half gallon of cran-raspberry juice in the trash. I also noticed that the ten or so cans of Wolfgang Puck soup — the ones that had moved from the kitchen to the workshop — were now gone. Evidently he threw them away, too.

In the house, I noticed that Trester still had most of the corn dogs I got him last time. I asked him if he liked them. "They have goop on them," he said. I asked him if he wasn't going to eat the rest. "They're the wrong brand or something," he said. Then he offered them to me.

When I asked Trester where he wanted to eat, he named the Tyler Galleria mall in Riverside. Then he said we shouldn't eat in Riverside. Then he said we should go there anyway. As we drove, he told me to go to Norco, a nearer city, and eat at a steakhouse. Just as I was about to turn off, he said we should go to Riverside. He wanted to go to the Galleria to have his picture "put on a mat," by which he meant a mouse pad. As I've noted earlier, he has six or eight of those already. We did end up at that mall, and had some nice mahi mahi at the food court.

After lunch, we looked for the photo kiosk, but it wasn't there anymore. Instead, Trester bought a candle holder and a ceramic artichoke at a store. He later said they had klonked him while he was inside.

When I asked how he was feeling, he said he slept better than usual and that his heart still bothered him occasionally, but that it was better than before. I made my usual suggestion about medical attention and got the usual answers: "No," and, "I'm all right."

I was happy to note that Trester was not hallucinating as much as he sometimes does. He did stop walking and look back a few times, but he was not "under attack" as is sometimes the case.

Sunday, February 05, 2006

I took Trester his groceries Saturday, mostly the usual items, just adding some turkey lunch meat and some different soups to give a little variety.

As we drove toward lunch, Trester squirmed a bit. I asked if he felt okay. "There's a big round thing in me," he said.

I said, "It could be a tumor. Do you want me to make an appointment for you to get checked?"

He said, "No."

We ate at the Mexican restaurant we've been to a few times. Trester had a coupon, so we got a little discount. He ordered a Margarita and a fairly large plate of food: a taco, Chile relleno, two enchiladas, rice, beans, and I think one other item. He ate about half of it. Later, in the car, I overheard him in conversation with his imaginary audience, saying, "Sorry, I ordered the wrong food or some deal."

After lunch, we walked over to a store to browse around, but Trester didn't want to go in. He said, "Let's go find Gordon's smoke shop in town." Before Trester became too ill to work, he bought a small tobacco shop in Anaheim, called Gordon's. Now he seems to think it exists where he lives in Corona. Before we left for lunch, he called directory assistance to get the phone number, but of course, there was no such store. Two or three more times as we drove around, he mentioned wanting to find it.

As we walked from the store back to the car, a truck

with that deep pounding bass and rap music drove by. Trester waved at it and said, "Yes."

We got in the car and I asked where he wanted to go. He said, "Let's go home." We started home and then he said, "Let's go shop at the one-dollar store on Main Street." So we started that way. Then he said, "Let's go home." When we got near the turnoff to his street, he said, "Do you want to shop at the one-dollar store? Let's go there." So we drove down town to the dollar store. About two blocks before we got there, Trester said, "I forgot. They don't want me to shop there."

I said, "We've driven this far, so let's go there anyway." There may have been a bit of exasperation in my voice. So we parked. Trester hesitated at the door, but I told him to go in, and this time he did.

I went in to get him a couple of toilet brushes while he looked at some plants. He had said he wanted bird seed. When I got outside, he was already there with his purchases. I asked him if he had gotten bird seed and he said no. "I couldn't find it," he told me. So I went back in and got him a bag of bird seed.

As we left the parking lot, Trester asked me to drive down one of the main streets to look for his group's store. "I think it may be called Joy," he said. We drove slowly down the part of the street he named, but soon he said, "Go on home. It's not there."

Back home, as I was cleaning up a bathroom sink, I saw a sign (on a 4-by-6 card) taped near the switch to the thermal light. It said, "Warning! Don't use hot lights. Dangerous." That's at least the fourth or fifth warning sign in the house, now.

When I took the mop back to the workshop to hang up, I happened to notice some cans of the tropical fruit drink I had bought him last week for a change of pace. "How did you like the tropical raspberry drink I got last time?" I asked, just as I picked up a can and noticed that it was still unopened.

He said, "It was poisoned. It almost killed us. I had to throw it away." It appeared that most of the 12-pack was in the trash, unopened.

He once more asked me to help him get an airline ticket to the other Corona, saying they cost only $80. I told him I'd never heard of another Corona. He said okay.

He asked for another disposable camera, so I told him I'd get one for next time.

Saturday, February 25, 2006

On this visit, Trester wanted to find his group's store again. Once again he thought it was on Main Street. We drove downtown and parked at a spot along the street while he got out of the car and walked along the shops. The place we stopped was one of the old parts of downtown, and most of the shops were closed. Trester tried the door knob on one of them and then came back to the car. "It's not there," he said.

As we drove on down the street toward our lunch, Trester said (to his imaginary audience), "Hang the lady that did that." Then after a few moments, he said, "Get an attorney and sue them, then."

Next, Trester wanted to buy a radio, since the four or five radios he has don't get his group's frequencies. He said, "Let's go to Pep Boys and get a radio." I told him that Pep Boys sold auto parts, but he wanted to go there anyway. We stopped, he got out, almost made it inside the door, but came back with the usual story that "they don't want me to shop there." We had the same experience stopping by a shoe store where Trester wanted to get a new belt.

At the house, Trester had a 3-by-5 card on the kitchen table that said, "Home to Molokai or Maui Island." That was apparently his "to do" list.

This week on the way to lunch, Trester said, "See if you can get 201 on the radio." I told him that my radio probably didn't go down that far. I dialed the AM band down to 530 to show him. He said he needed to buy a radio that got 201.

I asked Trester where he wanted to eat lunch, and after two or three changes of mind ("they might leave us stranded if we go there"), he named Del Taco, a Mexican fast food place downtown. He also wanted to go by certain back roads and not go the shortest way (on the freeway).

When we got to lunch, Trester stopped before we went in and looked around with anticipation as if expecting someone. In one direction he turned, he spoke to one of his imaginary audiences, but I couldn't hear what he said.

After lunch we went to a small dollar store. After being inside less than a minute, Trester said, "I'll walk out the door and they'll put us in Jumpy's." He left while I looked around. In a couple of minutes I saw him again inside the store, holding some candles, laundry detergent, and fabric softener. After we checked out, he wanted to go to another dollar store to get some headline cards, so we did. He wanted the 4-by-6 cards this time, so he bought four or five packs of those and some "balm" — meaning mentholated petroleum jelly.

At the house, Trester had almost torn off one of the kitchen cabinet doors (a large one about 2 by 3 feet), so I had to finish removing it so it wouldn't fall on his head. He had taped it closed. The top hinge was torn off. His explanation was that someone was attacking him. I couldn't get a clearer story than that.

I saw the live-in mouse again. Trester is still leaving stuff out to feed it.

I cleaned up the counter tops this week. He still had four or five cans of corned beef hash and half a dozen cans of chili. I asked him if he had stopped eating corned beef hash for breakfast, and he said no. After a few more questions, it turns out that he doesn't like Hormel (corned beef hash or chili) but other brands are okay. So I have inherited a bunch of food. Seems that I'll be eating a lot of chili for a while. It's probably not the taste he doesn't like. He most likely has some delusion about Hormel being "the wrong brand" or not his group's brand or something.

Trester asked me if I knew whether someone had given him a checking account with money in it and a credit card. I told him I didn't.

After mopping up some spilled soda and miscellaneous dirt, I left for my next task. Trester was grateful as usual.

Monday, March 6, 2006

When I arrived at Trester's on Saturday, I was happy to note that everything seemed normal. Trester had called a few days earlier to say that the power was off. I called the electric company and reported it, but over the next couple of days couldn't get through to Trester by phone. Finally, he answered and said the power was back on. The most he lost was some ice cream, I think.

As I was unloading the groceries, I noticed a mouse scampering across the kitchen table. It disappeared but I didn't see it land on the floor, so I went over to investigate. I saw it hiding in a bag of pretzels. I grabbed the neck of the bag so the mouse couldn't escape and took it out to the workshop. Fortunately, Trester was not up and dressed yet, so he didn't see me catch the mouse or dispatch it in the shop. Otherwise, he would not let me hurt it. (He'd probably want me to let it go.) After all, he leaves food out for "the little critters," and throws away the mouse poison I buy. The mouse had nibbled on every one of the remaining chocolate mini donuts on the table (about a dozen, I'd say). I tossed out an open bag of chips from the table too.

When I said good morning to Trester while he was still in bed, I took a moment to count his mouse pad photos. He has eleven mouse pads, each with his photo on it, nailed to the wall of his bedroom. He also has an 8 by 10 regular photo there.

When I asked Trester where he wanted to eat, he said "Stone Canyon" and showed me a map. "It's right down the road," he said. I looked at the map and explained that it was actually more than 20 miles away. Then he said, "I need to buy a radio that gets the right frequencies." I pointed to a radio nearby and asked about that one. "It just gets stations far away. I want local frequencies."

As we drove out to eat, he mentioned that he had to walk home from downtown (by which he meant a shopping center about three miles away). Apparently, he gets around during the week. Considering his poor physical health, that's remarkable.

We ended up at a Mexican restaurant that also serves barbecue. We each ordered a barbecued pork sandwich. Trester ordered a beer, too. When the food came, Trester handled and looked at his sandwich with dissatisfaction. I said, "It looks good, huh?" and he said, "I got an icky one." I offered him mine. He refused. Finally, he started eating his and soon seemed to relish it. Later on when I asked him how his food was, he said it was good.

As we were walking back to the car, someone honked at someone else. Trester looked around and said, "Go that way. Someone's honking for me." He said we should walk over and listen to the music (there was a small band at the other end of the lot). I think it was a ruse to get him where he thought his friends were, because as soon as we got near the band he wanted to go home. When we got home, he said, "We should have stayed there. They were calling for me."

I may have mentioned that last week at the dollar store, one of the things Trester bought was a bottle of Snuggles fabric softener liquid. At the time he was buying it, I mentioned that it was fabric softener (since he doesn't normally use it). I asked if he was going to use fabric softener and he said yes. Well, when I mopped his bathroom this visit, I saw the empty bottle near the bathtub. It makes me think he used it in his bath water. In the past he has put some unusual things in his water, including hand lotion and after-shampoo conditioner.

When I asked Trester how he was feeling, he said he felt tired (as he inevitably reports) but that he was feeling better than before, with fewer and less intense pains.

As usual, Trester thanked me for coming, for lunch, and for helping him.

Sunday, March 12, 2006

I took Trester his usual groceries Saturday, adding some juice boxes to provide a bit of variety. When I put a bag of cheese popcorn on the kitchen table, I noticed about a third of a banana had been eaten by some "critter." There must be more mice around. I also noticed a bowl of water by the back door, likely a water bowl for the critters.

Trester had some difficulty deciding where to eat this time. He first suggested one place, then another, then back to the first, then to a third, and so on. Sometimes he would name a place and then in a few moments say, "They really don't want me there." Then he would say, "We really should go out and find Stone Canyon, near here." Finally, he mentioned a place I'd never heard of, so we drove downtown to see where it was. I was mildly surprised to find out that the place actually existed—a little Chinese takeout almost next to one of the dollar stores we have visited often. We ate there (it was quite acceptable) and then went to the dollar store.

At the store, Trester bought some cologne, some headline cards (about 1500 I think), shampoo, candles, and five photo albums for the pictures he keeps taking around the house. He also bought a box of band aids.

On the way back home, Trester wanted to look for the Omni store again, along the same street as before. We drove down it slowly while he looked. Then he asked me to drive down another street so he could see if his "Palm Tree Nursery" was there. It wasn't.

We then drove to Target, where he bought two T-shirts and a disposable camera. He wanted to get some underwear, but said Hanes wouldn't sell to him. I pointed out Fruit of the Loom and the store brand, Merona. He seemed almost ready to buy the Merona, but decided not to. So he bought the other items and a magazine. The T-shirts were yellow ones, in keeping with his preferred shirt color.

Not surprisingly, back in the car, Trester said, "They klonked me back there and tore one of us off." Then he said, "Should I wait by the store and smoke a cigarette and maybe they'll put us back together?" He shook his right hand in a trembly motion (which he sometimes does when uncertain about what to do) and said, "I don't know what to do."

We headed home, where Trester took a couple of pictures of me and had me take several pictures of him, standing and sitting in various places.

During our day, Trester complained of pain in his testicles, and when I asked him if they were enlarged, said yes. I tried three times during the day to get him to agree to medical attention, but each time he said, "I'll be okay," "Maybe I'll be all right," or, the first time, "It's a ghost deal sticking me." A large source of my anxiety is knowing that he has several things wrong with him physically, but I can't get him to see a doctor.

Tonight Trester called me breathlessly to ask if I was all right. I said, "Hi, Trester."

He said, "This is Auy." Then he said, "My name is Tyby now." When I asked him why his name keeps changing, he said, "We're all getting our new names." He said he just called to see if I was okay. I told him I was fine. He said there was a huge war going on and that the whole place was being blown up by bombs. I told him I didn't hear any bombs going off here. After a few minutes, he calmed down some and repeated that he just wanted to find out how I was.

I continue to pray for Trester.

Saturday, March 18, 2006

I woke Trester up when I arrived today, and he got up while I unloaded the groceries. When he was getting dressed, he picked up one of his shirts and asked someone other than me, "Should I wear this shirt?" He put on a yellow shirt. Then he took it off and put on a blue one. Then he took it off and put on the yellow one again. Then he took it off and put on the blue one again. Then he asked the same person or persons, "Do you want me to wear the yellow shirt?" Soon he took off the blue shirt and put on the yellow one again.

Trester asked about going up to the mountains. "That's pretty far away," I told him. Then he said, "Do you know where I can get a checkbook with some money in it like I had before? I guess I spent it too fast. And I need to get a car. Then I can drive there myself."

We ate at the big Chinese buffet where we've been several times. It was great, as usual. Afterwards, Trester wanted to go to Sears to buy a radio "that gets channel 201." So we headed that way. On the way he asked, "Do you know where the killers and attackers are coming from?" I said I didn't.

Trester saw a mini-mart and asked me to pull into the parking lot. "Is that one of our stores?" he asked. When we pulled in, he said, "Not today." So we headed on to Sears, where once inside, he said "They don't want us here. We have to leave." So we did.

We went to one of the dollar stores where Trester got some birdseed, candles, mentholatum, band aids, and coffee cups.

When I asked about his health, he said his heart was feeling better but that his legs hurt sometimes. He said they felt okay now, though.

I noticed that he had some cigarettes on the coffee table. I said, "I see you have some cigarettes left over." He said, "I bought those myself at the gas station." So, he does get out and get some exercise.

He seemed cheerful by the time I left.

Sunday, April 9, 2006

Last week, I went to see Trester as usual. After I unloaded the groceries, he said, "Where can we shop where I can get some T-shirts? I need some new ones." I asked him where the two T-shirts were that he got the week before. "I had to throw them out," he said. "There was a complaint. They didn't want us to buy them."

We went to a small Chinese takeout place for lunch. Afterwards, we shopped at a nearby dollar store. As we drove home, Trester said, "They klonked me back there in the store." Then he added, "They tore one of us off back there. Maybe we should wait for him. Maybe he needs a ride."

When we got home, the phone rang and Trester listened for a minute or two, and then said, "Thanks for calling." He turned to me and said, "There's one of us at the Savings and Loan. Can we go down and get him?"

This week, I realized that Trester is making me into a philosopher. The wisdom of the week is, "It is difficult to obtain what does not exist." He still wants to buy a radio that gets 210 or 201 on the dial. The second bit of wisdom is, "It is difficult to find what exists only in one's imagination." Trester still wants to find the Omni store, also called the Jumpy store. I keep telling him to get the address so we can go to it.

As we drove to lunch this week, Trester said, "See the Penske truck? That's one of our brothers. There's a whole bunch of them, and they're all truck drivers.

As we passed a gas station, we heard some tires squealing. Trester turned his head around and said, "They had someone calling for us back at the Shell station. Can we go back after lunch and see if they need us?" A few blocks down the road, he added, "They're under the Shell station in a crypt deal."

After lunch at a regular buffet, Trester wanted to go to Home Depot to get a magazine. He decided against the one near where we ate, so we drove to another across town. Just as we were about to get out of the car, Trester took two quarters out of his pocket and said, "Do you want to trade some regular quarters for some government message quarters?" I said okay, so he gave me two of the commemorative states quarters in exchange for two of the older eagle quarters.

I went into the store while Trester drank a soft drink before entering. I came out with my purchase (fertilizer) and found Trester by the car. "Did you get a magazine?" I asked.

"They didn't want me to shop in the store. I heard the announcement over the loudspeaker system." So, he didn't get a magazine.

I sprayed some weeds that were coming up in the driveway. Trester thanked me for coming and I left.

Saturday, April 15, 2006

When I arrived at Trester's today, he was already up and dressed, and he opened the door for me. I brought in the groceries and noticed that I had to walk around some large artificial flowers in a tall vase on the floor (standing a total of perhaps four feet high). "I rearranged the furniture," Trester said. As I looked around, I noticed that he had moved his bed into the family room where a small sofa had been. The sofa was to one side and the table that had been near the back door was now across the room. "I wanted to sleep in the light," he explained. "I want more light when I sleep so the ghosts won't attack me in the dark." The family room has quite a bit more light than his bedroom, and at night the porch light shines into it also.

When I asked Trester how he slept, he said much better. The new sleeping room must be working, because he said he had slept very well and felt rested, too. He usually says he feels exhausted, "like an old man" all the time. (He did say that moving all the furniture was almost too much for him. He had to take the bed apart and move it piece by piece.) When I asked if he had any pain today, he said he felt pretty good.

The TV was moved from the family room into the living room, where there is no antenna connection. Trester had an FM radio antenna hooked to the TV.

I brought Trester two new yellow shirts. He asked me, "Should I put one of these on?" and I told him it was up to him. Then he said, "I'll wash them first." He asked, "Is this Sunday?"

And I said, "No, it's Saturday."

Then he said, "Okay, I'll do the laundry then." And he started the dryer. (He won't do laundry on Sundays or days he thinks are Sundays. In a former entry, I think I mentioned that he believed there were several Sundays in a row at one time, keeping him from doing any laundry.)

I noticed that one of the family room windows had a large crack in it. Trester said he didn't know how it got cracked. I made a note to call the glass company on Monday.

Two or three times when I asked Trester a question, he asked me to repeat it and said, "I'm half deaf. They put out a deal here that made everybody half deaf."

We ate lunch at a small Chinese takeout place and then visited a dollar store, where Trester got his usual supply of headline cards (3-by-5), candles, laundry detergent, dish washing liquid, and some other items.

Back at his house, I took the opportunity to vacuum the bedroom that was now without the bed and side table (the table is now in the living room, replacing a side table that is now in the family room). Both vacuums choked. I cleaned up the bagless vacuum, but will have to take apart the other one later (I noticed a bunch of lint coming out of one side). I mopped a bit as usual and then said goodbye.

Saturday, June 17, 2006

Since the last entry, I've continued to visit Trester each week. His preoccupations remain largely the same. He still wants (nearly every week) to buy a radio that gets "the 210 band" but we can't find one that does. He still wants to find the Omni store and Jumpy's store, but doesn't know where they are.

Two weeks ago, Trester said, "Let's go to the farmer's market and take the old highway instead of the freeway and see if there's one of us dead lying along the road." For some reason, he changed his mind and we ended up downtown at an Islands restaurant. As we were about to walk in, he said, "They don't want us here." I told him they did. Then, just before our order arrived, he said, "They don't want us here. Shall I leave?" I told him no and our food arrived. As we later left, Trester turned around outside the front door and said, "Where's the sign that they don't want us here?" He seemed to point to the blue handicapped accessible sign in the window.

Last week, Trester still wanted to take the old highway to look for the body of "one of us" so we drove out to Tom's Farms, the farmer's market. He looked over the road carefully in some spots and ignored other parts. When we arrived at the restaurant he picked out, he said,

"They don't want us here." Then, to my surprise, he added, "Let's go in anyway." That is a first.

Last week also I noticed on the kitchen table two athletic shirt and short sets in the toddler size 2T. I asked Trester about them and he said he bought them at the sporting goods store in the nearby shopping center. They are for his kids that he might adopt, he said.

Last week further, Trester said that he needed to borrow money from one of his stuffed animals in order to buy something. Each of his stuffed animals (teddy bear, panda, platypus, etc.) has a couple of dollar bills nearby and sometimes a five or ten. This week as we left the house for lunch, Trester said, "I owe the panda bear twenty dollars." I asked him what his stuffed animals do with money. He said, "I don't know. They spend it."

Today my recurrent suggestion about going to the A&W root beer place finally paid off. If you recall, in the past every time I would suggest that place, Trester said no because "they took away my car." Today he seemed to think it was under new ownership. It's half a fish place, so he enjoyed some shrimp.

We went to a dollar store and Trester got some jar candles and headline cards. We drove to Walmart and he got some magazines and a disposable camera (but no radio that gets the 210 band).

I left after I mopped the kitchen. Trester seemed to be feeling better and was in pretty good spirits.

Sunday, June 25, 2006

I visited Trester as usual this week, taking him his groceries. He complained of hurting all over, especially in his back. I was unsuccessful in getting him to take any aspirin and he shrugged off the doctor suggestion as usual.

We had lunch at the little Mexican place on the old road — the place you'd drive on by if you didn't know how good it was. Then we went to Target to get Trester some shirts and underwear. Unfortunately, none of the shirt brands were the correct ones and then Trester decided that he wasn't wanted in the store, so we left empty handed. Trester asked, "Do you know where Jumpy and Jarry's store is?" I told him I didn't. He thought it was on Main Street, so we drove downtown and looked on Main Street. "This is the wrong area," he said. "We should have taken the back road instead of the freeway." Apparently, he thinks we arrive in different towns depending on the route we take.

On the way home, Trester said, "How do you get the spooks off of you or some deal? Go away!"

After looking in a strip mall for Jumpy and Jarry's store, Trester said we should go to a one-dollar store, so we did. He bought detergent and candles. He later said he forgot to get birdseed and headline cards.

Last week we went to Walmart where Trester bought a disposable camera. We had gone there for shirts but none of them were the right brand. And then, "They don't want us to shop here." So he went outside to smoke while I finished my shopping. There was a man giving out free copies of the *LA Times* and offering subscriptions outside.

Well, this week in his mail there was a bill from the LA Times addressed to Tibby Saldikik. Since Trester has told me his name is now Tyby, and since he has mentioned Sandkik Island, it wasn't hard to conclude that he had somehow subscribed. I asked him if he had subscribed and he said no. I asked if he was getting the paper and he said "Someone has been delivering it." After a few more questions, he said, "Maybe one of the others subscribed."

I mopped and pulled a couple of weeds. When he was well, Trester had been quite the gardener, but all he does now is spray the driveway with the hose. He no longer trims anything.

As I left, he waved.

Monday, July 3, 2006

It was close to 100 degrees when I got to Trester's on Saturday, but he still had not turned on the air conditioner. He had a box fan going in the living room. The house itself felt cooler than outside.

As I unloaded his groceries, Trester asked, "Can we go shop at Mike's store?" I asked him where it was and he said it was in the shopping center nearby. So I said okay.

After some of his usual questions ("Do you know where Stone Canyon is?" "Can I fly to the other Corona?" "Can I get a cheap car so I can drive?") and some preliminary indecision about where to eat, we ended up at a strip mall Chinese takeout place near one of the dollar stores. We ate and then shopped at the store. Trester got some headline cards, Epsom salts, body powder, and rubbing alcohol.

Just after we got back into the car, Trester pulled out a dollar and said, "I'll be right back." He walked back to the store. When he came back, I asked, "What did you do with the dollar?" He said, "It's right here. I was going to give it to them for pulling one of us out."

He again asked to go find Mike's store so he could buy a radio that gets 210. As we drove back toward home a leaf hit the rear side window. "Someone just got klonked on the window," Trester said, turning around and looking hard in that direction. He turned back and looked two or three more times.

On the way home, we detoured down another street to look for "our group's store" but didn't find it. Back home, Trester went to the workshop to sit (where it was rather hot) instead of in the house where I had turned on the air conditioning. He asked me, "Do you have two fives for a ten?" I looked and I did, so we traded.

I asked, "What are you going to do with the two fives?"

He said, "I don't know. I just wanted two fives." I'm sure he has something in mind, such as giving the money to his stuffed animals or putting it in one of the brass bowls, but he often won't tell what he's thinking.

Trester seldom tosses out the magazines he buys. I've mentioned before the shelves crammed with magazines. He still has a *National Enquirer* (from around 1997) with the headline, "Cops Shred Ramsey Alibi," and another (from around 2002) that says, "Laci Peterson's Final Minutes," so you can see what I'm saying.

Trester was still in quite a bit of back pain this week. I encouraged him (two or three times) to take some aspirin and he said he might. The offer to take him to a doctor was again rebuffed with, "I'll be okay."

He seemed to be in relatively good spirits when I left. We waved as usual.

※ ※ ※

45.61 L.A. – – –[?] etc So Cal Headlines: Killers of Imperor surrounded & shot & Killed etc— "Willy Ken hanged for it..."

45.62 Hold 3 days. City & Fam Headlines: New Cops are back in city again—gunman shoots car & cop too from "green" along road—& off freeway too—

45.63 Our —-[?] Pond etc City Headlines: Oil S——-[?] Law Suits are huge & win all the time over 2 [?] & loose here! Have [?] to give one to some 10 million Lunatics [?] too!!!

45.64 Other company Indited—Shell too & Birchers on Island are butting into other country's Island

45.65 Headlines: Here: ABC looses their license here—& 10,000 requests for that too—

45.66 Oil Not Farly [?] Problems: Congress USA Headlines: Yarboro's son shoots up the Congress again like down south yesterday—

45.67 News — —-[?]: Headlines: Scandal Page—Monico small area in Europe & Arab type area over here—was City Attack on South — —[?] & People aloong with 3 others etc—

45.68 Islands Here: No Entry Island down here is real warm & misty & 1/2 tropical all year & beautiful— Ideas: Have a large 1.00 flower garden too!! for tomato— "See if they tramp it up!"

45.69 Headlines: War Declared on 10,000 Countries again—

45.70 Answers in the News: Inside News Info: Masons were Washington's Builder family & co etc

45.71 Fam & group need help! Hope ok! all— Attack on our up 10 level group almost chopped arms off & hurt them badly—kroker device was used—

45.72 Headlines: 2 Kidnap Charges too & 3 President kids murdered— 8 Million Generals hanged Publically yesterday overseas—for personal — — —[?] while keeping an united[?] war going etc etc

45.73 House Headlines: Horrendous Attacks on us here continue—bombs, guns, killers nightly with zappers & poisons [crossed out] etc — —-[?] too!

45.74 Ideas: "Dr. Pi" cures everything!

45.75 Bad Headlines: Tonight: Frogs Shoot everybody in Australia—real world Crisis—war overseas against Buchley's — —-[?] etc—

45.76 Get our Ed Course out—like Farmer's Almanac—copy later with prints[?] on hundreds of topics & for sale essays & etc on zillions of historical & other topics...

45.77 Killer "surgeons" under house kroke one & 1/2 head off others here—

45.78 City Crackpots: Headlines: "Booze Nuts Mass Multiplied: ... Zillions of each on local phony law booze etc claims—never in courtroom lost first day—

45.79 Answers in the News: Spain ran "Lada" thing on the Enchilada— etc— "Same as before in old anti-crime Book"

45.80 Personal: Horrid carve up head lunitic here hurting us—"Spook head kroker off needed—-"

[71 and 80 show the kind of mental anguish and perhaps physical pain that schizophrenics can experience. A doctor once told Trester that his pain was "psychogenic." That didn't make it stop hurting.]

※ ※ ※

Sunday, July 9, 2006

When I got to Trester's yesterday with his groceries, I was met with a furious ant swarm in the kitchen—countertops and kitchen table, as well as interstate highways across the floor. I did my best to dispatch a few thousand of them (using diluted pine cleaner in a spray bottle), but they returned pretty quickly. They were in everything: fruit, candy, crackers, pretzels, and especially a half-eaten can of corned beef hash that was left open on the countertop. Some of the ants were inside a bowl containing about a third of the cherries I had gotten for Trester last week or the week before. The cherries were now liquefying and growing mold. I tossed out all the contaminated food I could find.

When I asked Trester how he felt, he said he was tired from not sleeping at night. He said he had to nap during the day. He did say that he was not having any pains, though, which I thought remarkable. He said his back had hurt earlier, but he felt okay now.

We ate at a small Chinese takeout where we had eaten once before. On the way back to the car, Trester threw up in the parking lot. After that, he seemed to be having trouble with the ghosts choking him. He kept clearing his throat and telling them to go away. As we drove out of the parking lot, Trester said, "We should wait here for a while. I think they left one of us back there." However, I was already in the street, so we didn't wait.

Trester asked to return to the mini mart we almost went in last week (but he had to get home to use the restroom), so we drove over. I parked in front of it and (since my back was bothering me) told him I would wait in the car. He got out and walked away. I noticed he didn't go into the market but couldn't see where he went. In a few minutes he returned.

"I thought you were going into the mini mart," I said.

"I was, but it was the wrong store."

"Where did you go?"

"I went to another store, but it was the wrong store, too."

"What store were you looking for?"

"I was looking for the Omni store, our group has."

Next, we went to a dollar store, where Trester got some

headline cards and candles. When we got to the car, I opened the trunk so he could put his stuff in. He said, "Last time they switched it. I'll put this up front with me." And so he kept his bags with him in the front seat.

On the way home, he asked to stop at a drugstore, where he bought a couple of magazines and a disposable camera. As we drove, he said, "They charged me way too much money. They're robbing me." Then a bit later, "They took a five dollar bill out of my wallet." A bit later, "They klonked me and tore half of my head off."

Trester said, "Let's go back on the street we came down [that is, back toward the restaurant] because there are little pieces of us floating around there." So we drove back on the same street. As we approached the intersection where the Chinese takeout spot was, Trester asked, "Do you see one of us standing around?" I said no. He looked intently at the area as we drove by.

Nearing his house, he asked me if I knew how to drive to Yibi-Corona, and once again, I said I didn't.

Back at his house, the ants had sent in several divisions of reinforcements, so I did battle with them. Trester had spread cleanser around some of the countertops (a remedy our mom used to try), but the ants seemed impervious to it. I wiped up a few more thousand. I also took the anty trash out and put the big trash can out by the curb.

Saturday, July 15, 2006

When I arrived at Trester's today, Trester was asleep on the sofa. He got up and dressed while I unloaded the groceries. The kitchen countertops and table were aswarm with ants again. Apparently, they preferred the watermelon rind and the powdered sugar donuts Trester left out instead of the ant poison I left out. I cleaned up a few thousand ants and put out some better bait traps. I told Trester that the ant problem would not go away if he left food out. He said okay.

On the way to lunch I asked Trester how he had been sleeping and he said, "I sleep like a baby. I sleep all night and half the day. I was zonked out when you came."

As we drove, I asked him if he was keeping cool on these hot days. He said the air conditioner didn't work very well, so he used a fan. (Later back at his house, I noticed that all the windows were open six to twelve inches. I closed them and the air conditioner started working much better.)

We ate at a buffet since Trester couldn't make up his mind about what kind of food he wanted. Then he wanted to find "our smoke shop," which he thought was on a particular street. We drove down to that street and stopped at a smoke shop where he has bought cigarettes before. "Is this yours?" I asked.

"I don't know. Should I buy one pack of cigarettes if it isn't ours?" I said he could do whatever he wanted. He soon came back with one pack of cigarettes.

"Was it your smoke shop?" I asked.

"No," he said. "Somebody else owns it now."

Then he asked, "Do you know how to get to Jumpy's store?" I said I didn't. So he asked to go to the dollar store we went to last week. We did. Inside, Trester said, "Should we ask to go up one level to Jumpy's store?" I asked him whom we would ask. He said, "The checkout person." I told him he could ask but that the checkout person might not know what he was talking about.

Trester bought some candles, headline cards, birdseed, and orange drink.

Back in the car, Trester started complaining about his

heart. "My heart stopped," he said. I asked him if he was feeling pain. He said yes. He was holding his hand on his chest, the way he does when he has pain there. I asked him if I could take him to a doctor. He said no. When we got home I tried to get him to take some aspirin, and he said he would do that "later." He was about to light another cigarette, so I told him that at least he should stop smoking, since smoking was bad for the heart. "No, no," he said, "these are good for you."

I stayed longer than usual to keep an eye on Trester, but he soon fell asleep, so I decided to leave (after cleaning up a few thousand more ants and mopping the floor).

There are a few new signs around Trester's house. You recall one on the back door that says, "Be careful! Guru attack out behind shop at nut tree. Avoid place. Please. Love, Auy." Now there is another that says, "Don't go to the local stores anymore. They don't like us." Earlier there was a sign written on a paper plate taped to the inside of the front door: "Zapooie Warning: No Out at Night. Air gun blows away. Dangerous." A sign on the walk-in closet door reads: "Warning. Don't use. Dr. Botts around. End up in Africa."

Saturday, July 22, 2006

I arrived at Trester's about noon today and found him napping on the sofa. He got dressed while I unloaded the groceries. He had asked for Cokes instead of Pepsis this week and I also got him some orange ice cream bars. Otherwise, his groceries were pretty much the same. I did avoid getting him anything sweet (like powdered sugar donuts) until the ant problem was under control.

Trester said he was feeling better and sleeping better,

and he didn't complain of the pains he had felt last week.

Speaking of ants, there were only a few thousand streaming across the kitchen countertops this week, so I thought that the trusty ant bait I have found (Max Attrax) works better than the stuff I got at the dollar store. However, I also brought out some ant spray this week, and — as my grandfather used to say — I fixed their wagon. I sprayed up under one of the countertops where they seemed to be nesting. By the time we got back from lunch, there were only two or three stragglers wandering around.

I asked Trester where he wanted to eat, and he first named the City, a mall 35 miles away in San Bernardino. I told him it was too hot to go that far. Then he suggested the Tyler Galleria mall 15 miles away in Riverside. Then he asked where we could eat, so I named several places and he picked the big Chinese buffet we like. Then he asked me, "Do you know where there's a Jumpy's restaurant?" I said I didn't. He said, "There's supposed to be one over by Walmart, but it's not there."

As I finished cleaning up a few ants, I noticed the flash of something large and furry go under the dryer. What I almost saw was too much fur to have been a mouse, I think. I asked Trester, "Do you have rats in the house?" He said, "Oh yeah. We have all kinds of critters around here." I went to the car where I still had several packs of mouse and rat poison and brought them in. While Trester wasn't looking, I tossed one behind the dryer. I also put one under the sofa and one under a bed in the spare bedroom. (Perhaps I should mention parenthetically that Trester leaves the back door wide open much of the day, even with the air conditioning or heating on, and I think that allows the mice and rats free entry.)

We went to the Chinese buffet. On the way, Trester said we should go to the mall, so I told him we'd go there next week. He wants to have his photo put on a mouse pad, like the ten he already has. I've told him several times that the photo kiosk is no longer there, but I guess he will have to find out once again.

As we walked up to the door of the buffet, Trester said, "That red sign means they don't want us." The red sign was a neon sign that said, "Open."

We both had a great lunch as usual. Then we went to a dollar store where Trester got candles, headline cards, birdseed, notebooks, and orange drink.

On the way home, Trester said, "They keep tearing people off my head."

I asked, "What do you mean when you say that?"

He said, "Spooks or some deal." I asked what kind of people were being torn off. He said, "I don't know."

Back home I closed the windows and turned on the air conditioning. It was only 94 but felt much hotter because of the humidity. By the time I got back to the kitchen, Trester had opened two of the windows again. I closed them and told him the A/C wouldn't work very well if the windows were open. Then he went outside and left the back door open. I went out to the shop where he was sitting. He said, "It's too hot out here." Back inside, he opened one of the kitchen windows again. I think they were all closed when I left, but who knows how long that lasted.

Trester asked, "Is this Sunday?"

I said, "No, it's Saturday."

He said, "Oh, good." Then he turned on the washer and the dryer.

Just before I left, he took some leftover popcorn and put it outside for the "critters" to eat.

After I had been home for two or three hours, Trester called and said, "They're bombing the whole place around here. And they're murdering our group at the Reagan political convention. I can't seem to get to warn them. Can you warn them not to go?" I told him Reagan was dead. He said, "There are 400 more of them and they're killing us all over." Then he said, "It's raining here." (Which might have been true, since the weather was unstable and getting cloudy.) I told him I would warn anyone I saw, but that I didn't know where the convention was. Then he said, "I just called to see if you got home safely." I told him I did.

Trester is a caring person, always trying to help his imaginary friends in trouble, and concerned about me and my safety. It's amazing that he has time to think of others, considering the torture he experiences himself.

Sunday, July 30, 2006

I arrived at Trester's as usual yesterday, about noon. I took him his usual groceries, with some extra soft drinks and bottled water that he had requested. He said the heat was making him drink more. He thinks the tap water has poison in it, so he won't drink that.

There was not an ant in sight on the countertops this week, in spite of a slice of watermelon sitting next to the sink. The traps and spray did a good job. (I did later see two trails of ants outside near the back door, so I strafed them with ant spray before I left.)

Because we had searched in vain for the right store with the right underwear, I bought Trester some new boxers at Target during the week and gave them to him on this visit. He put on a pair and said they were "real nice." So, I hope that problem is solved.

I asked Trester where he wanted to eat, and he said,

"Let's go to the mall in Riverside." Then he added, to himself, "They want us to stay in town? I don't know." Then he asked me, "Where can we eat in town that we haven't been for a while?" I told him we could eat anywhere he wanted to. Then he said, "Can we go to our supply house first? It's down the street by the Home Depot. Then we can eat lunch." I said okay. Trester said, "Let me smoke first and then we can go." So he smoked two cigarettes before we left.

We got in the car and drove down to the street where Home Depot is. Trester looked at each side street. "Turn in here," he said at last. We turned into a side street in an industrial park area and he looked over each building. "It's not here," he said.

I asked, "What street is it on?"

He said, "I don't know."

I asked, "How do you know it's around here?"

He said, "It was on the radio." Then he added, "It was a subliminal message on the radio." I asked for the name of the store and he said he didn't know.

Trester said we should eat at "the Chinese place on Main Street," which is one of the little takeout places we've been to. So we headed on over. On the way, he asked, "Do you know how to drive to the other Corona?"

I said, "No, this is the only Corona I know of."

Then he asked, "Do you know where Jumpy's store is?" Again, I said I didn't.

We ate at the Chinese place and Trester remarked (when I asked) that his food was good.

After lunch I asked Trester where he wanted to shop and he asked, "Do you know where our supply place is?" I said I didn't. So he named one of the local dollar stores and we went there. He bought some candles and ammonia cleanser. He didn't find the bird seed or headline cards he wanted, so he asked if we could go to another dollar store he named. So we drove over there. On the way, he asked, "Do you know where Jumpy's store is?" I said I didn't. He said, "It's over by the one-dollar store."

At the new dollar store, Trester walked in about twenty feet and then said, "Put us up where Jumpy's store is." He walked back to the entrance, and then just inside the door, turned back around facing me inside, pointed up with his index finger, and gave a little jump. I don't think he was satisfied with the results, but he did come into the store and buy a few items—though there was no bird seed or headline cards at this store.

As we drove toward home, Trester said, "We need to find our place to shop. They keep saying it's there but don't do anything." His tone indicated his frustration. Then he said, "It's up one level."

Back at Trester's, I tried to do a little trimming, but noticed that the green waste trash can was missing again. I asked Trester, "Where's your green waste can?"

He said, "That isn't ours."

I said, "Yes it is. I put your address on it."

He said, "Oh, well, I don't know. It was out front." In the past, Trester kept putting the can so far onto the neighbor's property that I think they finally took it. Maybe the same happened again.

Overall, Trester was in good spirits this week and feeling physically better than he often does. He still seemed to have a bit of abdominal (or testicular) discomfort, but didn't complain to me and he said his heart was not bothering him. He thanked me a couple of times for bringing him his groceries and "for helping."

He took some pictures with the one-use camera I brought him and had me take a few pictures of him.

Saturday, August 5, 2006

At his request, I brought Trester some extra soft drinks and water (four twelve packs of soda and 24 bottles of water). I also brought his usual lunch meat, TV dinners, ice cream, soup, and the like. I brought his usual four large boxes of Kleenex. (He's quite a nose blower.) As usual, he opened all four boxes at once.

Trester asked me, "Do you know how to find the supply store our group is supposed to buy from?" I said I didn't. He said, "I walked down there where it is supposed to be, but it wasn't there."

I said, "Well, if it wasn't there, maybe it doesn't exist."

Trester said, "Well, can we go down there and look for it anyway?" I asked him how we would find it. He said, "Maybe it's on a different street or in another city." Then a minute or two later, he said, "And we never did find Stone Canyon where we were going to buy a place."

I might mention here that Trester often thinks he is supposed to live somewhere else. Sometimes he will say that he really lives in the other Corona ("Yibi-Corona"). Sometimes he will point to a large building (occasionally a church) and say, "We were supposed to live there." And of course, in the past, he's wanted to fly to "the Main Maui" and live there.

At first Trester wanted to have lunch at the Tyler Galleria mall, but then he decided on a chain Mexican restaurant, where we had eaten several times before. We drove over. Just outside, Trester said, "They don't want us here. Should we eat somewhere else?"

He was turning to leave when I said, "No. Let's eat here."

We got inside the first set of double doors and Trester said again, "They don't want us here." He paused, so we let another couple go on in. I told him to come on in, and he did. The food was quite good. Trester said he liked his plate when I asked.

Afterwards, Trester put two dollars on the table. "Is that the tip?" I asked.

"No," he said. "That's to get our friend out from under." Apparently one of his friends was trapped or imprisoned under the restaurant and the two dollars was the bail. He wouldn't let me put it with the rest of the tip, but wanted it left on the table in its own spot.

We next drove down the street next to Home Depot (same as last week) and pulled into the same industrial park area. Trester looked at the signs on the buildings, but didn't find what he expected.

We then drove to a dollar store, where Trester got some laundry detergent, some lemon and orange flavored mineral water, some oxygen cleaner, a pillow, and some hand lotion.

On the way home, Trester was muttering, and I could make out only some of what he said (and can remember even less). One thing he did say clearly was, "A bunch of screwballs run the world." (He's in the company of many sane people with that sentiment.) He also said that "they were getting murdered again," but I missed the context.

Back at his house, I was getting ready to mop the floor and remembered that last week he had bought two half gallon jugs of detergent ammonia at the dollar store. I thought I'd mop with that. I didn't see it anywhere, so I asked Trester where it was. "I used it," he said.

"All of it?" I asked. "On what?"

He said, "All over the place. In the shop, on the floor, and in the vents." Later I looked down into some of the floor vents (his house has floor vented heat and A/C) and noted that at least two had puddled liquid in them.

I mopped and vacuumed a bit and then headed home.

This week Trester was in pretty good spirits and was once again in very moderate pain. He said his heart didn't bother him anymore and he didn't complain about his back at all. He seemed fairly cheerful by the time I left.

[Undated]

Trester called a few days ago to ask if I would be coming out the next day. I told him it was the middle of the week and I would be out Saturday. He said, "I want to shop at our group's supply house, where we can get some dope smokes and stuff."

I asked him how he had been sleeping, and he said not very well. "Some subliminal device insults us all night long." I asked him if the radio helped. "They insult us on the radio, too," he said. "I have to turn it off."

He asked me if I had heard that "Bob the attorney" had won a big lawsuit. I said I hadn't. He said he just called to see if I was okay.

Last night Trester called again. When I recognized his voice, I said, "Hi Trester" as I always do.

He said, "This is Tibby," as he usually does. (Sometimes he says, "This is Auy, or Tibby" seeming a bit unsure of his name.

Anyway, Trester asked, "Are you all right?" I said I was. He said, "I got a message that you got blown up driving out here, so I wanted to see if you were all right." I assured him that I was. He said bombs were going off all over the place and that he had nearly been killed, and "they" were blowing people up all over the place. I told him things were quiet where I was.

I asked Trester if he wanted any special groceries for

the next day, and he said, "I almost ran out of food this week." He asked for some butter and spaghetti and spaghetti sauce and the usual lunch meats and soft drinks.

We talked a few more minutes and said goodbye.

Sunday, August 13, 2006

The weather was much cooler when I visited Trester this week. And I noticed that the ants were still gone when I unloaded the groceries. After Trester got dressed, I asked him how he was feeling. He said, as he often does, that he was feeling tired. I asked him how he slept, and he said okay. Then he added, "They sprayed poison oil in the house and almost killed us." I asked him if he felt all right now, and he said he thought so. He said, "I thought it was in the water, but apparently it wasn't."

The decision about where to eat for lunch took a while, as it often does, with Trester at first changing his mind, then settling on a place, then forgetting what he settled on and asking me where we should eat. We finally decided on the combination fish and root beer place that Trester had refused to visit for so long, but has recently agreed to patronize. On the way down, his smoker's cough began acting up. Every time he coughs, he says "Don't!" or "Stop!" to whoever is making him cough. (He's already told me I'm wrong to think it's the cigarettes, because "they're good for you.")

As we ate, I asked Trester how he liked his food and he nodded with a bit of enthusiasm and agreed it was good. I noticed from looking over the receipt that the cashier had given us both a senior citizen's discount (we both have gray hair). I mentioned this to Trester and he said, rather matter of factly, "We're getting old." This time, the "we" sounded as if he meant him and me rather than his usual "royal" we.

After lunch, Trester started hallucinating more than usual. He said, "There's a spook deal on my head," and he made those throat clearing, clicking noises that he does when he's trying to pop the ghosts away and keep them from choking him. In spite of this, he wanted to look for his group's supply store again, in the same industrial park as before but this time approached from a different road. So we drove over, up a different road and into the same street. The store was still not there.

He decided that we should go to one of the dollar stores (this one on the far end of town), so we headed over. On the way he said, "They klonked me back there at the toy machine." He had bought a little toy from a vending machine at the fast food place.

We shopped at the dollar store. While I was buying some deodorizer for the dog laundry, Trester finished his shopping. I met him back by the car and we started home. "They klonked me on the head," he said, "and I threw up a little bit."

On the way home, Trester had quite an animated conversation, though I couldn't understand much of what he was saying. He did complain to me that he couldn't shop at Sav-On anymore. He said, "They don't want me to shop there." I asked him how he had learned that. He said, "They tell me when I'm about to enter the store, on a loudspeaker deal."

I was encouraged again this week by Trester's saying that he was not having the pains he has often had in the past. He seemed to be feeling relatively good, considering his condition. He thanked me as usual for coming, for helping him, and for bringing him some good things to eat.

Sunday, August 20, 2006

Trester was still asleep when I arrived, though he was dressed. He had gotten up and dressed, but then fell asleep on the sofa. Not long after he woke up, his smoker's cough hit him. "I'm getting choked by these bogey men," he said. "Little spooks are getting in my throat all the time."

One of my weekly checks is to go into the bathroom at the front of the house (which is the farthest distance from the septic tank) and flush the toilet a couple of times to keep the sewer line from clogging. This week, as is often the case, I had to scoop out a huge amount of toilet paper first. For some reason, Trester sometimes leaves a mountain of TP in the toilet, which I'm afraid to flush down. (We've had lots of plumbing trouble at that end of the house over the years.)

When I got back into the kitchen, Trester said, "Oh, hi," in a tone of voice as if he were greeting me for the first time that day. A few minutes later, he said, "Sorry. I've been zombied. I was asleep when you got here today."

As we got ready to leave for lunch, Trester told me, "I need another five-dollar wrist watch like the one you got me." (As I recall, it was about $13.)

I asked, "Where's the one I got you?"

He said, "The lady that sent it to us didn't like us."

I said, "But I bought that for you."

He said, "Yeah, but they switched it." He eventually put the watch on before we left.

We ate lunch at a strip mall Chinese takeout (and eat in) place that Trester calls "the Panda Bear" because Panda is part of the name and a bear is part of the logo. Trester ordered only a one-item combo this time instead of the more usual two-item.

After lunch, we had to wait a minute in the parking lot because Trester said they pulled somebody off him and he wanted to see if whoever was pulled off was going to come with him. We were near a dollar store but Trester didn't want to go in. Instead, he wanted to look for his two supply houses. He directed me down a frontage road and around a street, pointing out a particular building. "It's supposed to be right there," he said. It was a Salvation Army thrift store. We pulled into the parking lot, but then Trester seemed convinced it wasn't his store, so we left without going in.

Now, Trester wanted to go back to the dollar store, so we did. He bought quite a bit of stuff there, about 30 items or so. I can remember only some of it: 3 bottles of baby powder, 2 small jar candles, 3 tall jar candles, 10 stick candles, 5 packs of 250 3-by-5 cards, 2 composition books, 2 small vases, 1 box of Epsom salts, 2 bottles of rubbing alcohol, and one bottle of dental rinse. Before we went in, he showed me his shopping list, where he had "off my body powder" listed twice. The baby powder apparently is to keep off or remove the ghosts (?) or something from his body. He wanted mentholatum, too, but the store was out.

Next, we drove over to the same industrial park we had been to the previous two weeks, to look for the other supply store, but as in the past, we didn't find it. So we headed home.

On the way, Trester said, "We were supposed to go through the main gate and go home." He doesn't believe that where he lives now is his home. He also said, "I hope we didn't leave one of us down there back in the place."

He thanked me twice and with a sincere tone for my help. He seems to be getting just a little more mental clarity at times. His only physical complaint this week was that "they keep sticking me" in the groin. He was cheerful when I left.

Saturday, September 2, 2006

    Last week, Trester asked if we could drive to the civic center after lunch and go to the mayor's office. I asked him what he wanted there. "The mayor's office has a gate where you can go through to the other Corona," he said. So after a pastrami sandwich lunch, we drove over to the city hall. I pointed to the sign that said "City Hall," but Trester said, "No, it's in the other building." Then he said, "Oh, I don't know what I'm doing. Let's just go home." I asked if he wanted to go to a dollar store and he said yes. First, though, he said, "Let's go down to the [Salvation Army Thrift] store and see if they put our store in. We drove down and determined that his store was still not there. We went to a dollar store. Outside, Trester said, "Do you know how to go up one level? Jumpy's store is there." I said I didn't, so we went into the dollar store. After we shopped, Trester said, "They had a goon poop in my pants." I told him there was a bathroom at a nearby fast food restaurant, so he went over.
    After the dollar store, Trester wanted to look at the same industrial park we have been to before to find his group's store. We drove down the same streets and found the same things. As we continued on toward home, Trester said, "One of our brothers is down at the dollar store."
    This week, I discovered that getting Trester a birthday cake last week was probably not a very good idea because the ants were back in full force, streaming all over the countertops and enjoying the uneaten cake and other food that was sitting around. I wiped up a few thousand before

we left for lunch.

As I was unloading groceries, Trester said, "I need something to put all the trash in." His kitchen wastebasket was overflowing and the three trash cans in the workshop were full.

I said, "Well, your trash can is out front." I was referring to the big can the trash company picks up. It was empty and out by the curb.

Trester said, "I was going to bring it in yesterday, but it was dangerous."

I asked Trester if he was ready to go to lunch and he said, "I have to sit down a minute. I'm going to croak." He sat down and soon felt better. While he was sitting, I went out front and brought in the big trash can. Then he said, "Before we go, let's take some pictures." So he took two of me and I took two of him. He said, "Take one of me with Platty," which is his stuffed animal platypus.

In the workshop, when I emptied one of the smaller trash cans into the big can, I noticed that Trester was throwing away two jackets, two or three pairs of jeans, and some Dockers. I asked him, "Why are you throwing away all the clothes?"

He said, "Everybody was doing it, so I thought I would, too." I told him that if he threw away his clothes, he wouldn't have any to wear. He said, "Those belong to someone else."

Again this week Trester asked to go to the civic center "so I can go to my homeland." And he added, "If not, let's go shopping." We had lunch at a little Chinese takeout and then headed to the civic center. As we drove I asked Trester about his health. He said he was tired (which is his usual complaint) but when I asked about pain, he reported having almost none. We stopped by the civic center. Trester got out and walked around a bit, retracing his path as if in doubt about whether to continue, but then walking over. He soon came back. "I don't know what I'm doing. Let's just go to the dollar store," he said, just as before. So we did.

After the dollar store, I took advantage of one of Trester's many coughing fits and said, "You know, if you stopped smoking, you wouldn't cough so much."

"No that's not it," he said. "They keep sending a deal in my throat that makes me cough."

Back home, I tried to turn on the light in the kitchen but it didn't come on. "Is the kitchen bulb burned out?" I asked.

Trester said, "I forgot to tell you, all the lights blew up. Maybe it's the device in the ceiling." Trester's house has push-button lighting, run by solenoids and a transformer (the device he referred to) in the attic. I thought I might need to order a new one (it has gone out a few times over the years). I tried pushing a few lights but none worked. Then in the workshop I noticed that the patio light button was smashed in and jammed. I took the switch apart and disconnected the control wires. Trester came out about that time, so I asked him, "Did you jam this button in? See, it's all broken."

Trester said, "No, someone from overseas pushed it." At any rate, the lights started working again after the switch was disconnected—it had been jammed in the on position, preventing any of the other lights from working. I was glad at least to be spared a hot hour in the attic.

Trester took my picture as I got in the car to leave. He waved as I drove off.

※ ※ ※

61.1 Shot in Back here

61.2 A lot of guys left today —

61.3 Go thru gate to yevy Corona tomorrow —

61.4 Another Lunatic attack here — our state Authority is suing them again —

61.5 They claim that they own marijuana now on radio too —

61.6 USA and Outlying Area Headlines: More Crooked Cops beat up 10,000 Candidates — all over the place —

61.7 Ideas: As before too!!! for our Group to run and own! Get together a real nice "our stuff" & general magazine like pub. — for our group!

61.8 More Ideas: Put our Records [?] music [?] flowers & plants & movie [?] BICS [?] & TV things in etc —

61.9 Monopoly America leaves [?] for our District etc —!

61.10 Europeans move continent to wrong place —

61.11 Corona Area Headlines: Valley Bombed again & really destroyed —-

61.12 Australia blown up real badly in huge Air Attack — may start another war.

61.13 Guru & other outside churches move in to Australia already!

61.14 Missy [Smith] died — she ran the Attack —

61.15 [Jones] goes to "Sub-way" now — not Nor-way!

61.16 "Deal Cancelled!" More valleys blown up just now — was government order against it — please tell them to stop —

61.17 Local Headlines: 8 million planes blown up after mass bombing attack over here —

61.18 World Headlines: Main Australia Invaded now — way over seas...

61.19 More of ours Attacked around houses here by secret double agent phony cops etc —

61.20 Mrs. Johnson others shot: Frogs kill — — —-[?] off — —-[?] several hundred anyway — "Buckley was Thrown out."

61.21 Magazine Ideas today etc — News & Features lots of full page color pictures etc

61.22 Special Products Advertiser mag type pub —

61.23 Mag Pub Ideas: 14 features like Gardening flowers plants as one & others around city and country & etc

61.24 Food Ideas: — — —-[?] too: Orange juice plant group for foods & foods with one flavor base for fancy eating place! etc.

61.25 Newspaper ideas: Special pages for stick [?] in when needed — string of articles down one page either end etc — or mid-sections in row — other USA's etc- like — — — [?] news

NNN

Friday, September 29, 2006

A few weeks ago, Trester wanted me to take him to the Village apartments, which he had discovered while riding the bus. "I want to go through the gate and go home," he said.

I asked him, "If you go through the gate, does that mean I won't see you anymore?"

Trester said, "I don't know. I guess so." We went to the apartment complex where he went inside and got a brochure. Apparently no one was there at the time.

The next week at the dollar store, Trester said, "I want to buy a dollar button so I can go up one level and move around." Then he said he wanted to go back to the apartment complex we had visited the week before to "go down underneath the ground where Jumpy's apartment place is." At the apartment complex, he said, "I'll ask how you get to Jumpy's deal." He went inside the rental office after much hesitation, and came out soon. I asked him what he found out. "They don't know," he said. "Let's go home."

The ants were back but this time streaming along the floor instead of the countertops. A couple of weeks ago I put an ant trap on the floor near a stream, but the trap was gone by the next week.

At the dollar stores, Trester has been buying his usual supplies: bird seed, laundry detergent, rubbing alcohol, ammonia, soft drinks, talcum powder, candles, hand lotion, mentholated petroleum jelly. The talcum powder had again (after several months respite) been spread over various surfaces (desks, tables, and the floor). The floors are somewhat slippery in places now. I try to mop up what I can.

Trester's health varies. Two weeks ago he was feeling great, no pains, rather cheerful. Last week he complained again of pains in his heart (angina, evidently). I told him to take aspirin, but doubt that he did.

He is well enough to do quite a bit of walking, since the bus he takes lets him off more than a mile from his house, and the walk back is all slightly uphill.

Sunday, October 1, 2006

When I arrived at Trester's yesterday, he was still sleeping, but he got up and dressed in short order. As I unloaded the groceries, I took a minute to spray the ant trails along the kitchen floor. (None on the countertops now, just along the floor.) I also noticed that the last remaining peach on the kitchen table had rat gnawings in it. The rat poison behind the dryer is only six feet from there, so I wonder why there are still signs of rats. (The teeth streaks looked too big to be mice.)

Trester asked his usual, "Do you know where Jumpy's is?" so I told him no, but that if it existed, he could get the phone number from directory assistance. I left to get the green waste container (which has miraculously returned after several weeks' absence), so I don't know whether he called. He didn't say anything when I got back.

Trester wanted to eat at Tom's Farms, the farmer's market type place (home of nominal food), so we went out there. He was going to order a pastrami sandwich (which I had sworn off because of its quality), but they said they didn't have them anymore. So he ordered a chili burger. (I ordered chicken tenders to be as safe as possible.) When I asked Trester how his food was, he said, "It tastes all icky." He kept wiping the bun off with napkins and pulling out the onions and some of the chili meat.

There was a party near us on the grass and at one point a balloon popped. Trester stared over there for quite some time, and, sure enough, when we were leaving he said, "Can you see if we got shot at?"

We went to the candy store at the market and Trester got some salt water taffy and chocolate orange sticks.

We then proceeded to one of the dollar stores where Trester got his usual supply of cards, candles, lotions, and so forth.

Back home, I decided it was time to cut up a few of the dead tree limbs around the place, so I got out the electric chain saw and went at it. Later, when I had several limbs on the patio, I asked Trester if he would help me cut them up. He said okay and held the limbs while I made fireplace sized pieces. I was greatly encouraged by his willingness to help and I think the dose of reality (need to pay attention while I was sawing) was good for him. I hope he will help again next week, because there is much more to do. I told him we could have some nice fires when the weather cooled and he agreed.

I can't quite say why, but I get the feeling that just the tiniest bit of rationality is beginning to break through into Trester's mind. Something seems to be getting better, in spite of his constant hallucinations and ongoing delusions.

Monday, October 9, 2006

I arrived at Trester's as usual on Saturday. As I unloaded the groceries, I told him, "I got you a different brand of bologna to see if you like it." I usually get Oscar Mayer but this time got Bar S.

Trester said, "Don't buy that kind. You're not supposed to eat it if you're a socialist, and we're real liberal." ("Bar-S" means "barring socialists"?) This was an interesting comment because when Trester was sane, he was politically very conservative. He seems to have had some reversals in his mind about many things, including politics, religion, law, etc. (He had "dope smokes" on his shopping list again.)

After he was dressed and we were ready to leave, Trester asked, "Can I get a radio that gets 210? Would they have one in the next town? 210 is a teenage rock and roll station." I once again told him that I've never seen a radio with 210 on the dial.

I suggested Chinese, and Trester liked the idea. I let him choose the place so he picked one of the take-out type places we like. Then he asked, "Is there a Jumpy's place to eat down there? It's on the second Main Street." I said I didn't know where that was.

As we got in the car, Trester asked, "Do you know how to operate a control in your car to go down a third or half a level? There's a Jumpy's underneath the Terrace Apartments." I said I knew of no such control. We drove to lunch and Trester asked, "Can we go to Jumpy's store by the industrial park?" I said we had looked for it three times already. He said he had walked down there recently and couldn't find it.

We had a tasty lunch as usual at this place. The owners are unusually polite and friendly, and I always appreciate that because Trester has a rather disheveled appearance and a strange look that causes stares and sometimes a cool reception.

After lunch, we walked to one of the dollar stores so Trester could get some headline cards and candles. The store didn't have the candles he wanted. As he checked out, he asked the cashier, "Can you put me up one level to Jumpy's for an extra dollar?" Of course, she didn't know what he was talking about.

At one point she asked, "Do you want your total to be nine dollars instead of eight?" Trester asked his question repeatedly in order to clarify what he wanted, but, as you might imagine, it's hard to clarify being "put up a level." Finally, she said she didn't understand what he wanted and he gave up asking.

We went to a second dollar store for candles, but the tall glass kind (novenas) he likes all had pictures of Jesus or saints on them and he wants blank ones. He won't buy "guru" candles.

Back home I brought out a new chain saw and asked Trester to help me cut up branches again. He helped till the first pile was cut and then helped again when I had gathered more branches. I brought out eye protector goggles for both of us and Trester wore his, too. After he finished helping I tackled some dead trees for a while. I didn't have time for house cleaning as a result. I did notice that the bathtub had spots in it from some substance he had repurposed for bathing. (He has used all kinds of things in his bathwater, such as hair conditioner and skin lotion. If he gets an idea that the product is medicinal, he will use it no matter what it's really for or what I say.)

Trester was in pretty good spirits this time and said he had been sleeping better. He did seem to have a bit of lower abdominal discomfort, but was otherwise okay.

Sunday, October 15, 2006

I brought the usual groceries to Trester on Saturday, and as usual asked him how he was feeling. "I feel like my heart's about to stop," he said.

"Are you having pain?"

"No."

"Dizziness?"

"No."

"Faintness?"

"No."

"Can I take you to a doctor?"

"No. I'll be all right." I tried to clarify his symptoms, but all he would say was, "I think my heart's about to stop."

We had our usual discussion about where to eat lunch, and after I made a couple of suggestions, Trester came up with his own: "Let's go get a pizza pie." (If you're old enough, you'll remember that pizza used to be called pizza pie.) So we agreed to do that.

While Trester was in the bathroom, I noticed a sign

taped near his small refrigerator: "No go to the mail station or the stores at center here. It said so on radio our whole group. Mandatory. Don't shop. Killed there one of us today."

We drove down to a local pizza parlor that has a weekday buffet, but this being Saturday, there was order only available. We ordered a medium The Works for about $20, which, to his credit, Trester recognized as "too much money." For someone who thinks he can get a Lexus for $300, he sometimes recognizes a high price when he sees it. Thirty minutes and two trips to the counter later, we finally got our pizza. It was good, but I mentally wrote off the place. (Five minutes to stick on ingredients and seven minutes in the oven. . . .) Trester left a fifty cent tip anyway, probably to get some of his friends or relatives out of jail.

As we got in the car after lunch I asked Trester if he felt any better and he said he felt much better. He was acting a bit cheerful and seemed to be physically feeling well.

We shopped at a dollar store nearby and headed home. Back home, Trester said, "We need a hole in the garage ceiling to let the cool air come up into the house. Someone plastered over it. Can you make a big hole in the ceiling for me?" (The house is a split level with the garage underneath, so a hole in the ceiling of the garage would open to the floor of the house. There was a plastered over hole from a plumbing repair many years ago.) Trester asked me twice, and I tried to explain that the covered area was from a repair and that the weather was getting cooler anyway, but I didn't make any more impression that I usually do with my explanations.

I continued this week to clean up some of the branches and palm fronds. I burned some more palm fronds in the fireplace, and in the process noticed that the ash shovel was all banged up, as if it had been whacked against things. The ash bucket was similarly bent out of shape. Trester continues to buy coffee mugs at the dollar store and there continue to be mug fragments in unusual places, especially in the kitchen. The life of a mug at Trester's house must be "nasty, brutish, and short."

I cut down some of the volunteer bushes that are springing up from root runners all over the property. At one point Trester said, "Don't cut down the trees." I told him the place was growing out of control.

Many of the usual issues came up this week too. At one point, Trester asked me if I knew where his group's store was, where he could get a radio that gets 210, if I knew how to adjust the car to go up (or down) a third or half a level, if we could go to the Terrace apartments and go down to Jumpy's, and so on.

I reminded Trester about the leftover pizza in the fridge and headed on home. He thanked me for my help and had some feeling in his words. We waved as I drove off.

Wednesday, October 25, 2006

When I arrived at Trester's on Saturday, he was already awake and the back door was open, so I hauled the groceries in without delay. When I asked him how he was feeling, he said he was feeling better. Then he added, "I have a long shopping list. I need some new shoes." I told him we could get him some.

As I entered the hallway, I ran upon a large metal shelving unit (four feet wide, six feet high, a foot deep) that had been in the garage. When I had a chance, I asked Trester what the shelf was doing in the hallway (making the trip down the hall a lot narrower). He said, "It's to ground the house better. We've been getting zombied again."

With his groceries, I got Trester a disposable camera. He started taking pictures right away and had me take a couple of him and then he took some of me. He took it with him on our lunch-and-shopping outing and took pictures of the places we visited, together with some surrounding stores. He had taken all 27 pictures by the end of the day. (At first, he gave me the camera to take in for developing, but then he took it back and said he wanted to keep it for a while.)

We ate lunch at a Mexican restaurant. The food was good as usual. After lunch, Trester left a quarter on the table. I asked him what that was for. "It's the fee for using the restroom," he said. Then he left two dollars on the table and said that it was the fee for "getting a friend out."

We went to Target to look for shoes, a yellow shirt, and some underwear. However, he wouldn't buy anything with the Cherokee brand because "I'm not a Cherokee," and he wouldn't buy Hanes underwear because "They won't sell to us." He couldn't find any shoes he liked and the other brands of undies didn't seem to appeal to him. Finally he said, "They don't want us here. Let's go." So we did.

Outside I saw an Old Navy store, so I suggested we look there. "That's only for Navy people," he told me. So we got no shoes or clothes. We went to a dollar store where he got some cleanser and candles, but, "They told me to leave, so I didn't get any bird seed or cards."

We drove by the Salvation Army Thrift store once again to see if his supply house was there "and where the Sandkik stuff is." But it was just a thrift store.

In spite of his (regular) disappointments, Trester was in

pretty good spirits when I left.

Monday, October 30, 2006

    Trester was lying on the sofa when I arrived Saturday. "How are you feeling?" I asked.
    "Okay, I guess. I just got nuked a few minutes ago," he said. Then as he got up, he asked me, "Do you know when it will stop?" He was probably referring to the war he thinks is going on. I told him I didn't.
    As I unloaded his groceries, I noticed a dusty, unopened bag of Cheetos on the table. I asked him if he didn't like Cheetos, but he said he thought they were okay. I was going to take them home to eat until I noticed the "turn to poison" date of April 18. They were likely a bit stale by now. Anyway, I had brought him some cheese flavored popcorn and some nacho Doritos as replacements, so he should be fine in the munchy crunchy department.
    I asked Trester where he wanted to eat and he said, "Somewhere where we can get a lot of food. I'm hungry." So I suggested a couple of buffets and he chose one. We ate there and he (and I) enjoyed it. At the end, he put a quarter and a couple of dimes on the table. I asked him what that was for and he said, "It's a tip. Do you want to add some?" So I put in a couple of dollars. I thought that forty-five cents might look like a negative comment on the food or the service (such as it is at a buffet — they just come to take the old plates away).
    I had found the last short sleeve yellow shirt in the store at a Mervyn's, so I gave that to Trester, together with some boxer undies that he has been saying he needs for several weeks (he never will buy them though, when we go to a store together). Unfortunately, the shirt was an XL

and Trester is a medium, but he washes his clothes in hot water most of the time, so the shirt may fit by the time he wears it. (He washes all his new clothes before wearing them.)

We visited a dollar store where Trester got candles, bird seed, Comet cleanser, headline cards, orange drink, and some other items.

Trester made his usual number of comments to his hallucinated audience. One that I could understand was, "We've got to get away from that Siamese snake pit."

All in all, he seemed to be doing pretty well. He did say he was not going to walk downtown any more. I asked him how often he had done that and he said about once a week. It was getting hard on his joints now, he said.

As usual, he thanked me for the help and we waved goodbye.

Sunday, November 5, 2006

Trester was awake and dressed when I arrived. As I unloaded the groceries, he looked at the photos I gave him (the ones he took with a disposable camera a week or two earlier and that I had developed for him). I asked him how he was feeling and he said he was feeling better and sleeping better. He seemed to be in good spirits.

After he returned from the bathroom, he said, "A ghost scraped my bottom in the bathroom." Soon, though, he asked if we could drive down to see if we could find Jumpy's place. He asked if I knew where it was, and I said I didn't.

As I put some groceries on the kitchen table, I noticed a sign next to the telephone. It said, "Telephone fee, $100. Call Melvyn Belli's Law Office for telephone money."

As we headed toward lunch, we took the city streets because the freeway was jammed. At one intersection, a truck coming the other way braked with that squeal that means there is little or no brake lining left. Trester turned and looked in that direction and sort of waved. Down the street a ways, he said, "Someone was calling for us back there. You should have stopped. Can we go back there and see if one of us has to walk home?" I told him I didn't see anyone.

We ate lunch at a fish-and-chips place, and when I asked, Trester said his food was good. After lunch, Trester wanted to go to one of the dollar stores, so we headed toward the one he described. On the way he seemed to be pretty cheerful. For a bit, he hummed the theme from the movie Charade, and then later sang some unrecognizable song.

At the dollar store, Trester spent $38, his all-time high. In the car he said, "I spent too much money there."

Back home, I worked on the outside (piling firewood and palm fronds, cutting and shredding brush) and then mopped the kitchen. I then discovered that two of the three toilets were stopped up (I've mentioned that Trester uses large amounts of toilet paper). I unstopped one but couldn't get the other with the toilet snake and didn't have the tools to open the cleanout under the floor, so it will have to wait till next week. I told Trester to use the toilet near the back door (closest to the septic tank) and that might avoid blockages.

I was glad that he was feeling so good. We waved as I left.

Friday, November 24, 2006

    This entry is a composite of the last three visits to Trester.

    Trester has a habit of talking to himself or others (those in his imagination) in a near mumble, so I can't always make out what he is saying. A couple of weeks ago, he was talking rather harshly about something, but all I could make out was "ten mobsters and a guru cult." In a minute he said, "They ought to get a lawyer and sue them."

    I asked, "Who are you going to sue?" and he mumbled an answer.

    At lunch he left an extra dollar tip "to feed one of us who wants to eat also."

    Two of the three toilets were stopped up. I've mentioned that Trester uses a lot to TP and this is the result. The next week I brought out the tools to unstop them, but they were working all right. I asked Trester if the toilets were okay now and he said, "Yeah, most of them corrected themselves." I was glad to save the job of cleaning out the sewer lines.

    Last week when I asked Trester where he wanted to eat he said, "One of our group of brothers called from over in the next town. Let's go over and eat there." Then when I asked again, we had another discussion about where to eat. Places that came up included Wendy's, Quizno's, Del Taco, the Mad Greek. Trester decided on Del Taco and then asked, "Do you think they'll give me a car?" He still mentions getting a car, sometimes a "$300 Lexus" and sometimes "just a klunker for a few hundred dollars." I always remind him that he needs a driver's license.

    After lunch, he asked, "Can we go to the next town to see if one of our other brothers needs to be picked up?"

    I asked, "Do you have other brothers?"

He said, "A whole bunch of them." But soon his mind changed and he wanted to go to a dollar store, so we did.

Trester continues to have less pain than he often does and he reports that he is now sleeping well.

Monday, November 27, 2006

There were two new warning signs at Trester's when I arrived, one inside near the back door (the door itself sports two or three signs) and one on the workshop door. The sign near the back door read, "Warning! Don't go downhill to shop or look around. They shot one of us real badly. Sandkik and Auy Family." There was some other tiny writing at the bottom, but I couldn't decipher it.

When I asked Trester where he wanted to eat, he said, "Do you know where Jumpy's restaurant is?" I said I didn't, so he named a Mexican restaurant we occasionally go to. The buffet was closed, so we ordered off the menu. Trester ordered a beef burrito which he didn't like and ate only a third of. I ordered a chili Colorado burrito, which was good. After lunch, Trester said, "They lifted off the top of our head or our body when we went to the bathroom back there" at the restaurant.

I asked him where he wanted to shop and he said, "Can we go down this street and go down half a level and go to Jumpy's? Do you know how to signal to go down half a level?" I said I didn't know how to do that. So we went to the dollar store nearby. I took longer looking around than Trester, and when I got back outside, he said, "They're blowing up the place around here." I asked him if he got the headline cards he wanted and he said they didn't want him to buy them. I asked how he knew and he said, "I got the Colorado message." So he didn't get all the items he wanted. He said, "They sell cigarettes in there if you knock on the wall." Then he asked if we could go to another dollar store where he could get the candles he likes.

We got in the car and started to drive over. Trester said, "Let me get a newspaper." So we drove over to the rack of newspapers. He bought a Spanish language paper. "Do you want to look at it?" he asked. I said I didn't read Spanish. "I don't either," he said. "It's not written in Spanish. It's in the upstairs language."

After we left the second dollar store, Trester thought we should wait for one of his friends or relatives. Then he said to go home. He changed his mind a couple of times, then twice on the way home and once after we got home, he said, "We should have waited for five minutes. One of us was calling to us back there."

Trester's most mysterious action this trip was to take out of the trash a pile of cigarette butts sitting on an empty TV dinner carton and pour them onto a small, swept-together pile of butts on the shop floor. There was evidently some reason for this, but all he would say was, "I'll sweep this up later."

Trester said he has been sleeping well and had only some discomfort, but no severe pains. He seemed to be doing better than he often has been in the past.

Saturday, December 16, 2006

When I arrived at Trester's today, he was already dressed, but lying on the sofa. He said he did not sleep well last night and was tired. After I unloaded the groceries and asked him where he wanted to eat, Trester said, "I have the address of the Jumpy store." He held a 3-by-5 card and read the street address, together with the cross streets. I asked him where he found the address. He said he got it from directory assistance.

He said we could go there after we ate. I suggested a restaurant near the address, but Trester wanted to go to Tom's Farms, so we did. As usual, the food was perfunctory. We each had a "world famous" hamburger. World infamous is more like it. And the usual amateurish pop band badly singing 60s retreads was present, and as usual, making up in volume what it lacked in quality. But we lived to tell the tale. Trester poured a beer over ice and drank it. After lunch, he bought some candy, and then we headed back down the freeway to Jumpy's.

Jumpy's turned out to be Jump, a "dance and performing arts center." A look inside at the girls in tutus leaping about caused Trester to remark, "That's not our group." As we drove away, though, he asked me, "Do you think I should have looked further inside?" I told him the place was a dance studio, not a supply house.

So we went to a dollar store where Trester got some items. As we left, Trester asked me, "Which store was going to have three packs of cigarettes for a dollar?" I said I didn't know.

On the way home, Trester complained about all the money people had stolen from him, saying, "They're all cheats and thieves." At another point, he asked me, "If the sign has a red O on it, who does that mean they don't sell to?" I asked for clarification, and he said, "Like the Mobil gas station." Again, I said I didn't know.

Some changes at home: Trester's 19-inch TV was moved into the kitchen from the living room. There was no reception because the rabbit ears were not sufficient to bring in a signal. A sign taped in Trester's living room says, "Leave Platty doll on chair, not in study, please." In the kitchen, I asked about the many cans of soup, and Trester said all the canned soup except chicken noodle tasted "horribly icky" and I shouldn't buy any more canned food.

Trester seemed to be generally in good spirits today and said he had been feeling better except for the sleepless night.

Saturday, January 20, 2007

This posting features events from several trips to visit Trester.

Trester showed me an advertisement for health screening showing a drawing of an exposed carotid artery (that the scan would examine). He asked me, "Does this mean they're torturing us and ripping us in pieces?" I told him no.

On the way to lunch, Trester said, "It feels like your tires are all flat." I told him I'd check them.

On one trip, I noticed that Trester has removed all the security rods from the windows and put them outside on the ground. They had been lying in the window track so the windows could not be slid open from the outside.

Last week, we went to a strip mall with a dollar store. Trester saw another store called "Kid's World." He asked me, "Do you think they have clothes for me, too?" I said I doubted it. He walked over and went it anyway. He soon came back and said it was a kid's store.

Today, after lunch, Trester threw up in the parking lot. He apologized to me and said, "I got choked by Ronald Reagan." Then he added later, "I'm being choked by some ghost deal."

Trester still wants to find Jumpy's. He said he thought

it might be at "Fourth and Main." Since there is such an intersection in town, I said we could go there. But that's when he threw up and wanted to go home.

I noticed that the kitchen linoleum continues to develop new gouges. I asked Trester, "How does the floor continue to get more and more pock marked?"

He said, "I don't know."

The floor was getting increasingly slippery from all the talcum powder and perhaps cleanser Trester has sprinkled around, so I mopped the family room as well as the kitchen today.

When I asked him, Trester said he slept really well but had trouble getting to sleep. He also said his heart was not bothering him the way it had been. He did complain once of being konked on the head during lunch, but one such complaint is fewer than usual. He is increasingly emphatic in his thanks for my help. Today he even said he didn't know what he'd do without me. (But he still doesn't help unload the groceries!)

Monday, February 5, 2007

When I arrived at Trester's Saturday, a piece of his refrigerator was lying on the floor. I opened the door and discovered that the part belonged to one of the door shelves. There was a broken spot in the plastic on the lower corner. Much of the inside of the fridge has broken or collapsed over the years. The vegetable drawer now sits on a shelf, the slides and surrounding supports long ago having broken.

Perhaps I should mention that the refrigerator was made and installed in 1959. Thus, it is 47 years old. It has seen a lot. Trester sometimes slams the door. I use a heat gun and a ball peen hammer to defrost the freezer compartment (carefully, of course). It just keeps chugging along. And that's good, because when I offer to get Trester a new (self-defrosting) model, he always declines.

We ate at one of the Chinese fast food places Trester likes, then shopped at one of the several dollar stores, where Trester resupplied his inventory of cups and mugs. Then he wanted to return to the drugstore where he bought his wristwatch last week. He said he wanted to buy a *Maxim* magazine, but I told him we had looked there three other times and the store didn't carry it. We went in and Trester walked up to the checkout counter and showed the clerk his watch. He said to her, "I don't want the $18 back. I paid for the watch and it's okay. I'm going to keep it and I don't want the $18 refund." The woman was confused, of course. Trester later told me that "they" told him he was supposed to ask for his money back.

Trester didn't find a *Maxim* magazine, but bought a gardening mag and a *Newsweek*. I told him that the grocery store next door might have the magazine he wanted. We went in and before we got to the magazine section, Trester said, "They don't want us here," and walked out.

Back in the car, I heard him say, "Everybody in the world has a lawsuit against us." He believes that lawsuits are preventing him from being paid the billions of dollars owed to him. He thinks he is owed quite a bit of money from selling water, though I haven't gotten the details.

This week we recited one of those common scenes:

"My heart hurts."

"Did you take some aspirin?"

"No. I need some heart pills."

"Do you want me to take you to a doctor so you can get some heart pills?"

"No. I'll be all right."

His pains seem to have stopped by the time I left.

Monday, February 19, 2007

Trester and I have one thing in common. Both our lives are pretty routine. He asks me what I did this week and I usually say, "I just worked at the office." He doesn't understand much about computers and software since he has been ill during that time, so he wouldn't know what I was talking about if I described some of what I do. On his part, I ask him how his week went, and he is usually either noncommittal or tells me how "they" blew up the area with nuclear bombs.

When I visit him, our routine is usually the same. The last few weeks we have been looking on the same street for the Supply House. This week, as we drove down the street, Trester at least looked on the other side of the street.

Last week Trester had a coupon (saved from the junk mail) for a juice bar. So we went there. It was a few miles away, and at one point he said we had gone too far. After we ordered, he said they didn't want him there, but I told him we had already paid. The juice bar served smoothie type drinks and had some sandwiches too.

This week we ate at the big Chinese buffet on the west end of town. It was good as usual, though some of the food was not as hot as it should have been.

We stopped by one of the dollar stores and then headed over to a drugstore where Trester bought $30 worth of magazines (including two computer magazines!). On the way home, he complained that he had spent too much on magazines and that "they shouldn't charge so much." I got the impression that he thought two of the magazines were a dollar each. They weren't.

I didn't get the sewer pipe cleaned out because the cleanout cap would not budge with reasonable force. It hasn't been opened in 45 years, so I guess the cast iron has rusted together. Next week I'll try a different remedy. Meanwhile, two of the three toilets still work.

The weather was very nice and Trester seemed to enjoy the day. He seemed surprised when I told him I had to leave. Bless his heart.

Sunday, April 8, 2007

Not much is different in Trester's world. Here is a compendium from the last several weeks.

We still have trouble getting into a store where Trester can shop. A few weeks ago, he wanted some shirts, so we headed over to a Target. Outside, he said, "They don't want us to shop there." I asked him how he knew that, and he said, "The Target sign is red." I told him it was always red. He said, "It used to be orange." So we couldn't shop at Target. There were similar rejections of four or five other stores that day.

Trester is still looking for a radio that gets 200 or 210 on the dial.

The sewer pipe is still not fixed. I'm using an enzyme cleaner to eat away at whatever is blocking it, adding more each week. Might test it next time.

There was another case of brakes squeaking and Trester turning and waving and saying, "Hello there!" and later saying we should have stopped because they were calling for him. Honking and even car alarms also seem to suggest the same thing.

Two weeks ago I developed two rolls of film for him from disposable cameras. The pictures were mostly of himself (holding the camera at arm's length). A few pictures were of the area around the house and a strip mall or two.

Trester's usual dollar store purchases: candles, birdseed, headline cards (3-by-5 index cards), mentholatum, a vase, mug, or other ceramic, rubbing alcohol. Occasional items: glass paperweights with laser images inside, odd sodas (like lemon water).

We continue to search for places that do not exist: "our supply house," "Jumpy's," "the smoke shop where the old pharmacy used to be." Part of the problem is that some of these stores are "half a level down" from where we are, and I don't know how to "signal with your steering wheel lever" to get there.

"If I pay a dollar at the bar, I can go to the Jumpy's store a level below here."

"They ran over one of our kids on the street above. Let's go check it out. They're calling for me."

Trester can be surprisingly alert for someone in so much mental confusion. Yesterday as we were leaving, he said, "Let me turn the heater off while we're gone."

Yesterday at the dollar store, I saw Trester jump up and down once, probably in an attempt to change levels.

Yesterday was the first time I persuaded him to take some aspirin, too. He was complaining of his heart hurting, so after his usual rejection of my offer to take him to the doctor, I suggested (about five times) that he take some aspirin, and he finally did. It bothered his stomach but he later said he felt better.

Trester was doing better by the time I left. He thanked me and waved, as usual. I wish I knew how to love him better.

Saturday, April 14, 2007

I visited Trester today as usual. Things were pretty much the same except that the kitchen floor was incredibly dirty. I asked Trester about it and he said he spilled some soda pop and some buttered popcorn. The soda was thoroughly trampled all over the kitchen and had glued down the cigarette ash that falls from Trester's smokes. Mopping took longer than usual, as you might imagine.

Have I mentioned that Trester is something of a pack rat? If you open the "junk drawer" in the kitchen, you will have to pull out several fistfuls of Band-Aid wrappers before you can get to the pliers or batteries you want. When Trester puts on a new Band-Aid, he leaves the wrapper and the adhesive protectors in the drawer. Similarly, when he trims his fingernails, he trims them into a desk drawer.

He now has hundreds of old magazines groaning on several shelves and stacked on the floor. (But he does eventually toss out old newspapers.) His hundreds of soda cans finally got tossed into the recycle bin.

Today we drove down the same street and looked in the same location to try to find the supply house, but it still was not there.

Outside the restaurant where we had lunch, Trester asked to borrow two quarters to call his house to see if anyone was there. No one was, so he got his quarters back.

Trester said he was tired a lot and that his heart bothered him earlier but he felt okay today. After lunch he wanted to go to "that big store in the next town" (by which he meant an old Kmart which is now a Sears Essentials). We drove over and when he found out it was a Sears (instead of his supply house?), he told me to go to one of the dollar stores he named. There he bought his usual supplies: candles, headline cards, bird seed, laundry detergent, and some other items.

He was feeling pretty good when I left. He gave me four single-use cameras to get developed. His last roll of film (that I took him today) was similar to the others: pictures of himself, the area around the house, and nearby shopping areas. I was tempted to ask him why he took pictures of the same things, but settled for, "You like taking pictures, don't you?" He said yes.

✷ ✷ ✷

45.81 Bomb set off at house—ruins plant collection & 10 buildings too—

45.82 Ideas: Greese for horridest people in town or even net[?] is needed—one rope, bandrobbery or torture or worse is all needed—

45.83 Headlines: Major family Infringements Cause problems—Headlines: "Children Snatched" from their mothers!!!—in City here & other areas!!!

45.84 Ideas: Celebrations etc. Flower Days for City—get desert plants with real nice & rare desert blooms that grow in hot dry weather etc.

45.85 Notebook: 800 million washytors[?] killed someone[?] & stoled a property—

45.86 Lunitic Society Dismissed: Trillion dollar/yr products being sued[?] to own here—(USA NOT locals)—

45.87 Headlines: Local Island: Island blown up again—everybody killed in one end almost—Real problem with continual Attacks—

45.88 Get a test against groups after legit[?] wealthy people—

45.89 City headlines & News Info: Krokers Kill peoople in Neighborhood—foreign leaders here kill people too—

can't shop in Circle K store —

45.90 Kemed[?] (group) is president in other country

45.91 Local Headlines: British moore Invasion here is real big — Attacked almost all the children in San Diego over — — -[?] more[?]

45.92 City Headlines: Here Today — Guards & Policemen here were Attacked today to — is midnight down south —

45.93 City, North of Our Island — Prices still real high here — for cigs & so on —

45.94 City Headlines: Attack continues in store. Konneyer[?] owns Circle K store here & half of Walmart!!!

45.95 Store take over krokes customers here — Ex Dem V.P. too!!! is for Democrats only???

45.96 American — — —[?] were Expelled yesterday & have to leave & sell out —

45.97 Local cops shot & old guard on store too —

45.98 Mrs Moore Hanged overseas —

45.99 Bush group Attacked on Island — other all shot — - just now —

45.100 Local Leader was hurt in Circle K store yesterday — Charges already filed —

※ ※ ※

Monday, May 28, 2007

I guess you could say Trester and I are in the same routine. He seems increasingly appreciative of my help (which may mean that he is getting just a bit more aware of reality), since he thanks me, sometimes almost earnestly, for "helping."

The other slight change in his behavior is that he now

walks down the hill to the supermarket to buy disposable cameras. When I get to his house, there will be one, two, three, and once even four cameras, all with their 27 photos taken. Often he wants to take them to the one-hour photo to be developed right away, but more often I take them in for processing. A look over his shoulder as he reviews the pictures shows that perhaps a quarter of them are photos of himself, camera held at arm's length. The others are photos from around the house or of the nearby shopping center.

A week or so back when he did take the pictures in to be processed, he wrote on the processing envelope that his last name was Axle and that his first name was Vatuy. Later when we returned to get the pictures, the clerk asked for his last name and he didn't seem to know what to say. She looked at the envelope (there apparently weren't any other pending orders) and read off Axle, to which Trester assented.

As we headed for lunch this week, we stopped in some traffic and Trester said, "There are dead bodies stacked on that truck." The truck appeared to be closed in from what I could see, so I don't know what triggered that thought.

When we returned home, Trester showed one of the photos of his stuffed animal panda bear to the panda bear. Since he also talks to and pets (and covers) his stuffed animal platypus, he evidently has personified them. (I may have mentioned in a previous entry that when I was a graduate student eating in a fast food restaurant, I saw a man having lunch and interacting with his stuffed animal alligator. That was before I knew much about mental illness or schizophrenia.) The platypus, by the way, is as far as I can tell, the only animal with a name, Platty. Trester calls the others "rabbit," "panda bear," "moose," and so on.

I mentioned to Trester that I wanted to bring in a gardener to cut down some of the weeds, especially the locust trees sprouting everywhere. He said, "I like the trees. Don't cut them down. I want a forest around the house."

Last week when I mopped, Trester said I should put some ammonia (that he had bought at the dollar store) in the mop water. So I did. He evidently likes the aroma.

This week we ate at the buffet. Trester had some ice cream for dessert and commented that it was really good. We stopped by one of the dollar stores for the usual candles, bleach, detergent, and this time photo albums.

Trester still complains of his heart hurting, but said it was somewhat better. As usual, he attributes it to a "sticker" that "they" have put in him. And when his smoker's cough kicked in a few times, he kept saying, "Stop it. Quit. Go away," attributing the cough to the ghost chokers.

I brought Trester a couple more small boxes to put his headline cards in. He has quite a collection now.

Last item. He doesn't seem to be wearing any of the pants or the shirt I bought him recently. He may have thrown them away. I'll check, but last time I found clothes in the trash, he said, "Those aren't mine."

Saturday, June 2, 2007

Today when I arrived at Trester's house, he was already up and dressed. I asked him, "How are you today?"

He said, "I feel better." There was even a bit of enthusiasm in his voice. In another unusual move, Trester helped unload the groceries, making two trips to the car and back. He was more alert than I have seen him in a long time.

The bed was gone from the family room and the metal

shelf was gone from the hallway. I asked Trester where they were and he showed me. He has moved both into one of the bedrooms near the front of the house (empty of furniture until now). I asked him if he was sleeping better in the new bedroom and he said yes, because "they kept using a zombie attack machine on me" where the bed used to be. Later I asked him again why he moved his bed and he said he did it to get away from the "swirly squealies."

I asked Trester where he wanted to eat and he asked me if I knew where Jumpy's restaurant was. I said I didn't. Then he said we should go to the mall to eat. We got ready and as we were about to leave I double checked, saying, "So we're going to the mall?"

Trester said, "That's where they want us to go."

I said, "Don't pay any attention to where they want you to go. Let's go where you want to go."

So then he said, "Let's get a hamburger. Where can we get a hamburger?"

"What about Carl's Junior?"

"They didn't like us there."

"What about Tommy's?"

"They didn't like us there, either."

"Well, there's McDonald's, Wendy's, and Burger King. Do any of those appeal to you?"

"Let's go to the Panda Bear."

This exchange took about five minutes, since Trester was thinking or listening to his voices or something. He is quite indecisive because of the complexity of his decisions.

We ate at a Chinese fast food place, though when we were in line, Trester said, "They don't want us here. Should we go eat at another Chinese place?" I told him they did want us there, and we ate lunch. Trester said he enjoyed his food.

We shopped at two of the dollar stores because the first

one did not have headline cards (3-by-5 index cards) and Trester was out. As we drove, Trester experienced some of his common hallucinations: "There was a little kid calling for us back there." "Was that a bump in the car or is something following us around underneath?" "The other one of us flew off the top of our head. Do you want to wait while I smoke a minute and see if he shows up?"

Trester wanted to go talk to someone at an apartment complex to see if he could "go home" to the other Corona where he thinks his real home is (a kind of alternate universe sort of thing). He will point to a building and say, "In the other Corona, that building is one of our houses." When he discovered that the apartment complex we stopped at was for retirement living, he said it was the wrong building.

Trester bought two more disposable cameras and gave me two others to have developed. (There are now six or seven cameras at the processor.)

I cleaned up the dust bunnies that were left when Trester moved the bed and then mopped the kitchen.

I was happy to see Trester in such relatively good shape. He even said his heart was feeling better.

Saturday, June 16, 2007

When I got to Trester's today, the ants had returned, streaming on a multi-lane highway (eight or ten lanes or more in places) from the kitchen wastebasket (where they had found a paper plate with some uneaten food) all the way to the back wall, a distance of about 25 feet. I couldn't find my pine cleaner sprayer, so I had to use multipurpose cleaner on them. That took longer but it did the trick.

Trester said he wasn't feeling very well today, though I

couldn't get many details. He said, "I feel like I'm getting a disease." After lunch I asked him if he felt any better and he said, "Not much. I feel like I'm getting some quick die disease." As we walked toward the entrance to a dollar store, he said, "We need some Cure Aid drink." I asked him if they had it at the store, and he said he didn't know. I mentioned those vitamin water products, but I couldn't understand his mumbled reply.

Last week he had asked to visit the apartments again "so we can go through the gate and go to the other Corona where we live." But then "half of us flew out the window" and he wanted to go home. On the way home then, he said, "Maybe they'll let us leave if they drop the lawsuits against us." And a bit later, "This whole place is controlled by voodoo cults."

This week, he once again said he wanted to visit the "big apartment buildings" to see if he could go through the gate. I said okay. Trester got dressed in some of his quite worn clothes, with grime on the slacks and holes in both shirt and pants. His shirt pocket was torn. If anyone should ask, "I wonder why that poor man is so shabbily dressed?"

I would reply, "It's because he throws his new clothes away." He tells me they belong to someone else.

Before we left for lunch, Trester said, "I need some perfume on," and proceeded to spray something around his hair and head. (Since I have very little sense of smell, I can't report on any scent.)

We ate lunch at a Chinese takeout and shopped at a dollar store. Then we drove to the four-story retirement apartment building he wanted to visit, and Trester went inside. A few minutes later he returned. I asked him what he found out and he said, "There are a bunch of Americans in there today. The gate isn't open there." So we went home.

Back home, I pointed to one of the bowls of dollar bills sitting around and asked Trester if he wanted me to put the money in the bank for him, because otherwise someone would eventually steal all the money. His stuffed animals have five or ten dollars each, and there are three or four bowls with a dozen or two dollar bills in them (to get his "kids" out of jail or something). He said he might put the money away in envelopes.

Some items revealing more about Trester: In the workshop where he sits and smokes and writes headline cards (and sometimes listens to the radio) he always has a neat pile of cigarette butts on the floor—50 or 100 I'd say—all swept into a circular pile about ten inches across. His bathtub is almost always stained with some of the bizarre items he bathes in. Last week I made it slightly less dirty than it usually is. This week it had green water in it. In spite of his sign, "Don't go to the local stores anymore—they don't like us," he had four more disposable cameras on the kitchen counter. He has several envelopes addressed to imaginary relatives and friends, some addresses are places he used to live. Some of his headline cards are rubber-banded together in sets of about 100.

Before I left, Trester had me take a couple of pictures of him and he took a couple of me.

Sunday, July 1, 2007

When I arrived at Trester's last week and this week, my first task was to spray the pine cleaner on the ants. By careful observation, I have calculated that I'm killing between 5000 and 7000 ants on the first pass, and when we return from lunch the ants have rebuilt their forces to approximately 2000 more, which I also spray.

Trester was feeling about like usual these last two visits, which is to say not extremely well. After I unloaded the groceries Saturday, I asked him where he wanted to eat lunch. At first he suggested the mall, but by the time we left he wanted to visit a particular Sizzler restaurant. As we drove down the freeway toward it, he saw a sign off the side of the road that he thought said ROLEY'S. He said, "Let's go there." We pulled off the road and drove into the parking lot of a Polly's and had lunch there, even though at one point he said, "This is the wrong place." While we were looking at the menu, Trester said, "All these restaurants have the same food."

I asked him, "What would be an example of a different food?"

And he said "I don't know. They have all the same stuff here like fish meals." This place was a restaurant and bakery, and I counted more than 50 types of pie on the menu.

Just before our food arrived, Trester needed to go to the restroom. When he returned, he said, "They almost killed me in the bathroom with a zombie noise, like a high-pitched machine gun rat a tat tat. They shot a dart into my gut too." Later he added, "They zombied me so bad in the bathroom, I disappeared into a different person again."

Trester had an open-faced salmon sandwich, which he said was okay though the fish didn't cover the bread, and I had a perfunctory hamburger that was inferior to any $2.95 hamburger you can get at a fast food restaurant. Worse, it was $8.95.

Outside after lunch, Trester asked, "Where did the other one of us go?" As we walked to the car, I noticed a Roto-Rooter type of plumbing truck on the side of the building near the bathroom, and wondered if the noise he heard came from the clanking of a plumber's snake in the pipes.

When we got out of the car at one of the dollar stores, a car alarm was sounding. Trester looked over in the direction of the alarm and waved. He continued to stare in that direction until the alarm stopped. At the dollar store Trester bought his usual supplies of candles, headline cards, knickknacks—and a peacock feather.

On the way home, Trester said, "Three of us were mashed together with another person back there and I don't know what to do about it." Later down the road he said, "We were supposed to go to the discount store back there to see if we could go to through the gate and go upstairs." Later he said, "Can you find out how to go through the gate so I can go where the rest of us are?" I asked him if he had someone to take care of him there. He said, "Oh yes, I'll do fine. I'll get married. They keep pulling half of us off here."

Trester continued to mutter on the way home, but all I could make out was the phrase "the screwball nut society."

Back home, I mopped up the dead ant bodies, and I placed four ant traps in strategic locations. Trester seemed to be in good spirits as I left.

Sunday, July 15, 2007

When I arrived at Trester's on Saturday, he was sleeping on top of his mattress without any sheets or blankets. I asked him, "What happened to your bedding?"

He said, "They were coming apart." Later he told me that he had put them in the laundry because they were dirty.

Last week, Trester said he wanted to go to the discount

store to see if he could go through the gate. He said it was over by the dollar store. So we drove over there and he walked into a store named Discoteca Jalisco. As its name implies, it was a Mexican music store. He soon came out and I asked him what he had found out. He said, "It's been taken over or some deal." This week he wanted to go to the store again to see if he could go through the gate to "go home."

I asked him, "If you go through the gate, does that mean that I'll never see you again?" He mumbled an answer I couldn't understand.

This time, I went into the store with Trester just to hear what he said to the clerk. Trester walked up to the counter and ask the man, "Do you have some teenage boys to help put us through the gate?" The man looked as if he had never heard of that musical group, and he said no. So we left.

Trester had called me during the week to tell me that he had eaten at a restaurant and had forgotten his wallet. So when I arrived Saturday, I asked him if we needed to go pay. He said he had walked back down and paid the bill. Then on the way to lunch, he said, "When I was eating lunch at that restaurant the other day, somebody came in with a machine gun and killed everybody in the place."

"While you were eating?" I asked.

"Apparently," he said.

The last two weeks the ants have been down to the mere hundreds or low thousands and confined mostly to the countertop area in the kitchen. There is no longer a 20-foot stream from the back door to the kitchen sink. I did my usual mopping, and cleaned out about five fistfuls of empty Band-Aid wrappers from the drawer next to the refrigerator. I threw away three peaches that were rotting and liquefying on the kitchen table.

This last visit, we drove to the Tyler Galleria mall in Riverside and ate at the food court at a place that has some nice fish. We both had the mahi-mahi. This is the mall where Trester used to get his photo made on a mouse pad (which he calls a mat), but that vendor is not there anymore.

As usual, Trester asked me if I knew where Jumpy's was. Last week, we drove around several streets looking for it, and this week we took a long way back home doing the same thing.

We visited one of the dollar stores as usual, and Trester bought his usual supply of candles, bird seed, headline cards, and baby powder. I think he also got some rubbing alcohol and a notebook or two. He did not buy any new photo albums this time, even though I took him some more photos. In his workshop I counted 25 photo albums.

Physically, Trester was having some pain this week. His back especially seemed to be bothering him.

He was in better spirits when I left, as he usually is.

Tuesday, August 7, 2007

When I arrived at the house this last week, Trester was still sleeping in the back bedroom, and he was still sleeping on his bare mattress. His sheets were near the foot of the bed, so I later made his bed for him. When I asked him how he was, he said, "The place was being attacked by spooks all night so I couldn't sleep."

While Trester got dressed, I noticed huge bleach spots in his striped shirt, and some holes where the bleach had eaten through. I told him to change his shirt and he picked up a torn yellow shirt and said, "This one is all ripped up." Then he said, "I need some new shirts." I asked him where the shirts were that I got him recently, and he said, "They're in the laundry." He walked over to the dryer and pulled out a shirt from the pile on top.

I also noticed on the kitchen table that he was getting junk mail addressed to Avy Pollaxik, which was the name he used when he signed up for the newspaper a few months ago. (It is a version of the name he sometimes calls himself, Auy Poll Axils.)

On our way to lunch, Trester said, "Do you know how to get down south here in the real world to Jumpy's place? It would be real nice." Later he added, "Let's see if we can go to the store under Mervyn's that the kids own."

For the third time he wanted to go to the discount store (the Mexican record store) to see if he could go through the gate and go home. When he returned from the store, I asked him, "What did you learn?"

He said, "I don't know. It was a foreign language."

As we drove, Trester said, "I got klonked on the head by a couple of spooks last night. I don't know how they got in. They must fly through the walls because the windows were closed." Later he asked, "Will you cut a hole in the garage ceiling so that air can flow up into the house? It would be nice and cool."

At one point, we were discussing what kind of TV dinners I should get him and I asked him if he liked the Marie Callender's lasagna. He said, "Don't get anything with the name lasagna on it. That lady doesn't want to sell to us."

Trester wanted to eat at a particular Chinese restaurant where we hadn't been for a long time. So we went there. The food was okay but nothing to brag about. Genghis Khan must've commented on how fresh the noodles were that they served him before they served us his leftovers.

After lunch, we went to Mervyn's so Trester could look for some shirts. The security strip on the back of his watch has still never been desensitized, so on entering Mervyn's it set off the alarm which was quite piercing. Of course, no one paid any attention, but a few minutes later Trester said, "They killed my head back there." In fact, it hurt him so much that he wanted to leave the store soon thereafter. I warned him in advance that the alarm would sound again when we walked through the sensors. But he didn't make the connection, and complained again when we got outside (after the alarm went off as we left).

On the way home, Trester engaged in one of his conversations with his imaginary audience. He said, "All the attorneys are two-IQ idiots. Every attorney in the country sued us." Later I overheard, "He was eaten by sharks on Bora Bora or some island like that. They arranged the whole thing." Later, "They cracked our head and threw us out the window."

Overall, Trester was doing about like usual. He didn't complain of any pains other than his head being klonked and killed. He continues to express heartfelt gratitude for my help (even though he still seldom helps unload the groceries!).

Sunday, August 26, 2007

Here are some comments and events in Trester's life over the last few weeks.

"Can we go to Critter TV so I can go through the gate?"

"I want to smoke a dope smoke first." [referring to a specialty brand of cigarettes he had]

At a recent dollar store visit, Trester did a little bounce on his feet to try to get up or down another level. Seems that everything important is "down half a level."

"Did you ever think that smoking is what's making

you cough?" I asked.

"No, it's spooks attacking me."

"I can't eat at hardly any restaurant in town because of all the lawsuits."

The chair I often sit in while Trester dresses was recently covered in talcum powder, so now I just stand and wait. Trester uses talcum powder or baby powder as a disinfectant.

I brought Trester another new shirt and he said, "Don't buy me any more shirts. I have plenty now." After lunch we went to a drugstore where he bought himself a shirt. At home, he said, "I should have bought several of these." The one he bought had thin yellow stripes (among other colors) in it. Seems that yellow is the acceptable color.

This week, Trester complained of an upset stomach, for which he has been taking the pink bismuth medicine. He said his heart pains were not bothering him much this last week.

At about 10:30 Saturday night, Trester called to ask if I were all right. I said I was fine. He said, "They said you got shot." I told him "they" were wrong.

Sunday, September 23, 2007

When I visited Trester this week, he was feeling about the same, and thinking about the same kinds of things. He wanted to go down to Pacific Sales to see if he could go through the gate. Apparently Pacific Sales has a gate the same way that the Disco store supposedly does. He also wanted to find Gordon's smoke shop (which is the name of a tobacco shop he ran for a while when he was first becoming ill). And he wanted to go to the CVS pharmacy to find out whether his watch was paid for. I have told him on several occasions that I paid for his watch myself, but he still occasionally wants to go to find out.

Trester wanted to look for Gordon's on the way to lunch, and he thought it was in a particular shopping mall, so we drove through the parking lot and looked around to see if we could find it. We did this two weeks in a row, but Gordon's failed to appear on either occasion. The first week when we didn't find the smoke shop, Trester said we were "half a level too high."

As I unloaded his groceries, I noticed a dozen bags of microwave popcorn (that had been there the week before) were now missing. I asked Trester, "Did you eat all your popcorn this week?"

He said, "It didn't taste good because somebody switched it." That probably means he threw it all away.

In a chair in the family room was a sign that said, "Don't sit here. They jump through the window right at us."

We ate at a small Chinese takeout place, where Trester said that "they" switched his food. He continued to complain about this after we got home later. But right after lunch, someone honked in the parking lot. Trester said, "The horn said for us to wait a minute and they'll take us home."

After we got home, I was in the kitchen manually defrosting the freezer (of his 1960 model refrigerator), and Trester came inside the house and said, "The workbench was on fire." I walked out into the shop and saw a small area about 6 inches across in the middle of the workbench that had burned down at least an inch deep.

I asked Trester, "How did that happen? What were you doing when this started?"

He said, "I don't know. Some guy came in and started it right here, I guess. There are guys going around burning houses down all over the neighborhood." I had him clear everything off of the workbench and we pulled up a layer of melamine and poured water into the burned area. I told Trester that if he burned the house down he would not have any place to live.

Since I haven't posted for a while, I guess I haven't mentioned that a couple of weeks ago I was about to mop the small bathroom near the back door when I noticed that the floor was all wet. After a little investigation, I noticed that the toilet tank was cracked and leaking. I asked Trester if he knew the toilet was leaking and that the floor was all wet, and he said, "Oh, yes." I told him that he should have told me about it. At any rate, I drove down to Home Depot and found a "toilet in a box" that just fit into the trunk of my car. So I installed the new toilet for him. I have checked the last two weeks and it seems to be working well and not leaking. Trester said he likes it because it's quiet.

Saturday, October 13, 2007

Trester was feeling better than usual last week, he said. He has taped double sheets of aluminum foil to some of the windows and on the door of the small refrigerator and a couple of walls. These are pieces about a foot and a half long. When I asked him why he had taped the foil up, Trester said, "They were zapping me with a ray gun."

I noticed that one of the windows was cracked in the lower right corner. (This is the same window that I had had replaced awhile back.) I asked Trester how it got cracked. He said, "They had a spook deal that came with a long deal that cracked it and I saw them do it."

There was a new sign on the shop door last week:

"Don't leave the house. Don't go downtown or to stores anymore."

This week Trester said his back and heart were not hurting very much at all. (This in answer to my specific inquiries.)

We ate at a Mexican restaurant we occasionally patronize. Trester got out a $20 bill while we were waiting to order and said, "Two of us need to get out." That was bail money, I supposed. Later, he put the bill away (after deliberating back and forth a few times) and settled on three one-dollar bills. (I later made them part of a generous tip.)

Trester said his food was "not very good." In the parking lot, next to the car, he threw up. (This is the first time he has done that in a long time. For a while there, he threw up regularly after lunch.) I asked him if he was going to be all right, and he said, "Somebody like Reagan peed in my mouth." He then said he would be okay.

We drove over to Best Buy where Trester asked about "an old fashioned radio for $39 that gets a new station." They didn't have it. He didn't mention the 210 frequency this time, but might have been thinking of it. The helpful salesman looked on the Best Buy Web site and then even offered to look on the Circuit City Web site for us. Great customer service. Trester said to forget it.

We then went to a dollar store. Trester bought two pre-loaded, disposable cameras and took all 12 pictures in one camera in the parking lot of the store. He wanted to go to another dollar store (the one near the "Disco" store) so we went over there. He took 12 more pictures around the parking lot of that store and gave me both cameras to take in for developing.

On the way home, Trester said, "Let me know if they give us permission to leave anytime." Later, he said, "One of us got klonked last night, and I think they chopped him up."

Back at his house, I noticed that Trester had written, "Trash Okay" on the Green Waste recycling bin, and he had filled it with trash. I hauled it in from the curb and dumped it out on the patio. When he asked what I was doing, I explained that he shouldn't put trash in the green container. I shoveled the trash into the trash can.

When I was ready to leave, Trester thanked me as usual, and we waved to each other as I drove off.

Sunday, October 28, 2007

Last week Trester was feeling fairly well. I noticed that the back shelf in the workshop was becoming covered with empty soda cans again. I asked him if he wanted me to put them in the recycling container, and he said, "No. Leave them. They short out the zapper they're shooting at me."

When I asked Trester where he wanted to eat, he didn't know (we ended up at the buffet), but said, "After lunch, let's drive around the city and see if we can find Gordon's and Jumpy's." For the third or fourth time, on the way to lunch, he wanted to go first to a new strip mall center to look for Gordon's (a tobacco shop). (When he was first getting ill in the late 1970s, he bought a tobacco shop named Gordon's in Anaheim. That's where the name comes from.) We drove through the mall and, once again, did not find the smoke shop. Trester was talking to himself and said something like, "Everybody's suing everybody else, or something."

The buffet is never something to put in the Michelin Guide, but this time is was even more pedestrian than usual. Anyway, as we were leaving, Trester got out a handful of change.

"Do you want to leave a tip?" I asked.

"Yes," he said, "I want to leave some message coins." He carefully looked at both sides of a couple of quarters and a dime and left them.

This week I brought up the Southern California fires and said, "There's a lot of smoke and ashes in the air."

Trester said, "Somebody shot a missile and dropped the bombs on us again." I later tried to raise the same subject, telling him that there were fires burning, and he said the same thing about missiles and a bomb attack. I said that if the fire got near and he was asked to evacuate, he should call me. He said, "Maybe you can find out if it's okay for me to leave and go home. If you do, will you let me know?" I said yes.

The dollar store we patronized this week had not only Halloween items but Christmas items. Trester bought a Christmas stocking and hung it on the refrigerator door. I told him that Christmas was two months away. He told me that Christmas comes at different times in different places, and that at his home (the one he can't seem to get to) it was coming soon.

We had Chinese fast food. This week Trester said his heart was hurting him more frequently. I asked if he was taking aspirin and he said no. He seemed to be feeling pretty good when I left. He did say, "I like those stores where you can get a lot of things for not much money," referring to the dollar stores we always go to. I took him prints from five rolls of film this week, too, and he was appreciative, as usual.

Sunday, November 18, 2007

This week, Trester was feeling better than he sometimes does. By the time I finished unloading the groceries, he was dressed. He told me, "Some of us tried to drive to the other Corona on the 61 and got in a big crash. I don't know if they made it." Then he asked, "Can we drive out on the 61 and see if we can find them?" I told him I didn't know where there was a Highway 61 around there.

After the usual, "I don't know where we can eat; they don't want us to eat there," and so forth, we headed for lunch. On the way, Trester said, "One of our group started a restaurant. Let's go find it. It's on Main Street past the mayor's house." So we drove down Main Street. Trester said, "There is it right there."

I looked at the building he pointed to and said, "That's a pet hospital."

Trester said, "Do you want me to go and find out for sure?" I said okay and pulled in. Trester got out and went over to check. He came back and said, "That wasn't it." I asked him if he knew the name of the restaurant, and he said, "I'm not sure."

We went to the big Chinese buffet for lunch. It was good, as usual. After Trester finished his dessert, he said, "They're pushing on the barf spot in my stomach." He hasn't thrown up at the table for quite some time, but I expected the worst. Fortunately, he seemed to recover and there was no incident, not even outside.

We visited two of the dollar stores in town after lunch. Trester got his usual supply of jar candles, headline cards, something to drink, and several photo albums. (I take him a set of prints nearly every week. I took in three disposable cameras for developing last week.)

Back home, the entire family room floor was covered

with a white residue. I asked Trester what it was. "I put some bleach on the floor," he told me. "I didn't know it would leave anything." I mopped up the family room after I did the kitchen.

Last week, I fixed Trester's old turntable (the belt had slipped off) and hooked it up to his old receiver. (He had bought a new receiver a couple of years ago but threw it away because "they switched it.") He has a small stack of 45 rpm records that he started listening to. This week, Trester said the record player didn't work again. I checked it and this time the belt was broken. I told him it couldn't be fixed.

His collection of soft drink cans in the workshop continues to grow. Oh, I did get him a lower stool (at his request) so that he can sit more comfortably at the workbench. He really seems to prefer sitting there in the shop.

Trester didn't complain of any pains this week. He, as usual, thanked me for my help, and seemed almost cheerful by the time I had to leave.

Saturday, November 24, 2007

Trester was already up and dressed when I arrived today with his groceries. He told me that he hadn't slept all night, but that he had been snoozing on the sofa since about 8:30 a.m.

In addition to his groceries, I brought Trester an early Christmas gift. In keeping with my personal philosophy that "the best repair is a new everything," I braved the Friday after Thanksgiving sale crowds and got Trester a combination record player, radio, CD player, and tape deck, all in a wooden box similar to what I thought he had described to one of the store salesmen a few weeks ago when he was looking for a radio.

When I told him that it was an early Christmas present, Trester said, "Don't buy me any more gifts. I'm going to leave here soon." Later he added, "I don't want to live here anymore." (On the way to lunch, Trester said he sometimes walks down to one of the stores where he thinks there is a gate to the "other Corona" where he really lives. But, he said, it's always the wrong day or the gate is closed.)

The radio part of the new music system worked very well. The record player, though, wasn't exactly high fidelity. We played one of Trester's 45 rpm records and he asked, "Can they record two versions of a song on the same record?" He noticed the difference in the sound. Later, when I asked him if he wanted the system in the living room, he said, "I don't know. It doesn't sound very friendly."

Trester also asked if the radio got 210, so I looked and told him that the dial went down only to 540. I asked him if he had any music CDs (I had given him a few when I gave him a radio-CD-boom box awhile back — the one that soon hit the floor at high speed). He said, "Yeah, they gave us a computer deal that wouldn't play them. They have a lawsuit against us to swipe them, just like everything else."

We ate at a Chinese takeout place and visited two of the one-dollar stores. Trester got jar candles, headline cards (he now prefers the multicolored ones over the white ones), some Mr. Clean and some pine cleaner, incense, some lighted tree ornaments, several strings of mini tree lights, some hand lotion, and a few other items.

As we drove home, Trester said, "There was a pile of sand on one of these streets that looked like it had one of our kids all crunched up in it." When I mentioned that fires had broken out in Malibu again, he said, "Those are bombs."

Trester is still using talcum powder and cleanser to disinfect things, making quite a mess in the house. His aluminum foil in the windows is still present (for example, a one foot by two foot sheet taped in the middle of a three foot by four foot window). The last couple of weeks, I have turned off the 12-inch desk fan I got him in the summer because he has put it in an empty bedroom and left it running (by empty I mean no furniture at all).

When I gave him the prints from three disposable cameras, Trester asked me to bring him two more cameras next week. He usually buys them himself. Maybe he now thinks "they" don't want him to shop at the grocery store anymore (where the cameras are).

When I left, Trester was fairly happy. I'm sorry his gift was something of a dud. I hope he gets some use out of it.

Saturday, December 8, 2007

Last week was a usual trip to Trester's. I asked him how he liked the new record player and radio I had gotten him, and he said, "I wanted the one that had the songs on it our group had, and I got that one instead." The 45 rpm records sounded somewhat better, though still not quite the right speed. I found an old Elvis Presley LP and started playing that and it sounded fine—as far as Elvis can sound fine—so 33 1/3 seems to work.

As is often the case, Trester couldn't decide where he wanted to eat. "We'd better stay in town," he said (though to himself and friends). I suggested a couple of places we hadn't been in a while, and he chose one of them—a Del Taco (Mexican fast food). When we got near there, Trester named a local Mexican restaurant nearby, so we went there. The restaurant had just been remodeled and upscaled, and because Trester doesn't pay much attention to prices until after the fact, we spent $34 on lunch. After the bill, Trester said that it was too much.

We went to the dollar store near the Discoteca, and Trester asked as usual, "Can we go to our level?"

This week, Trester got up complaining, "They put a sticker in my back and I can't get it out." He showed signs of pain and groaned whenever he got into the car. I suggested aspirin repeatedly.

For lunch, I suggested the fish and root beer place I like, but Trester said, "The Rockefellers have taken it over."

Trester was again repeatedly talking about "going home." He said, "See if we can get us a car or some deal so we can drive on home." "Let's go to the Mayor's office and go down half a level so we can go through the main gate and go home." "Let's go down the 61 to the other Corona."

During our time together, Trester mentioned several times wanting to go to the Mayor's house (at the civic center) so he could go home through the main gate. He kept changing his mind. Once I asked him, "You said the gate was at the Disco store and at the Pacific Sales store. Is there more than one gate?" That seemed to confuse him.

We ended up eating at a pizza buffet. Trester liked it. After lunch he said it cost too much. (It was about $10 each with a soft drink.)

We visited one of the dollar stores, where Trester got six jar candles, two small Christmas trees (gold metal ones about 8 inches high), four packs of 250 3-by-5 cards (for headlines), some incense, a bottle of ammonia, some hand soap, and many other items—about 30 in all. (I need to pay closer attention to what he buys. Often his purchases seem nearly random, but he ascribes meaning to each one.)

On the way home, Trester said, "One of us flew off up in the air back there at the dollar store."

We stopped at a CVS pharmacy on the way home, where Trester had three of his disposable cameras developed with the one-hour processing. (I brought him prints from three other cameras today as well.) I took a nap in the car while Trester waited and shopped. He bought some more cameras.

Back home, Trester said the heater didn't work anymore, so I reprogrammed the thermostat to 68 degrees 24 hours a day. I told him not to open the programming door, but to use the up button for warmer and the down button for cooler. I had previously set the thermostat to drop back at night, but since Trester is up all night and sleeps much of the day, I thought a constant temperature was the best. Now, if only he will keep the doors and windows closed when the heat is on.

The house was warming nicely when I left.

Sunday, December 16, 2007

Trester was already up and dressed when I arrived yesterday. He said he was feeling better and that his heart was not hurting now. I unloaded the groceries while he smoked a cigarette.

Trester showed me a Christmas music CD a cigarette company had sent him. He said he couldn't play it because he didn't have the right machine. I showed him that the music system I got him had a CD player also. However, the CD was defective. Most tracks wouldn't play at all and the ones that would had chipmunk-sounding music. We tested the player with another CD to be sure the player wasn't defective.

Trester asked me, "Can we go to the civic center so I can go through the gate?" I said I would take him. He asked, "Can we go down half a level?" I asked him how to do that and he said, "I don't know. You signal on the steering wheel somehow."

I asked where he wanted to eat and he asked me where we could eat that we hadn't been for a while. I named a few places and finally asked, "Do you want to eat at the buffet?"

He said, "Okay, let's go up there. They won't let me eat anywhere in town." (Trester thinks the buffet is in Riverside, even though it's still inside the Corona city limits.)

On the way to eat, Trester said, "Our group bought Pandora's box." I asked him about that and he said it was a music box company, where you pay to hear songs.

We ate at the buffet and Trester had a hamburger, some spaghetti, mashed potatoes and gravy, and some ice cream.

After lunch I took Trester to the civic center and pulled up at the curb. I asked, "Is this where you want to go?"

He said, "Yes. I'll come back if they don't take us." He got out of the car and closed the door without saying goodbye. He left in the car a little rubber ball that he bought from a vending machine at the cafeteria. He walked toward the building and when he got about 50 feet away, he stopped and stared at it for a few minutes, apparently uncertain about what to do or where to go. Then he walked up to the door, but he stopped and didn't try to go in. He walked along the building and then stopped again, brushing his hair down and once again suspended about what to do. Then he came back to the car and got in. "I don't know what to do," he said, somewhat plaintively. Then after a bit he said, "Let's go to the dollar store where the Disco store is." So we did.

There were some small space heaters on sale at the dollar store (this store has items for more than a dollar—the heaters were about $13), so I asked Trester if he needed one for his workshop. "No," he said. "Someone fixed the heat so the temperature is real nice now." He was referring to the house, since the workshop is not heated. I asked again about the shop, but he wasn't interested.

After the dollar store, Trester wanted me to drive by the "Disco" record store slowly. He looked at it carefully, but then told me to go home. So we did.

While I mopped a bit, I noticed that Trester now has empty soda cans lined up in several locations inside the house. The shelf in the workshop (about ten feet long) is completely filled across and about six or more cans deep.

When I left, Trester seemed to be feeling content. He waved as usual and took a picture of my car as I drove down the driveway.

Sunday, December 30, 2007

Trester was already up and dressed when I arrived yesterday. He had called me a couple of times during the week and seemed to be feeling better then. So I was happy to find him saying he was still feeling well when I arrived. He was more alert than usual and said that his heart didn't hurt now.

We decided to eat at Wendy's close by to get some chili and a hamburger for lunch. On the way, Trester said, "After lunch, let's go up the other road and see if our supply house is there." A bit farther down the road he asked, "Do you know where Jumpy's or Jumbo's is?" I didn't. Then he said, "We should find Gordon's. Every time we look, it's not there." So many ideas crowd his brain that he keeps changing his mind about what he wants to do and where he wants to go. Schizophrenia clearly involves an over-stimulated brain.

As we were eating, Trester said, "Every time I eat, they tear half of me off and throw it up in the air." I asked him if this happened when he ate at home and he said yes.

After lunch, Trester wanted me to drive around the shopping center slowly to look for Treaters, apparently a store his "group" owns. As we drove, he read off the name of each store we passed.

We visited two of the dollar stores this time, where Trester got his usual supply: candles, birdseed, headline cards, some detergent ammonia, and a camera. He took about a dozen pictures of the parking lot at the second dollar store.

Trester's heater had broken down, so before we left for lunch I looked at it. In the past when it didn't work, it was the result of Trester's resetting the thermostat incorrectly. This time I discovered that the fan in the furnace was not working. So I needed to call the repair folks.

On the way home from the store, Trester asked if I could take him to Jumpy's, and I said I didn't know where it was. He said, "You signal or honk to go down half a level. Can't someone take us who knows how to do it?"

Trester had a piece of junk mail from the *L.A. Times*. It was addressed to Ms. Tibby Saldikik. That must have been the name he gave someone at some point, together with his address. Then the *Times* rented the mailing list. (It might have been his difficult handwriting, because he has said in the past that his name was Tvy (pronounced *tivy*) Sandkik (which he pronounces *sand cake*.)

I made a big fire in the fireplace and mopped a bit. Trester was in good spirits when I left.

Sunday, January 20, 2008

Trester is still trying to find the right radio to get the stations that his group offers. One of the things he asked for when I saw him three weeks ago was "a $20 radio." I asked him, "What about the radio I got you?" referring to the combination record player, radio, and CD player that I got him for Christmas. He told me, "They said it wasn't paid for." He said the same thing about the Christmas music I got him.

So I said, "I paid for those myself."

He said, "Oh you did?" (We have had this same exchange about three times.)

The stack of empty beverage cans in the workshop is once again about 10 feet wide by three cans high by several cans deep as Trester continues to collect them and not put them in the recycle bin. The cans are between one and 10 layers deep.

Once again, Trester showed his lack of understanding by asking about his aunt's phone number. He said, "They told me to call my aunt last night." I explained that his aunt had been dead since the 70s. Then he asked, "Do you know how to get to the kids' store?" Next, he suggested we go to the mall to get his picture taken on a mat, by which he meant a mouse pad. I explained, for about the 20th time, that that booth was no longer at that mall.

Two weeks ago, Trester was already up when I arrived with his groceries. He was complaining about chest pain, and this time I actually convinced him to take two aspirin, which made him feel better. (No luck with the doctor suggestion, as usual. It's always either "I'll be all right" or "I'm all right.") And Trester had already eaten breakfast but was willing to go out for some lunch anyway. He wanted to find Jumpy's and the supply house, which he said was on "Mackenna Street" in Riverside.

Trester again asked about getting a new radio, so I told him once again about the radio that I had gotten him for Christmas. He said, "That radio is owned by the country it came from." This time, we went to a sandwich place for lunch, but after we walked in the door, Trester said, "They don't want us here. Let's go somewhere else." So we went to a pizza buffet place where we had been before. However, when Trester noticed that the bill was $20 for two people he said, "That's too expensive." Guess we won't go back.

This last week when I arrived, Trester had moved his bed into another bedroom. I asked him if this was a better sleeping place, and he said, "I don't know. They didn't attack me as much in here."

I noticed that Trester hadn't eaten his Krispy Kreme doughnut holes that I got him the week before, so I asked him if he didn't like them. He said, "It looked like they switched them for something else." So I had to throw them away.

Trester asked me, "Can you find Gordon's? It's in one of those centers down half a level." I said I didn't know how to go down half a level.

In addition to the increasing amount of aluminum foil on the walls and windows, Trester this week had posted two 11 x 17 posters, handwritten. One of them said, "Balloon festival coming up soon. One dollar honorary membership." The other poster was something of a goodbye note, apparently written when he planned to leave, directing his group to follow him. I will try to get the exact text next week.

Trester wanted to eat lunch at a place we had not patronized before, so I suggested a few places and we ended up at a fast food restaurant where Trester had a meatball sandwich. He said it was not very good. Then, outside the restaurant he said, "I feel like I am about to throw up." I told him we could stay there until he felt better and that if he had to throw up he should use the grass or the trash can. After a while, he said he felt okay, so we walked over to the car, where he threw up.

Next, we went to a nearby dollar store, one of the ones that he likes to go to, but this time when we got inside, he said, "This place has been taken over, so they don't want us here. Let's go to the other dollar store." So he went to another of the dollar stores in town, primarily so he could get some more jar candles. However, inside that store Trester said, "They don't want us here either." He did buy a couple of items, though.

Next, Trester said, "Let's go by the CVS store and get some cameras." So we drove over there. Trester went inside but came out soon. He said, "They don't want us here. They told us not to shop there." I asked him how he knew that they didn't want him to shop there, whether someone came up to him and said that. He said, "I heard it on the radio loudspeaker." Many of the stores we go into have radio music playing over the sound system, sometimes rather loudly. Trester appears to take the songs as messages to him, usually with the implication that the store does not want him to shop there.

Finally, we went to the smoke shop where Trester got some cigarettes and then home.

I did my usual imitation of mopping the floors and then headed home.

Sunday, March 23, 2008

In a previous post, I promised to get the wording of the

other 11 by 17 handmade poster that Trester put up on the wall near the back door. Here it is: "Up to 9804 and home or other way. Please send all ours home. Sandkik diplomats all. Love you all and hope to see you at home soon. Tvy, Maui, and Ivy=Jr."

Trester bought (another!) new radio at the drug store, "but it doesn't get the right stations."

Trester's pants had a dark stain on the seat. I asked him how that got there and he said it was from putting oil on his bottom to ward off the ghosts.

I've mentioned Trester's taking pictures of the same things (including himself) over and over. He now has more than 35 small photo albums filled.

In the car: "Every deal around here is a spy group." I asked him what they were spying on. "I don't know. They steal everything."

I noticed an orange, yellow, and blue beach towel on top of the dryer. "Where did you get the towel?" I asked.

Trester said, "Somebody put it in the house to remind me to go pick up somebody in Baja."

One week recently, we ate at the Sizzler. I asked Trester how his food was and he said it wasn't as good as usual. Then we went, as usual, to one of the dollar stores. "They hit me three times on the head at that dollar store," Trester said. "Then they popped one of us off."

I asked him, "What does it mean when they pop one of you off?"

Trester said, "I don't know."

This last week, there was talcum powder all over again—on the windows, floor, furniture, the stereo set, base of the refrigerator, countertops. It seems to be a disinfectant or repellent of some kind.

We ate at a Chinese takeout this last week. My fortune cookie said, "Cheery company and a merry time are ahead for you." I was thinking that at last my life would turn around. Then, I looked at Trester's fortune. It read, "Success and wealth are in your future." So much for fortune cookies.

After we shopped at the dollar store this week, we were about to get back in the car when Trester said, "They said if I go back in and pay them a dollar, they'll take me up to Jumpy's. Should I try it? I'd better go try it. I'll be right back." Then after a bit of thought, he added, "If I don't come back—." He stopped at that thought. He did head over toward the store again, but changed his mind and we headed home.

Trester was feeling okay this week. No heart pains. Some usual insomnia. As usual, he thanked me "for helping."

Sunday, April 20, 2008

Trester had a new sign on a 4 x 6 card taped near the back door that said, "Don't go to local stores anymore. They will leave soon, probably."

As has been noted in these entries, Trester often has a problem deciding where to eat and where to shop. One week recently we ran through about 10 restaurants to find one that was acceptable. For one, it was, "They didn't want us there." For another it was, "They didn't like us." For another it was, "I didn't like the food." Once we decide on a restaurant, we get into the car and head for it, and it is not uncommon that Trester will change his mind two or three times more before we decide where to go. Then, if there is music playing near the entrance, he will sometimes say, "They don't want us here. Let's go somewhere else."

Two weeks ago, I noticed that where Trester has his stuffed animals placed in various positions in chairs and sofas there were, in addition to some coins and dollar bills, a few barbecued potato chips. So now his rabbit, panda bear, teddy bear, and other animals have a snack as well as spending money.

I think I forgot to mention that three or four weeks ago Trester scooped all of the empty soda cans off the back shelf in the shop and filled two or three trash cans with them, ready to go out for recycling. He has however, added more aluminum foil to the walls and windows, especially indoors.

Almost every week, Trester asks me if he can get a car. Two weeks ago he asked me, "Can we get the old yellow Mustang back?" He was referring to a 1965 Mustang that we used to own. I told him that it would be 42 years old if it were still around.

Every week he asks me if we can go to Jumpy's on McKenna Street, or find the supply house, or go to the Civic Center where we can signal down half a level and he can go home. These things are always on his mind.

During a recent phone call, Trester said, "Last night they came up through the mattress and tore the outer part of our body off. Now my head is being cracked."

This week Trester had two more rolls of film to develop and he wanted to have them developed at the one-hour photo instead of having me take them in. So we dropped them off before lunch. The clerk asked him what his name was, and he said "Tvy." She couldn't understand him even after he repeated it twice, so she asked, "What is your last name?" He said, "Sandkik." She wrote that down.

Two weeks ago, when Trester was checking out at the dollar store, he asked the clerk, "Do you know how to get to the main gate?" The clerk did not understand the question, and Trester repeated it a couple of times. In fact, the clerk came outside as we were leaving and asked, "Where did you want to go?" He thought perhaps that Trester had meant Main Street. As we walked toward the car, Trester said, "We are spending too much money. We've got to buy a used car and drive out of here." This week, by the way, he asked me again how much a used car costs, and we happened to be right near a used car lot. So I pointed to them and called out the prices, which ranged from about $3000-$9000. Trester didn't seem to like that. He had asked me last week if he could get a used car for $100.

One of Trester's idiosyncrasies is that he tends not to finish drinks. Whether it's a malt at the store or a glass of iced tea or a can of soda or a bottle of water, he always seems to leave some. In a twist to this, I noticed that he has eight almost wholly consumed pint bottles of water in the refrigerator.

A couple of weeks ago we ate at Marie Callender's. And as I have mentioned is typical, there was music playing inside the door, causing Trester to say, "They don't want us here. We should leave." I told him that they did want us there and that it was okay to go in, and after some more persuasion we went in. After we sat down and were about to order, Trester said, "Tell Robert not to make us come here when they don't want us here." After lunch, Trester asked, "Should I leave the dollar for a tip?" I told him that I had already left a tip. Then outside, he began to debate again, asking, "Should I leave the dollar?" I told him that I had already done so, and this routine went back and forth several times, with Trester getting out his wallet and pulling a dollar out and putting it back in two or three times. He finally decided not to go back into the restaurant.

Last week, we were eating lunch, and Trester had to

blow his nose halfway through. I said, "My nose runs now when I eat, too."

Trester said, "They're giving us bird poison. They switched the cosmetics I bought last week. It makes my nose run."

This week, Trester said, "I need a new shirt and a belt." The shirt he was wearing was ripped and torn in several places. I'm not sure how this happens to his shirts, but they don't seem to last very long.

I asked him, "Where is the new shirt I bought you recently?"

He said, "It's still in the wash. We had three Sundays in a row here and I wasn't able to wash it." (He doesn't do laundry on Sundays.) He asked, "Where can I get a shirt?"

I said, "We could go to Target."

He said, "They don't want us to shop there."

I asked, "What about Walmart?"

He said, "No, they stole it from our group."

So I said, "What about Mervyn's?"

He said, "That would be okay."

So, after lunch, we went to Mervyn's. We found a yellow shirt, but Trester said, "That's a military shirt." He pointed to the Dockers logo on it. We looked around a little further and finally found a shirt that was acceptable, although Trester didn't seem to be too enthusiastic about it. Then we looked at belts. The first rack had Dockers belts in it, and Trester said, "Those are military belts." So we went to the next rack and I found one that might suit him. He looked at it and said, "That brand doesn't sell to us." So we went to a third rack, and found a belt that was suitable, but then Trester said, "$25 is too much for a belt."

I told him, "It's on sale for $18, and besides, I'll buy it for you." We went back and forth a bit about the price, but finally Trester allowed me to buy it for him.

This week, Trester was complaining about heart pains again, so once again I suggested that he take some aspirin. After about the 10th reminder, he finally did, and later said he felt better. I brought up the subject of a doctor again, but he seemed uninterested.

Just before I left, Trester took my picture with one of the four single-use cameras he had bought at the drugstore. We waved to each other as I drove down the driveway.

Monday, September 1, 2008

Things are generally the same with Trester. At times he seems to display a glimmer of rationality and expresses consciousness of how much I am helping him (he thanked me three or four times last week), but then he begins talking about going through the gate to get "home" and how all his other relatives are there and so on.

I had a number of details on my pocket voice recorder to enter here, but it had some kind of failure and all were erased. So here are a few details I remember.

When I talk to Trester on the phone, I usually ask him what he had for dinner and whether he liked it (finding topics of conversation is a challenge). Recently he said he had a Salisbury steak TV dinner, which used to be one of his favorites. I asked how he liked it and he said he didn't, because "it had ground up people in it." He asked for more spaghetti and meatballs dinners.

The ants are back. There are little piles of potato chip crumbs on the counter and in the sink, which they enjoy immensely.

This last week was Trester's birthday (he has turned 60), so I suggested we go to the Sizzler and have a steak.

He said okay. Then the phone rang. Apparently it was a salesman or a recorded message, since he listened for a minute or two and then hung up. Then he said, "They don't want us to eat at the Sizzler. The lady on the phone said so."

So we went to the big Chinese buffet, which was better than the last time, though Trester said it was too expensive—quite a sane realization for someone who thinks he can get a Lexus for $300 and stay in a board and care home for $30 to $40 a month. He actually did bring up the board and care topic, but not as an idea of a place to stay, but as a means of "going through the gate to get home."

Trester's dollar-store purchases continue to include candles (jar and stick), incense, detergent, bird seed, headline cards, purple Fabuloso, green alcohol ("It's not alcohol; it's our group's chemical"), bleach, and cosmetic items. He appears to buy things not for their labeled use but because they are some special substance, such as a ghost repellent or anti-poison chemical.

The plumber has had to come out twice since my last posting, to unstop the mainline. Huge amounts of toilet paper, paper towels, and an occasional rag meet with roots and plug things up.

Trester's angina seems to come and go. Still can't get him to see a doctor.

He was feeling okay and was relatively cheerful this Saturday.

Sunday, September 21, 2008

Trester was feeling a bit more spry than usual this week. When he got up and dressed, he did complain about his back hurting him, but after lunch I noticed a little spring in his step.

When he got dressed, he asked me to take him to the mayor's office to see if the mayor would let Trester "go through the gate to home." This has been a frequent request, and a few times I have taken him to the civic center. Because I now visit Trester on Saturdays, the civic center is always closed. This time, I simply reminded him that today was Saturday and that ended the request. (Later, Trester asked me once again if he could get a car "and an income" so he could drive to the "other Corona." I usually tell him that he needs a driver's license and insurance, but this time I didn't say anything.

A few weeks ago, Trester put his stereo receiver out by the trash at the curb. He didn't want it because "it doesn't get the right channels" and because the channels it did get told him the wrong things. A couple of years ago he had a much nicer receiver that he also threw away. At any rate, for some reason no one picked up this item even after about three weeks, so Trester finally retrieved it and hooked it up again. (He still wants to buy a radio that gets 210 on the dial, but we can never find one.)

Last week, Trester had rearranged some of the furniture in the family room. He told me he was planning on moving his bed back in there, but he decided it was too much work.

He continues to pour bleach on the linoleum floor and down the heater/air conditioner vents (in the floor).

At the dollar store last week, a car alarm went off, and Trester stopped walking back to our car and stood there looking in the direction of the sound as long as it went off—which seemed like quite a long time. He appears to believe that honking, alarms, sirens, and other such noise are messages or signals to him.

Yesterday, while I was mopping, Trester said, "Everything here gets dirty in just a few weeks. I don't understand." This from the guy who half the time lets his cigarette ashes drop to the floor (not to mention wrappers, chips, grapes, toothpicks, and whatnot, all nicely glued down by spilled soft drinks).

The garden hose at the lath house (where Trester's cactus collection is) burst somehow, so Trester wanted another hose. After lunch we went by Home Depot and looked at the offerings. He said he wanted a yellow hose (probably because the old one was yellow), but he settled for a gray one. He got the economy model because he had only $10 left in his weekly allowance, and he turned down my repeated offer to subsidize a better hose.

We had Chinese food for lunch, which Trester said was good (while he was eating it) and not so good (when I asked him again half an hour later).

Trester bought the usual miscellaneous items at the dollar store, though some of the things on his shopping list (photo albums, a soup bowl) he forgot. He did get three bottles of green alcohol.

I was glad to see him in good spirits when I left.

Wednesday, October 15, 2008

When I arrived last week, Trester had posted a handwritten sign on the workshop door, "Smoke Old Golds." There was an Old Gold brand of cigarette many years ago, but I don't think it's still around. On the walls of the workshop, Trester has taped pieces of packaging (such as cut outs from six- and twelve-packs of soda) and product labels. There are labels from Wild Cherry Pepsi, Sunny Delight, Capri Sun, Basic cigarettes, a picture of a Cadillac from an ad, and a few others. As I think I've written before, the kitchen walls have a few similar items, including fast food cash register receipts, taped up.

When I entered the house, I discovered bleach poured all over the linoleum, with puddles in some places. Even I could smell it. I asked Trester why he did that and he said the house smelled funny.

Trester needed some new underwear, so we went to Target after lunch. We found the style he liked, but, alas, they were made by Hanes. "Hanes won't sell to us," Trester told me. I offered to buy them for him, but that didn't work. Then we found some undies by Fruit of the Loom. "Fruit of the Loom might mean we're fruit cakes," Trester said. After a few more false starts and hesitations and changes of mind, we ended up with a store brand.

We ate at the Chinese buffet this week. It was okay, but still not worth the money. However, Trester asked to eat there, and Saturday is his day. During lunch he said, "They switched my food and put ick in it," and afterwards in the car he said he felt as if he had to throw up. However, he didn't.

We visited two of the dollar stores in town, where Trester got his usual supply of green alcohol, candles, headline cards, and miscellaneous items. He's been buying vanilla wafers recently as a snack, too.

By the time I was ready to leave, Trester was humming to himself happily.

Friday, October 24, 2008

One of the manifestations of persecution in Trester's life is the delusion of being rejected or unwanted. Each week when I visit him, I hear him say things such as, "They don't want us to shop there," "They don't want us to eat there," "They told us they don't want us to listen to their radio stations," "They told us not to watch that TV." "We need a radio that gets our stations," he frequently tells me, because "they" don't want him listening to "their" stations.

When we do find a store that will allow Trester to shop there ("Do they want us to shop here?"), we have the next problem of the wrong brands. "That brand doesn't want to sell to us," I hear regularly. And sometimes it's not the brand. Last week at one of the dollar stores we were looking for candle holders for stick candles. I found a nice one, made of brass and ceramic. Trester looked at it and said, "That's a guru one. Find one that's not a guru one." Unfortunately, the only other one was a tall glass piece that would probably fall over and break quickly. So, Trester left without a candle holder.

I think I mentioned in an earlier entry that "lasagna" has become a prohibited word (taken over by Trester's enemies, it seems), so I can't buy him any food with that word on the label, regardless of brand. And meatloaf and Salisbury steak TV dinners are prohibited because "they have ground up people in them."

Finally, once we find the permissive store and the right brand, the goods often go astray: "They switched my camera," or, "They switched my food."

I might have mentioned this before, but will risk it again. I once suggested that for lunch we get some fried chicken. Trester said, "That's bird meat. I don't eat birds." The oddity in this is that he suggests Chinese food frequently, where he has various chicken entrées regularly. He will also eat chicken pot pies. But no turkey TV dinners at home and no chicken legs at the buffet.

Sunday, October 26, 2008

When I took Trester his weekly groceries yesterday, he said he wasn't feeling very well. I tried to get the *how*, but he wasn't responsive. (While he was still in bed, he told me a bomb just went off nearby. I asked him if he was okay, and he said, "I think so.")

We had another of those indecisive exercises when it came to choosing a place to eat lunch. Trester asked for some options, so I mentioned a few places. He said, "Where can we get some regular food?" So I suggested some coffee shops and the buffet. He said, "Let's eat in town. Is there a buffet in town?" I told him that the one we usually visit is still in town (though on the outskirts). So, he said the buffet was okay. Then a minute later, "Let's eat in town. Let's get a hamburger." I said okay. Then, "Let's go to the Mexican restaurant in the freeway shopping center." Okay. Then, "Let's go to the little Chinese place next to the big dollar store."

By this time we were in the car and heading toward downtown. "Where is it you want to go?" I asked. "I need to know soon to make the right turn."

"Let's go to the Mexican place." So we did.

After lunch we drove across the parking lot to one of the dollar stores. As we drove, Trester said, "Let's go to the Home Depot after we shop so I can go through the gate and go home." I said okay. I didn't point out that shopping would be pointless if he were to leave this level and go to another world right afterwards.

At the dollar store, Trester got the usual: candles, hand lotion, bleach, cleaner, incense, etc. He wanted headline cards, but the store did not have any. Similarly, he still wanted wood Q-tips, but this store, like the one last week, carries only plastic ones.

As we drove across the parking lot, I said, "Do you want to stop at the smoke shop since it's right here?"

Trester said, "I don't know if they sell to us."

I said, "They always have in the past."

He said, "What is the sign in the window?" We drove by the shop and Trester looked and said, "It's for blue liberals only." Since I was driving, I didn't get a chance to see what he was looking at. The "blue liberals" must have come from the blue state versus red state idea that's on the radio.

We headed for home and again Trester said, "Let's go to the Home Depot. See if they put us home." So we did. I waited in the car. Trester came back and said, "It didn't work."

So we headed home. At the house, I noticed the radio/CD player that I had bought him for Christmas last year was sitting in the shop (still covered with baby powder), with a note on it saying, "Take away please." The large office chair from his desk has also been moved — put out by the trash cans at the curb.

In the family room, Trester tripped slightly on a plastic sheet that was hanging to the floor from a chair. He glared at the floor and said angrily, "Knock it off down there! Get out of the house and leave or something!"

I mopped the kitchen floor (it was in particularly bad shape), cleaned the rear toilet with some hydrochloric acid toilet cleaner from the dollar store, and trimmed some more bushes to allow the septic tank pumper truck access up the driveway to the tank at the back. I made a bit of progress uncovering the lid to the tank, but it's covered with asphalt (the tank is under the driveway), so it was slow going.

Trester was again appreciative of my help. Recently he has been more emphatic about it. I always tell him I'm glad to help him. I only wish I could do more. But he's always been an independent and stubborn person. And being slightly paranoid still, he doesn't trust doctors and hates needles. I still ask him pretty regularly if he wants me to take him to a doctor, but he always says no.

He seemed cheerful enough as I left.

Sunday, November 30, 2008

Trester talks fairly consistently about wanting to "go through the gate so I can go home." The location of the gate varies. This last Saturday it was supposed to be inside one of the dollar stores. A couple of weeks ago it was in the Civic Center. Earlier it was at an appliance store, and before that it was at a music store. Once it was inside a senior citizens' apartment complex. Unfortunately for Trester, the gate is never there or at least not open when he visits.

Saturday Trester was already up and dressed when I arrived. I unloaded the groceries and we discussed where to eat. After the usual indecision and the usual "they don't want us to eat there" responses to a few suggestions, Trester decided on the big Chinese buffet. During lunch he had some angina pains, but they passed and he felt better.

We shopped at two of the dollar stores, where Trester got his usual supplies of candles, bleach, ammonia, purple cleaner (the color seems to be significant), incense, paper towels, napkins, lotion, rubbing alcohol, headline cards, miniature Christmas lights, and some cigarette lighters. He kept saying he wanted "laser" Christmas lights, but not finding any, he settled on the regular ones.

While we were driving around, he made a comment to the effect that he liked the dollar stores, where he could get so much stuff for his money. As usual while we were driving, he asked me to "signal down half a level" to get to the area where his group's stores and restaurants and smoke shops are.

I said, "Tell me how and we'll go there."

And, as usual, he just said, "You use that thing," and pointed to the wiper control.

(Last week, after shopping at one or two of the dollar stores, Trester was surprised that he was broke—that is, that he had spent all the money in his allowance. We went through what he had bought to demonstrate that indeed he had spent it all. Last week's expenditures included four disposable cameras and a few other items that added up pretty fast.)

Trester has a new practice of cutting things up into little pieces. He has done some trimming of a few plants, and he has cut the twigs and leaves up into pieces about three inches long. He has filled two trash cans with these pieces. When I arrived Saturday, Trester cut up a cigarette carton into pieces about one inch on each side.

A couple of weeks ago there was a brush fire in the area. I pointed to the smoke plume in the distance and said, "Look at the smoke."

Trester asked, "Is that a bomb?"

I said, "No, it's a brush fire."

He asked, "Where did it hit?" From then on, he referred to it as a bomb.

Trester was feeling fairly happy when I left. Earlier in the week when I had called he said he had been feeling a bit depressed. Considering the psychological burden a paranoid schizophrenic carries, it's a wonder he isn't always depressed. (I think I mentioned at one point that for years Trester would not leave the house because he feared being murdered by assassins.)

We waved to each other as usual when I left.

Saturday, December 6, 2008

When I visited Trester today, I finished unloading the groceries while he got dressed (as usual). Since I brought him three packages of his developed photographs, he wanted to look at them before we went for lunch. So I began sweeping the kitchen floor. There were the usual broken pieces of ceramic or stoneware in the corners. I asked Trester, "Are these pieces of broken plates I'm sweeping up? There's pottery around here."

Trester said, "I don't know."

I asked again, "You don't know what they are?"

He was preoccupied looking at his pictures, but said, "Uh huh" (rather than uh uh!). Then he added, "I almost stepped on some." I don't know whether he really had forgotten that he smashed the dishes (cups, usually) or whether he was being less than forthcoming. He is so confused about reality that he often doesn't know or remember what really is going on. But he can also be a bit misleading when he wants to.

I asked Trester, "Where do you want to eat today?"

Instead of getting the usual indecisiveness, he said, "Let's eat at Blimpie's." It took me awhile to hear the name of the place correctly. But he knew where it was, and it turns out he had a coupon for the place.

I said, "This gives us $5 off if we spend $10, so that's a good deal."

Trester said, "Don't use the coupon. They're just getting started."

As we drove, I asked Trester, "What kind of food does Blimpie's serve?"

He said, "I don't know." So we drove to Blimpie's. It turned out to be a Subway sandwich copy, right down to the $5 footlong specials. Before we ordered, Trester asked, "Should we eat here or go somewhere else?" I told him that he had wanted to eat here. He said something like, "Don't they have a regular meal?" I told him they had a combo that included chips and a drink. So we had some sandwiches.

While we ate, Trester said, "Let's find a place where we own a sandwich restaurant." Reading between the lines, I think Trester thought earlier that his "group" owned Blimpie's, and that's why he wanted to eat there.

After lunch we went to one of the dollar stores, as we always do. Holiday music was playing. After five minutes, Trester came up to me and said, "Let me go and see if they will put me through the gate. The man on the radio said they would."

I said, "Didn't you try that here last week?" (he had the same idea at the same store a week earlier).

He said, "It didn't work. They wouldn't let me." It evidently didn't work again, because when I left the store Trester was outside smoking away. We went back to the car, where Trester looked up and said, "Sandkik group, come over here!"

On the way home, we stopped at the mailbox (one of those collections of individual boxes with keys). Trester said, "I don't know if I want to open it now. It blows up sometimes." However, he did open it and retrieved what appeared to be several days' worth of mail.

I decided to work on the floors and toilets instead of trimming vegetation today, so I did that. The floors have dried something on them—bleach, cleanser, ammonia, who knows. (And there is still a combination of cleanser and talcum powder spread all over creation, with a little laundry detergent mixed in.)

I was about to put the used rags in the washer when I noticed it had clothes in it. "Are these clothes clean or waiting to be washed?" I asked.

He said, "It was Sunday twice, so I didn't do it."

As I got ready to leave, Trester said, "Thank you for taking us downtown. Sorry they were eating people at the sandwich shop."

I asked, "They were eating people?"

He just said, "Yes."

Sunday, December 14, 2008

Trester said he was feeling somewhat better when I visited this week. He said his heart pains were largely gone, at least for the time being, because "they keep sticking a sticker in my heart."

We discussed where to eat and Trester said he wanted pizza. So I looked in the phone book and found a place that has dine in. But as we started driving, he said we should eat at one of the Chinese places we've been to. So we started that way. Trester asked, "Do you know where Jumpy's is? We should go there." I told him that if he knew how to get there, we'd go. He said, "It's half a level down. You get there by signaling with the lever on the steering thing."

When we got to the Chinese place, there was a pizza place almost next door. I told Trester it wasn't too late to choose pizza, and he began in that direction. Then he stopped and said, "The owner doesn't want us to eat there." He then told me that the same "owner" ran all the places in the strip mall and that this person didn't want Trester to eat at any of his places. I more or less led him into the Chinese place anyway, and he went along.

After lunch we went to one of the dollar stores. As we walked toward the door, Trester asked, "Should I ask them if they can put me through the gate, so I can go home?" I told him I thought they would not know what he was talking about, and reminded him that he had asked the same thing the previous two weeks in a row at the same store. I went on in to the store while he smoked a cigarette, so I don't know if he asked.

In the car I had asked Trester what was on his shopping list, and he said, "Candles, headline cards, laser lights, green liquid, clear alcohol, and ammonia." He ended up buying green alcohol (the color has something to do with disinfecting or detoxifying things). He also bought birdseed, and some incense and some matches. He's been looking for "laser lights" for three or four weeks, but has found only standard Christmas lights.

On the way home, Trester wanted me to stop by a cigarette shop and asked where there were some. I named the three we have stopped at before. The one he used to frequent the most he said did not want to sell to him (though he bought some cigarettes there a week or so ago). He named the store he hasn't been to in a while, so we drove over there. I waited in the car while he went in. He soon came back empty handed. "They don't want to sell to us," he told me. "They're Democrats." This is the same store that "didn't want to sell" to him before because they had a blue sign in the window, and once even earlier because they had a doorbell that rang when he walked in. The "Democrats" comment seems to indicate that he has changed political sides again, and now no longer being a leftist, he is not welcome in establishments run by them.

At home it was a bit cool to work on the weeds outside, so I thought I would dust a bit. I had bought a few new rags at the dollar store to help with the cleanup, so I mixed some Mr. Clean in a spray bottle and went to work. The dust quickly turned to mud, if you need a clue about the state of things. After a bit, Trester wandered into the room where I was (he is always checking up on what I'm doing—at lunch he asked what I was writing on the placemat).

I asked, "Do you ever dust?"

Trester said, "Yes, there's a lot of dust." He is getting a bit hard of hearing now. The dusting rags got so filthy so fast that I didn't get very much done.

When I turned my attention to the microwave, I dusted it and wiped under it. Then it occurred to me to clean the inside. Let's just say that I had to use a putty knife inside on the ceiling.

For some reason, Trester thanked me several times during the day for helping him. He seemed to be a slight bit more lucid than usual, though he was still quite delusional ("One of ours got killed over there yesterday. I hope he's all right").

The heater has been acting up, so I need to call the repairman tomorrow. It was working when I left, but I've had to reset the high pressure cutout on the outside unit twice now. (It's a heat pump.)

Trester has continued to cut paper up into little rectangles. He was cutting up a cigarette carton when I noticed, and letting the pieces fall into a kitchen drawer. I asked him if he was going to do something with the pieces, and he dropped the scissors into the drawer and closed it.

Trester came outside and waved when I left.

Sunday, January 11, 2009

    This week I took Trester some shelving to put some of his magazines on and get them off the floor. It seems that he never throws any magazines away, so they accumulate on the floor. He has a few old shelving units that are all full, except for a very large one in his current bedroom. I vacuumed the carpet where I intended to put the new shelves. The vacuum filled up rapidly, telling me I have neglected vacuuming (something I neglect at my own house too).

    I put up the three units (four shelves each) and put most of the magazines from the floor onto them. I also cleaned off the large metal shelving unit in the bedroom and told Trester to use that for magazines. He said he would, but I won't know what he really thinks until I see what's what on the next visit.

    This week Trester said his heart was not bothering him (though he said a few days earlier it had been).

    We had the usual discussion about where to go for lunch. A hamburger sounded good to Trester, but of the four or five places I named, he said, "They don't want me to eat there." I also named a buffet, a couple of Chinese places, a pastrami spot, and one or two others. He finally said we should go to the A&W root beer place and get a hamburger there. It's also a Long John Silver's fish place (one of those combo restaurants), so we went there and Trester had a bacon cheeseburger while I had some fried fish.

    I have not mentioned it, but to my relief, Trester almost never throws up after lunch now. He seems to have outgrown that. He used to vomit at least half of the time after eating.

    After lunch we visited two of the dollar stores, where

Trester got his usual supply of candles, bird seed, notebooks, headline cards, talcum powder, cleaning products, and some candy and soda. (The soda—in bottles—is in addition to the 36 cans I bring him each week. He usually drinks all of it.)

I did a bit more dusting, but it's really difficult to dust through a thick layer of talcum powder on top of the real dust. When I get down to the surface, the rag comes up yellow-brown from all the cigarette smoke deposits. Poor Trester. Think of his lungs.

I had brought out a new chain saw to do a bit of work on the dead trees (Trester has stopped watering outside in most areas), but with the vacuuming, assembling shelves, and dusting —Oh, and mopping with a new mop—I ran out of afternoon and had to put that off.

Trester was still asking to go to Jumpy's to shop and also to eat, but I told him I didn't know how to get there.

As we drove to and from lunch and the dollar stores, Trester, as he usually does, pointed out various buildings and said, "I was supposed to live there." Then he would explain that someone else took it over. Sometimes he says, "I was going to buy that," or "That was supposed to be my house." He often points to a commercial building (such as a law office) or a church when he says that.

Back at the house, Trester gave me a couple more cameras to have developed. I filled a yard-waste container with weeds and then had to leave. Trester was fairly happy when I left.

Sunday, January 25, 2009

Trester was already up when I arrived with his groceries. He said he was feeling better and apparently had slept better than usual. (When I called the night before about 9:30, he said he had been in bed and was sleepy. Usually he's up until the early hours.)

Trester wanted to eat where we hadn't eaten before or at least not recently. I suggested a pizza place we had seen but not patronized, then mentioned some strip mall eateries we had not been to. I mentioned the buffet. Trester said that would be okay. Then as we drove he said, "Let's eat in town." I told him the buffet was in town, so he agreed. Trester had a plate full of items, including some spaghetti (one of his favorite dishes), and even some cherry cobbler for dessert.

After lunch it was off to the dollar store. Trester went back and forth between the Main Street dollar store (a 99-cent Only store) and the "Big Dollar" store (whose actual name is Giant Dollar). He settled on Big, but just as we reached the ramp for Main, he said to go there. I had repeatedly offered to go to both, but he wanted to choose one. At the Main Street store, he bought potting soil and some cleaning stuff. When I got outside, he said he wanted to go to the Big Dollar store, too, so we did. There he got some jar candles, headline cards, bleach, ammonia, paper towels, and ointment (for his sore ear).

He mentioned that he needed a new radio. I asked him why he didn't use the radio in the music set I got him over a year ago (the set that has a record player, CD, radio, and tape player in it). He said, "They told me it wasn't paid for." That's the same comment he has given me before about it. I think I mentioned in an earlier post that he had put it out with the trash for a while. But, of course, radios are now "electronic hazardous waste," and the trash men won't pick them up. So now the set sits in the workshop, still bearing the label, "Please take away."

I was planning to vacuum again (after long neglect) because the rain made it undesirable to use an electric chain saw on the dead trees outside. I have been a bit frustrated with the vacuum cleaner at Trester's (same model I have), because, even though it stops the dust, there are several filters and other parts that need regular washing. The sponge filter clogs up quickly in the tobacco-ash dust all over the place. Well, earlier at Home Depot I had seen a vacuum cleaner on sale for $30—bagless, only one filter to clean, 12-amp motor, automatic carpet level adjustment—so I got it and took it to Trester's.

The vacuum worked astonishingly well. It isn't very noisy, but the brushes loosen the soil and the suction grabs it. I vacuumed three rooms and two hallways, and (keep this confidential) filled about a third of a 33-gallon trash can with the dirt. There was a surprising amount of gray dust (from tobacco ash, I think). Lots of carpet lint (which seems at least in part to have been dug up by mice).

Now, the down side. When I brought the box in and started to assemble the vacuum, Trester asked, "What's that?" somewhat suspiciously. And after I'd finished vacuuming, he asked, "Where did you put the vacuum cleaner?" I showed him where it was in the closet. The potential problem, you see, is that the vacuum brand is Dirt Devil. Trester won't eat Deviled Ham, and is quite put off by devil anything. So, it may be that when I return next week, the vacuum cleaner might be standing out in the rain (as happened to a can of chain saw oil), or it might have disappeared altogether (having been put in the trash, for example). We will see.

I hope to be vacuuming more often in the future, in spite of my limited time at Trester's. It's difficult to mop, vacuum, dust, and cut wood all in one visit. Most of my visit time is spent with Trester on the way to or from restaurants and dollar stores.

When I left, Trester gave me two more cameras to have developed. It's usually at least one camera, and often two, sometimes three or even four in a week. The pictures are of ordinary items (bushes, trees, some of his cactus plants), himself (he takes a lot of self-portraits), and shopping areas (when we park at a dollar store or the drug store where he gets his cameras, he takes several pictures around the parking lot).

Trester waved as I drove off.

Sunday, February 1, 2009

Trester was feeling somewhat better this week. He didn't complain of any pains. Last week he said he had a hole in his head and that someone klonked him. He did say he felt tired, but I interpreted that to mean he is a typical human. I feel tired, too.

Trester asked where we could eat that was different, so I suggested the pizza place we had talked about but not been to. He agreed and off we went. On the way, I tried to make some idle conversation, so I told him I had reordered some of my medicines through the mail. "You shouldn't take too much medicine," he said. "I almost got killed." Then he added after a bit, "Too much medicine isn't good for you." Perhaps his belief that some medicine he took almost killed him explains why he is so hesitant to take even aspirin.

We arrived at the pizza place and went in. The TV was on, and Trester stopped and listened for a few moments. "They don't want us here," he said. "Should we eat at the Chinese place?" (One of the Chinese fast food places where we have eaten before was in the same strip mall.) I told him we could do whatever he wanted. I reminded him he had wanted pizza. Soon he said pizza was okay, then changed his mind and said we should eat at the Chinese place, reiterating the comment that "they" did not want us to eat at the pizza place. Any kind of music or voice (as with TV) seems to make Trester think that the owners of the store (whether tobacco shop, restaurant, or other store) do not want him to patronize their establishment. He seldom can be talked out of his conviction.

As we got in the car after lunch, Trester said, "There's a dungeon under the Chinese place with people in it. Maybe if I had left a dollar on the table, some of them could have gotten out." He acted as if he were waiting for me to say okay, so that he could go back and leave the dollar. But I didn't respond with any comments one way or another. He repeated this when we got a ways down the road.

After lunch we stopped by the Big Dollar store, where Trester got the usual—candles, paper towels, cleaning products, ice cube trays (several sets at his house seem to have disappeared), and so on. Outside, he saw a store that said, "Metro PCS here," and he interpreted it to be a ticket station selling tickets to a tram that would take him to the "other Corona" he lives in. I let him go check and he soon came back without a ticket. I could have told him it was a cell phone store but he (1) wouldn't know what that was and (2) wouldn't believe me.

Back at the house, I decided to vacuum some more, so I moved the sofa in the living room and vacuumed under it. I also vacuumed Trester's bedroom. At that point, Trester asked me to help him move his bed into the family room, so I vacuumed the family room (which has a linoleum floor), then mopped, and then we moved his bed. His bed has been there before, though on the other side of the room. Next week I will vacuum the floor of his now former bedroom.

I should mention that under his bed were three folding chairs, two wood panels (from sliding doors on a cabinet), and a metal wastebasket. All this is apparently designed to short out the electrical bolts and/or keep the ghosts from attacking him from below. Sometimes I glean from his mumbling to himself that he still hallucinates being anally raped (which apparently occurred when he was in the county jail in the 1980s I think it was). Once I asked him why he poured bleach all over the floor, and he said, "Bleach kills the involuntary bottoms." So all the junk under the bed (which in the past has included metal rods, a piece of railroad rail, and other metal objects) is for self-protection.

As I looked around thinking about dusting, I noticed that he has half a dozen strands of Christmas lights still lit, decorated with gold tinsel. Dusting the window sills would be quite a feat, having to move all that stuff. And there is the other inhibitor—the futility of knowing that body powder would soon be squirted back on the cleaned surface.

I used the rest of the time at Trester's to cut up some of the tree limbs that I had cut down earlier. Many of them were infested with termites—little white bugs with brown heads wiggling around. Some of the wood had gigantic (from a termite perspective) caverns chewed in it. There is a huge amount of work to do out there. I asked Trester if he watered the plants (so many of the trees are dying) and he said he waters a lot.

Trester was happy with the three rolls of photo prints I had developed for him. He bought two more disposable cameras on the way home. He asked me to take several pictures of him in various spots around the house, so I did.

Trester was in good spirits when I left.

Sunday, February 22, 2009

When I called Trester on Friday and asked him if he wanted anything special from the grocery store, he told me not to buy any more spaghetti. He has been on a lots-of-spaghetti kick for a while (after he wanted Salisbury steak and then tired of it), so it's about time for a change. He likes meatloaf now, as well as a variety of other TV dinners.

We entered the usual discussion about where to eat. Trester suggested fish, so I said fine. Then he said he wanted a hamburger, so I named six places. Finally, he decided on a Chinese place, where we did eat.

We went to two one-dollar stores (though the second one charges more than a dollar on many and an increasing number of items). At the first store, Trester seemed to be holding his chest more intensely than usual. I asked him if his heart was bothering him and he said yes. "They put a sticker in it," he said. I asked him if the pain was really bad, and he said, "No." I asked him if he had the pain during the week and he said, "Only a little."

Trester had left the first dollar store after buying only a few items because, "They don't want me to shop there." So we went to the second store, where he got a few more items, but forgot to look at his shopping list and left early because, "They don't want me to shop there."

I decided to mop the kitchen floor when we returned, so I got out the mop and filled the kitchen sink with water and Maestro Limpio (the Spanish version of Mr. Clean). I use the kitchen sink now because the laundry room tub has about a dozen bottles and plastic containers (filled with soapy water) in it and it's easier to use the sink. I pulled up the drain plug and the dirty water started to run out slowly. The usual problem with this sink is a couple of cigarette butts and some lint blocking the drain, so I reached down to grab it and promptly cut a nice gash in my left index finger. (Hence, typing this entry is slow, difficult, and painful.) I grabbed some Kleenex and asked Trester where the Band-Aids were. The blood was free flowing, but I got it stopped after the Band-Aid was soaked with it. After the water finished draining, I looked in and found a large piece of broken glass. I asked Trester where the glass had come from. He said it was probably part of a glass-jar candle that had exploded.

"Do they often break?" I asked.

He said, "Someone shot the candle through the window." I didn't bother to ask him why there was no bullet hole in the window.

So the first old lesson learned anew is, "Don't reach where you can't see."

Next, I wanted to wash off the furnace filter, so I went down into the garage and pulled it out. (It's the cleanable type, made of plastic mesh.) I headed out toward the hose faucet and promptly banged my head on the garage door. This is an old steel door that has rusted thoroughly, especially along the bottom, from the days when Trester sprayed it with the hose several times a day. Now it doesn't open completely without a good push, so I just left it half open, hanging in midair so to speak. I forgot to duck on the way out.

Lesson number two, learned anew, "Watch where you're going."

As usual, Trester thanked me several times and volunteered that he felt much better. His angina was evidently gone and he no longer held his hand over his heart.

He gave me two disposable cameras to get developed. I had brought him photos from four cameras the week before.

Friday, April 10, 2009

Here is a summary of the last few visits with Trester.

First, his health continues about as usual: he feels tired most of the time, has occasional bouts of angina, has some back pains, and doesn't sleep well at night (when "they" attack the most violently).

Trester has taken to cutting thin cardboard and some paper up into pieces about an inch square. He has a drawer full of pieces in the kitchen and a wastebasket full in the workshop. When I asked him what he was going to do with them, he said, "Confetti. For a party."

Random notes I've scribbled on slips of paper (it's difficult for me to remember everything he says or does):

As we drive down the road, Trester remarks on how the town has grown over the years. Then he asks, "What's the deal with the people moving in here? Do they want to ruin the world government?"

At lunch at a Chinese restaurant, with the numbered menu that has about 48 choices: "Number 77 is not on the menu."

Trester keeps complaining of getting klonked at the restaurant and some of the stores we visit.

He continues to put "wooden Q-Tips" on his shopping list. The dollar stores don't carry them.

In the family room: 5 bottles of hand lotion, 3 bottles of bath and shower powder. In the kitchen: 6 pump bottles of hand soap, 2 bottles of dish detergent.

Trester puts hair conditioner in the bathtub and hand lotion on his hair.

In addition to the aluminum foil on the windows, he has now put some metal tubing against two or three walls, taped down with aluminum tape.

I happened to meet one of the neighbors last visit and

asked him if Trester bothered them. He said no, but then added that Trester had been in the neighbor's house a couple of times. He said I should talk to Trester about that. (Quite a few years ago, with a different neighbor in the same house, he broke out all the windows during a rampage. He went through the county mental health system for a few months after that.)

I talked to Trester when I got back in the house and told him, "The neighbor says you have been in their house a couple of times."

Trester said, "Oh really? What did they swipe?" I reminded him that the police would arrest him if he did that again.

His "swipe" comment made me wonder if he went over there because he thought they had taken something that he couldn't find or didn't remember throwing away or never had in the first place. "They" are always suing him, stealing his $800 million, and otherwise absconding with his stuff and his people. He will often say, "They hurt one of us downtown" or something similar.

The debate about where to eat gets more extended every week, because Trester thinks no one wants him at the eateries we've been to. Last week, we went to a Wendy's we hadn't been to before and he seemed to be okay with it.

Last week I was pleased to see that the nearly one gallon of Round Up that I sprayed on the driveway weeds had produced the desired effect and left the weeds brown and ready to blow away. I've been sawing some of the dead wood into firewood sized pieces, but it's a long task. The real trimming that needs to be done around the house, Trester is against, so I just leave the bushes to grow for now.

Saturday, May 30, 2009

I haven't updated my visits with Trester in a while, although I continue to see him every week. He continues to say and do bizarre things, but the variety is limited. For example, each week he asks or says most of the following:
- Do you know where Jumpy's is?
- Do you know how to get to the teen store?
- I want to buy a $20 radio that gets station 210.
- They said they don't want us to eat [or shop] here. Let's go.
- Do you know how to get to our supply house? It's half a level down. You signal with that lever [pointing to the windshield wiper control].
- They klonked me on the head when I left there [a store or restaurant].
- Let me see if I can leave to go home. If I can, just put the shopping stuff in the house.

Occasionally, Trester will say, "Nobody in town wants us to shop or eat there." Hence, our difficulty in deciding on where to eat each week. He also will say, "They said we have a store near here. Can we go there?"

To which I ask, "Do you know where it is? Or do you know what it's called?" and he says no. I explain that we can't find a store when we don't know its name or where it is.

Other comments have been, "What do you do when they switch your food ten times?" and, "That popper almost killed me" — said when he hears a loud noise.

Trester's shopping list remains fairly constant: headline cards, novena candles (in the unprinted glass jars — he won't buy the ones with people on them because they are "guru candles"), photo albums, paper towels, potting soil, hand lotion, dishwashing detergent, bleach, ammonia, extra cigarettes, notebooks, pens.

At last count, Trester had 71 photo albums, almost all filled with the pictures he has taken with the one-use cameras.

The neighbors down the street trimmed back their very overgrown pepper trees, and now almost every time we drive down that street on the way to lunch, Trester says, "They wrecked the trees." I tell him the trees will grow back out and look great.

Trester continues to dissolve bars of soap in bathroom sinks filled with water. He has put up more aluminum tape on the walls (to short out the zappers). He continues to complain about "butt stickers" and says that pouring bleach and ammonia on the floor helps to ward them off. When he complains about chest pains (he has angina) and I offer to take him to a doctor, he declines with, "They put a sticker in my heart, but I got it pulled out."

So far, Trester has been hanging in there. He was stubborn before he became mentally ill, and he was resistant to dentists in those days, too. And, with his schizophrenia, he is suspicious of doctors and certainly of psychiatrists (even though in the past he has seen several).

Sunday, June 14, 2009

Trester was already up and dressed when I took him his groceries this week. He said he was feeling okay, though he was having a problem with intermittent pains ("They keep putting stickers in my heart, but they are out now"). I again told him to take some aspirin and he again ignored me.

Last time I mentioned that Trester has about 71 photo albums filled. Each album holds 96 photos, so that's about

6800 pictures of pretty much the same things: areas around the house, strip malls we go to, and himself. There's an occasional picture of me in there, too.

Trester continues his almost obsessive-compulsive cutting of thin cardboard (the kind that packages soda cans and cigarette packs) into rectangles and squares about an inch on each side. He has three or four baskets filled with the pieces out in the workshop and a kitchen drawer half full. The kitchen floor always has a dozen or two pieces on it from where he apparently spilled them when moving them from one place to another.

The kitchen ceiling and walls about three feet from the ceiling are stained brown from cigarette smoke. If I had the time and energy, I'd wash them. But cleaning at Trester's has a feeling of futility. It doesn't do much good to mop the family room, for example, because by the next week there is another white haze from the ammonia and/or bleach he's poured over it, and in several spots more baby powder.

Trester had the usual uncertainty about lunch this week. At first he wanted a hamburger, then the buffet, then, "Let's eat in town" (he thinks the buffet is in the next town, despite my repeated assurances that it's not), with the suggestion that we go to a Chinese place he named. So off we went. But then he decided on the buffet, so we finally ended up there.

After lunch we were heading toward the drugstore to pick up some more photos, when he spotted a Coco's. He said, "Can you take us there so I can see if they can send us through the gate to go home?"

I said, "Right now?"

And he said, "Yes." So we drove on over. He got out of the car and said, "Wait a few minutes and see if I come back." I waited for him and he came back out in five minutes or so. I asked him what he found out and he said, "They don't know what I'm talking about."

We were heading toward one of the dollar stores when Trester said he had to go to the bathroom, so we stopped by the library nearby. After he came out, he stood around the entrance, smoking a cigarette, for several minutes. I wondered whether he forgot where I parked or whether he was waiting for someone else to come and get him. Just about the time I started to go get him, he walked on over to the car. I guess I'm his last choice.

At the dollar store, he bought the usual—candles, incense, potting soil, and so on. Last week, he took a shopping cart instead of a basket, and got eight bags of stuff (lots of paper towels and napkins in addition to the usual). This week he took a basket. However, we needed to go to another dollar store to get the kind of candles (and ammonia, etc.) that he likes, so he still ran out of money.

Back at his house, I noticed that the door to the workshop now has little pieces of paper taped to it, each one with a message such as "Frog 1021."

Trester was feeling pretty good when I left.

Sunday, June 28, 2009

I arrived as usual with Trester's groceries yesterday. He got up and got dressed, and reported feeling okay.

When I asked Trester where he wanted to eat lunch, he said we should go to Coco's, so that he could see if they would let him "go through the gate to get home." I reminded him that he had asked them the last two weeks (week before last, he went in and asked, and last week we had lunch there, where he also asked). He said we should still go there, so we did. At the end of lunch, someone clattered some dishes nearby, and Trester thought he had been hit in the head, so he was not in the mood to ask if he could go through the gate to "Jarry Corona." (You might recall that in the past, Trester has referred to the other Corona as "Yibi Corona," but that has apparently changed.)

I got a bit of insight into this other town and "signaling down half a level" this week, when Trester said, "I was going to have you help me find Gordon's [the name of a tobacco store he ran for a few months in the late 70s]. It's two levels down south." I said I didn't know how to get there. He said, "You signal down with that [pointing to the windshield wiper control]. I once turned the wiper on when it started to rain and ended up 200 miles north in another realm." Whatever that experience was, it has stuck with him and he continues to think that we can signal down and get to another level of reality.

This week Trester wanted to get some mustard, so when we went to one of the dollar stores, I showed him a display of Moorehouse Mustard (regular, brown, Dijon, jalapeno, etc.). I asked him which one he wanted, and pointed out the regular and the Dijon. He said, "That's owned by Moore's group." He wouldn't have any of it. Later, we went to another dollar store, where he remembered seeing mustard, and we found the display. The brand was Koop. "They have a lawsuit against us," Trester said, and he refused to get any of it. I offered to get Trester some mustard at the grocery store next week, and asked what brand was acceptable. He said, "Just get a regular brand." I suggested Stater Brothers house brand, and he seemed to be okay with that.

Back home, I noticed that one of the stuffed animals had a glazed donut sitting in front of it, instead of the usual cash. Much of the cash in front of the stuffed animals has been moved, apparently to the two bowls.

This week I took the opportunity to copy the information on some of the notes taped to the workshop door. Here are a few, written on 3-by-3 pieces of paper mostly, though some are 3-by-5 approximately: "LADA 12141 Born 1214, Corn Dogs 8991 Registered, Laser 121105 18 Born 1211, Cheese 3855195 Born 3855, Corn 3151, Apple 1616125 Born 1516." In most cases, the word *Born* and the number after it are circled.

One anomaly I mentioned briefly earlier in regard to drinks is that Trester seldom completely empties drink cans and bottles. However I now noticed that this applies to all liquid containers. In his refrigerator are half a dozen 500 ml water bottles with half an inch of water left in each. On the kitchen countertop are two or three hand soap pumps with half an inch of soap left—and three or four relatively full ones. He sometimes leaves a little soda in a can, and the cleaning products often have similar fates. Perhaps he subscribes to the dregs-of-the-wine idea, thinking that the last bit of product is less pure.

This week I cleaned up the kitchen sink area a bit (a monumental challenge considering that virtually every square inch of countertop is covered with stuff), and then noted that I need to call the plumber tomorrow, because the mainline is once again stopped up. The toilet near the back door appeared to be working, so that is a relief.

Trester was sipping a cola as we waved to each other when I left.

Sunday, July 26, 2009

When I talked to Trester on the phone Friday evening, he told me he wanted to eat at Coco's again, to see if he could go through the gate. That would have been five weeks in a row. However, when I arrived yesterday, he first suggested the large Chinese buffet, and then the take out Chinese on Main Street. When we first started to eat, Trester said, "They switched my food." He ate some of it, but seemed dismayed that he was eating the wrong stuff. He mentioned something about getting potatoes as one of his items instead of what he asked for. I didn't notice when they dished up his order whether he pointed too generally or what happened. Anyway, he took home what he didn't eat, to save for later instead of throwing it away.

Not to get ahead of myself, when I arrived, the ants had returned en masse, running their four to six lane thick highways in various directions. I hit them with some diluted Mr. Clean in a spray bottle, and that fixed their wagons for the time being. I checked the toilets to see if they were working. The sewer line has been stopped up twice in just over a month, so I wanted to be sure things were working. They seemed to be. I once again tried to suggest some practices to Trester that would keep the line from clogging with too much TP, but he didn't seem interested. He said something like, "They blocked it for a while, but I think it's all right now."

This reminds me to report a brief conversation to demonstrate how difficult it is simply to chat with Trester.

Me: "Do you use scissors or an electric beard trimmer to trim your beard?"

Trester: "No. The other one burned out. It turned out to be a British spy thing. It started talking to you."

On our way to one of the dollar stores, I asked Trester what was on his shopping list. He read it to me:

candles
incense
paper towels
computer convention cigarettes

Kleenex

fizzy stomach pills [meaning something like Alka Seltzer]

a move-around button

color bandaids

ointment

I asked him if "computer convention cigarettes" was a brand name, but he said he didn't know. I'm not sure where that idea came from.

This was the second time a "move-around button" got on his shopping list. When I had asked the first time what such a button does, Trester was not very clear but apparently it allows one to move from place to place without the need for a car or bus ride. I would pay a dollar at any dollar store for such a button.

The last three weeks I have been taking cedar planks out to Trester's and we have been replacing the shelving in his lath house, where he has many cactus plants. Many have died, but he is beginning to take a bit better care of them now, I think. We took out the rotted, termite-eaten boards and cleaned off the redwood support two by fours. Many of the boards had some viny plants growing all over them, and Trester wanted to save every piece of it, including small sprouts growing out of the wood. This week he finally explained that the plant was his group's only plant, and that it could be sold for a profit.

Week before last, Trester said he was "going to the smoke shop and try to leave" (since Coco's has been a bust). As I had done once or twice before, I said, "So I might not ever see you again?"

And he said, "Yeah." The thought doesn't seem to bother him.

Random items from the last few visits:

Trester is putting Barbasol shaving cream in the toilets.

He once remarked in the kitchen, "It smells like a dentist's office." [He hasn't been to a dentist's office in at least ten years.]

Previously, Trester had at least a dozen bags of microwave popcorn on top of the microwave oven. Then one week it was all gone. I asked him what happened to it and he said, "I threw it away. It was the wrong company." Most of it was Orville Redenbacker, but some was another brand or two. I never know what gets eaten and what gets thrown away.

Working on the shelving was a good thing, because it gave me an opportunity actually to do something with Trester. I had him move plants, take the old boards outside, carry boards, and so forth. I hope it was mentally good for him.

This Saturday, Trester complained of back pain, but not of chest pain or any other problems. It was at least 95 degrees and humid, so we went back into the house for a rest after working on the lath house. He was fairly cheerful when I left, and he thanked me as always.

Sunday, August 9, 2009

Those who joke about mental illness often say, "The definition of insanity is doing the same thing over and over again and expecting different results." That definition took on some cogency yesterday when I visited Trester. When I asked him where he wanted to eat lunch, he said, "Let's go to Coco's and see if I can go through the gate and go home." Even after a gentle reminder about the lack of success five times in the past, and after my suggesting that we eat somewhere else and then go to Coco's, Trester wanted to eat there. So we did.

We were seated near a dish collection area, and as usual, the busboy clattered the dishes as he dumped them into the bin. After a particularly loud dish slam, Trester made a face and asked me, "Did you get croaked by that?" I asked him to explain, but he didn't say anything. He kept turning his head around to look behind him (where the collection area was). At one point he asked again, "Did you see where they zonked the thing at us?" A bit later he put his hand to his ear while his face had a pained expression. I asked him if his ear hurt. He said no, it was "that klonker thing."

We had lunch and went over to the cash register to pay the bill. Trester asked, seemingly of no one in particular, "Can we go through the gate?" No one said anything, so we left.

The sewer lines were clogged again this time. That's three times in about two and a half months. I asked Trester if he had been trying to use less toilet paper. He said, "It's not that. They kronk the inside deal some way through the wall. Some guy wrecks it." Some people think everything bad is their fault; others think that nothing bad is their fault. Trester is in the latter category. Either someone (human, ghost, whatever) did it or else he doesn't know. Maybe the ability to accept responsibility for misadventures or errors is a sign of mental health.

At the dollar store, Trester bought candles, paper towels, note pads, ammonia, hand soap, and so forth. He now has ten half-gallon jugs of ammonia, some partially filled. As I have mentioned, he likes to pour ammonia out on the floor to prevent "them" from coming up from under the floor.

Speaking of under the floor, Trester again asked me to "signal down half a level" while we were in the parking lot of the dollar store, because "we have our stores there."

I asked him how and he pointed to the wiper lever. So I operated it to its various positions and we waited to end up near Gordon's or Jumpy's or the supply house. But we remained in the parking lot.

On the way home, we picked up some film Trester had left for developing last week.

Back at the house, I made another attempt against the ants, who are having a massive party. They even got into the fresh grapes I had just brought from Stater Brothers. (I had to submerge the grapes in a bowl of water to float the critters out.)

As I left, I again told Trester that the air conditioning would work better if he didn't leave the back door and the windows open. He said okay and did nothing about it. He was feeling okay this week, not complaining about any back pain. He said he slept better the last couple of days. The weather was better, too, being in the high 80s instead of the high 90s.

For the first time since I can remember, Trester didn't come out and wave goodbye to me as I drove out.

Sunday, September 20, 2009

Trester has been much the same since my last posting. We have still been going to Coco's for lunch almost every week. Except for twice in the last 10 or so weeks, lunch has been at Coco's. Yesterday, after lunch as we stood outside the restaurant, Trester asked me earnestly if he could go through the gate and leave. I told him again that I didn't know how that could be done. He must feel disappointed and frustrated trying to leave for the "other Corona" where his family lives with all his kids in a nice house and so forth. It's really sad that they exist only in his imagination.

He showed me pictures of a vacant lot a few blocks from his house and said that it was where he was supposed to build a house to live in. I think I've mentioned before that he often points out a house, business, or church and says, "I was supposed to live there, " or "That's one of our houses."

Yesterday when I was getting ready to leave, Trester asked me, "Do you know how I can get registered, so that I can leave?" I asked him what he meant by getting registered, and he said, "So that they know that I exist and can go home." He also asked me how he could get some money. I think he feels constrained with the little allowance he gets. (However, it prevents him from buying airline tickets to distant destinations, as he has done in the past.)

The last several weeks I've had a helper—let's call him Mike to protect his privacy—come out and work on the landscaping and housecleaning with me. We've also been working on the very weathered and partly termite eaten woodwork around the living room windows. A couple of weeks ago, I bought a gallon of Kilz 2 to prime the scraped off woodwork. Last week it was gone. I immediately thought that Trester had seen it and, because it said "Kilz," he had thrown it away. He is phobic of anything that suggests poison. So Mike and I turned over a couple of trash cans and found the gallon can in the bottom of one of them. Needless to say, we have hidden the can and turned it around so the label doesn't show.

We have now primed the three window areas and are ready to paint. This week we also installed a fireproof desktop for Trester's workbench out in the workshop. We primed and painted the surface to make it more pleasant.

At the dollar store, Trester was looking for "two way pens," by which he means pens that are a combination ball point and highlighter. I haven't seen him highlight much, but then I haven't looked at his headline cards recently, either. He also had on his list again a "move around button." I've mentioned in the past that this handy device would allow one to move instantly from one place to another and even go up and down levels, if I understand Trester's explanation correctly. We all could use one of those, and if they are ever available at the dollar store, the price couldn't be beat. Occasionally Trester asks if the dollar store sells cigarettes, and one time (as I've mentioned), he said that one of the stores has them "three packs for a dollar." When I ask him who told him that, just as when I ask him who said he can't eat at a particular restaurant or shop at a particular store, he doesn't answer clearly.

On this trip, Trester bought more ammonia, dishwasher detergent, candles, incense, headline cards, facial tissue, and some colored foam craft squares. He asked me about antacid again, but the dollar stores carry only the kinds he doesn't want.

Trester walks around quite a bit, evidently. He seems to have walked down to the shopping center near his house and gone into one of the stores, perhaps Best Buy. At any rate, he told me last week that he wanted to buy a "looker screen," by which I guessed he had seen a netbook or notebook computer. He said he could communicate with his group with it.

This week Trester complained of a queasy stomach before we left for lunch, but he managed to eat a French dip sandwich and fries without any problem. He did complain about some angina for a bit, but was feeling good by the time I left. I got him a supply of Gatorade to help keep him hydrated along with his bottled water.

As usual, Trester thanked me for the help and waved goodbye as I rolled down the driveway.

Thursday, December 24, 2009

Some time has passed since the last entry. The fact is, there is not really much new in Trester's life. I continue to visit him weekly with his groceries and take him to one or more of the dollar stores. He continues to look for a "move around button," and in both restaurants and dollar stores he asks if they can take him home or to the "other Corona." He has recently begun to offer the other person $20 if they will oblige.

Once and still again we ate at Coco's last week and when he asked to be taken to "the main Cocos" or "home," the cashier told him where there was another restaurant down the freeway. Who knows—we might end up there this weekend.

Trester's life of futility continued by his looking for more things that don't exist: a string of laser lights, Gordon's dollar store, a radio that gets 210 on the dial, Jumpy's, the city "down half a level," and so on.

At the house, I have been cutting up an enormous branch (20 inches in diameter) that broke off a big pine tree there.

A week ago, I installed two new fluorescent light fixtures in the workshop. I happened to notice the light switch was on but only one bulb in one fixture was lit. I asked Trester about it and he said that was the way the lights were. I told him he should tell me when things don't work and he said okay (as he always does). At any rate, the new lights really light up the shop.

I got Trester a new wristwatch and an auto-setting clock radio with a huge digital clock on it for his Christmas presents. He likes both of them (I gave them to him early).

Trester is still pouring ammonia and bleach on the family room floor and sometimes the kitchen floor, creating a white film that takes a while to mop up.

Tuesday, December 29, 2009

When I arrived on Saturday, I asked Trester, as I always do, how he was feeling. He said he was feeling better. (Later in the car I learned that he had been up all night earlier in the week fighting off ghosts, so that his feeling better meant he was being persecuted less in the middle of the night.)

When I asked Trester where he wanted to eat lunch, he said, "Let's go get an enchilada." So I suggested Del Taco (a fast food place) and a regular Mexican restaurant. He chose the latter. At least being interested in Mexican cooking took his mind off of Coco's, so that we didn't have to eat there for the fifteenth or twentieth time. So off we went.

As usual, Trester doesn't have a sense of prices until after the fact. I don't want to challenge his ordering in advance since he has so little enjoyment in life as it is, but I sometimes point out the cost of what he orders so cavalierly. This time he ordered a Margarita ($6) along with his food.

The food was really good. Trester had an enchilada and Chile relleno with rice and beans. Just after he finished his food and the waiter took his plate away, Trester threw up. I pushed my plate over for him to catch the barf. I asked how he was and he said OK. He went to the restroom to clean his beard and wash up.

This is the second or third time he has barfed right after lunch. He did that after a big meal at Marie Calendar's a couple of weeks ago. My guess now, which I told Trester, is that he doesn't realize that he is overfilling his stomach. When we eat at restaurants with smaller portions, he seems to do fine.

For a while he threw up regularly after lunch. Just before he did, he would say something about feeling like throwing up. Afterwards he always responded to my question by saying that he felt okay.

At the house, I checked the new fluorescent lights in the workshop, and they are working fine. But before we go there, I should say we visited two of the dollar stores, where Trester got more candles, some home decorations, more ammonia and bleach, and foot powder. He still has "move around button" on his shopping list each week, but can never seem to find one. (I mentioned earlier that such a button permits instant travel from one place to the next.)

I spent part of the time at the house cutting up dead trees (some smaller ones than the huge branch I have told you about). Then I mopped the floor of the kitchen. The dried ammonia or bleach makes mopping quite a bit more involved than would starting with a regular floor surface.

Trester didn't seem to have any angina this week, which made me feel less anxious about him. What makes me the most frustrated are two things. One, as I've mentioned many times, is that I can't get him to see a doctor, dentist, psychiatrist, optician, barber, etc. Second, he keeps asking me to do impossible things (go half a level down, take him to the other Corona "down south," take him to Gordon's or Jumpy's, help him go through the gate, buy a radio that gets 210 on the dial, find his supply house) or do things I know will not be good for him (take him to the airport and get him a ticked to Hawaii), or do things that are both impossible and would not be good for him (buy him a $300 Lexus so he can go driving again). The upshot is that I feel bad that I keep denying him what he wants.

Perhaps we are all victims of our own imaginations to some extent, but the sane among us, upon reflection, can realize that, while Trester cannot.

The only other thing I can think of this time is that I continue without success to get Trester to close the back door when the heat is on. I will come back from cutting up some wood and see the back door wide open. I close it. Five minutes later, I come back and it's open again. I tell Trester that he should keep it closed or turn the heat off, and he sometimes says okay. But a few minutes later, it's open again. Good thing he doesn't live in North Dakota.

Case in point: When I left, I closed the back door, said goodbye to Trester, got in the car and followed the driveway around the workshop, where the back door came into view, and it was wide open again.

At any rate, except for the lunch episode, Trester seemed in reasonable spirits and seemed to feel physically no worse than usual. He, as always, thanked me for coming and for helping.

Sunday, January 3, 2010

My helper and I arrived a little after nine o'clock this week, so that we could continue to make progress cutting up that huge branch that fell from the pine tree. I inadvertently woke Trester up when I unloaded his groceries, but I told him he could sleep till noon if he wanted. He got up about 10:30, I think.

I decided to give Trester my old digital camera, thinking that it would ultimately save money over the purchase of disposable cameras and the processing charges. I showed him how to use it briefly, and he started taking pictures. I told him the current card would hold 83 pictures, so he had plenty. He very alertly asked, "So this camera doesn't use film?" and I told him it was electronic. Later on, while I was cutting up wood, I saw Trester roaming happily all over the property taking pictures. When we were getting ready to leave, Trester asked me, "Do you have the book on the camera?" He wanted to know how to use all the features.

So, just because he is mentally ill, and just because his brain is awash in way too many neurotransmitters, don't think he's dumb. He can't think straight half the time, and he is extremely confused, delusional, and hallucinatory, but the Trester who has to live with that dysfunctional brain is still there and fighting to think and learn. I've argued in the past for mind-brain dualism, that the "I" in us, our thinking mind and being, is separate from our brain, and we have to deal with the limitations of our brain to a greater or lesser degree. I might have mentioned that irritating occurrence when we can't think of the right word. Our mind knows what we mean, but our brain is letting us down.

Speaking of delusions, Trester wanted to eat at Coco's again (how many times is that, now?), so we headed on over. Trester had a prime rib sandwich and a "Corona Cerveza," as he calls it (instead of a Corona beer). This time he didn't overeat and didn't throw up.

At the end of lunch I went to the necessarium, and when I came out, Trester was talking to the cashier about going through the gate. The conversation was just focusing on the issue of whether the other Coco's in town had a gate. The poor cashier did not understand, of course. I came up just when Trester asked, "Does it have a gate I can go through?"

I looked at her and said, "We'll see." And we left for the dollar stores.

Trester got his usual supply of items at the dollar store, including four half-gallon jugs of ammonia. I got him some extra batteries for the camera, since he forgot. (And I noticed that he was forgetting to turn the camera off when he was finished with it, so he will be needing batteries.)

Next week I will swap memory cards with him and print off the pictures he has been taking. We'll see what he has shot.

Monday, January 18, 2010

Trester was already up and dressed this week when I arrived about 12:15 from the grocery store. He was wearing a ripped yellow shirt (his favorite color). I asked him if he still had the shirts I got him recently and he said yes, he was wearing them and they were in the laundry. I made a note to get him some more yellow ones, if I could find a brand he likes.

I asked him where he wanted to go to lunch, and he said, "I can't decide between a hamburger and pizza. I mentioned the usual suspects, In-N-Out, Wendy's, and so on, and then looked up pizza places in the two-year-old yellow pages he had. I offered to call Round Table to see if they were still in business, but Trester didn't say anything. Then he suggested (shudder) Coco's again and added, "Maybe they can help me go home through the gate." I told him that they hadn't helped him do that the last twenty times we were there and he seemed to remember that.

So, we ended up at Wendy's where we had a hamburger and some chili and French fries. I told Trester not to over eat so he wouldn't throw up, and he said okay. Fortunately (or blessedly) he didn't throw up.

Then we went to the "big dollar store," as he calls it,

taking the non-freeway route so Trester could look for another lot that he had bought (in his imagination) to build houses and stores on. He also said that his group was going to move into a large area one level down from us and asked me to take him there. Once again, I told him I didn't know how to go down a level.

Trester bought his usual supply of candles and ammonia and incense. Then he wanted to stop by the Fresh-n-Easy store to get some Brie cheese. So we did. He got some Brie and some artichoke hearts and some Muenster cheese too. We also stopped by a smoke shop so he could get "some extra smokes."

Last time, Trester had filled the memory card on the camera, so I took it and printed about 90 photos for him and gave them to him. He liked them. He also gave me the new memory card (I have two that I can alternate) which has twice the capacity. He said it was full, so there must be about 180 photos on it. That's a lot for a week's shooting.

In addition to my usual mopping, I took a few minutes to look through Trester's canned goods and refrigerator supplies, and tossed out the expired stuff. There were a few cans of soup dated June 2008 and some applesauce dated September 2009, so I tossed them out, together with some dehydrated cheese that had been left out of the wrapper.

Trester's complaint this week was that he had "stickers all over." It was more of a comment than a complaint of current pain. He did say at one point, "I need medical attention," so I took the opportunity to ask him if I could take him to a doctor. He said, "No, I'm all right." He appears to think that when he can move to the "other Corona" or go down a level or through the gate or into a new house, that he will meet up with his group (and his relatives?) who will help him with whatever ails him. As much as he thanks me for helping him each week, Trester doesn't seem to think I'm much more than a butler who won't be missed once his services are no longer needed.

At any rate, Trester was cheerful enough when I left and as usual thanked me for helping him.

Thursday, June 10, 2010

Trester is still pouring ammonia and bleach on the floor, leaving a white haze that is difficult to mop off. He adds body powder in some places, making the cleaning task even more of a challenge.

After perhaps 20 trips to Coco's in a row, Trester has occasionally wanted a pizza instead, and last week he took me up on my suggestion of Chinese food.

I bought him 10 pairs of white athletic socks because his others had holes at the heel. He looked at the package and said, "Hanes won't sell to us." I told him they sold to me and I gave him the gift. So after a few minutes of indecision, he put on a pair.

He continues to cut up thin cardboard (such as that packaging soft drinks, cigarettes, and grocery items) into one inch pieces. They litter the floor in the kitchen and in the workshop as the drawer and baskets are full to overflowing.

The workshop door is covered with tags such as "Corn Dogs 11562" or "Buy Old Golds."

He continues to want to buy a new radio that "gets our stations." The radios he owns don't play his music and don't play any stations that haven't been taken over by adversaries. For a while he said that the current stations wanted him to pay a fee to listen.

In addition to the socks, I got him two pair of pants. He

looked at them and said, "They switched them." So I don't know if he will wear them or not.

A "move around button" is still on his shopping list.

He won't drink Dasani water because it comes in a blue tinted bottle. "I don't want to turn blue" he told me.

At the dollar store he wanted to get some body powder. I found some, with the label Purity After Bath Powder. I showed it to Trester and he wouldn't have it. "That's for cats," he said, referring, as I learned after asking a few questions, to the name Purity, which suggested Purr and hence cats to Trester.

He rejects so many things that it's becoming harder to shop for him.

Saturday, January 15, 2011

For the most part, things have remained the same with Trester since the last entry, but here are a few items of note.

First news is that in November, Trester got into so much back pain that he wanted to be taken to the hospital. Considering his phobia for doctors, this was remarkable. I told the emergency room doctors that Trester did not have any insurance, but they graciously accommodated him anyway. The entire visit took five hours (once again making the term "emergency room" quite an oxymoron), but in the process, Trester did get a good examination.

His pain was the result of a spur on his spinal vertebrae. The doctors offered him a pain pill and he took it without hesitation. You'll recall that I can't get him to take even an aspirin at home. Anyway, he was given an X-ray, a CAT scan, a bunch of blood work, and the usual physical. His blood pressure was slightly high, and one or two blood results were slightly out of range, but considering his general chronic poor health, he was in better shape than I had imagined.

What I thought was Trester's testicular tumor turned out to be a hernia. The doctors told Trester that there was a hospital that would surgically repair it without charge, but Trester said he didn't want any surgery. The doctors wrote two prescriptions for antibiotics and one for pain pills. I filled them on the way home. Trester never took a single pill of any kind. His back pain eased, though, so now he is back to feeling pretty good.

After perhaps 30 straight weeks eating at Coco's, Trester finally agreed to branch out again, and we have eaten at the buffet and at Del Taco, and a pizza place. We almost got to Wendy's, but once we got inside it was the old line, "They don't want us here," so we had to leave.

Trester's microwave oven burned up, quite literally, so I got him a new one for Christmas. The previous oven lasted at least ten years, so I guess it had lived its life. I did ask Trester what he was cooking before it caught on fire, and he said a chicken pot pie. So it evidently wasn't a case of putting a metal item inside. Microwave ovens have gotten really inexpensive, and I found Trester one that has a stainless steel exterior. When I asked Trester how it worked, he said it was really nice. (Asking him was to make sure he had figured out how to use it, since the controls are just a bit different from those on the old oven.)

Trester still hears voices. I once asked him how he knew that a store didn't want him to shop there, and he said, "The man whose voice comes from the refrigerator told me." Another time, when I asked Trester what was on his shopping list (something I do every week), he read off these items: Candles, incense, headline cards, combo pens, a move around button, powder, a $20 radio. (Combo pens are the ones that have a highlighter on one end and a ball point pen on the other. The move around button is on his list every week. It would let him transport himself from place to place and level to level instantly.) Now, as for the clock radio, I had gotten him one just a few months before. When I looked, I noticed that it was gone, so I asked where the other one was. He said, "They insulted me so badly that I threw it away." He bought some Christmas lights that fairly soon ended up in the trash, because they flashed wrong.

I've mentioned in other posts that Trester throws away many items I get for him—pants, shirts, jackets, radios, food, and so on. The reasons vary: those weren't paid for, not my group's product, they told me not to wear or use them, those weren't mine, those are for girls, etc.

The Change

By now you are familiar enough with the mental and physical experiences that have made up the life of my brother for close to 40 years. After I no longer made entries in my Weblog, things continued much the same. Trester developed a fondness for a pizza parlor ("Two-topping special: Large pizza $8.99") and for Five Guys hamburgers ("all the way"—that is, with a dozen different toppings—of course).

In spite of my constant worry (and nagging) over Trester's angina—afraid that he would any day have a heart attack—his heart was not to be the ultimate issue.

But around late February or early March of 2014, Trester suffered an apparent stroke. He lost most of his ability to speak, both in finding the word he wanted and in pronouncing it. By April he was getting worse, and could barely dress himself. His pants showed signs of incontinence.

I finally got him signed up for Medi-Cal (he has been more willing to sign documents than ever before); however, he still refused to see a doctor or dentist or go to a hospital.

He shuffled when he walked and fell down or stumbled on stairs. He acted as if he couldn't understand what I was saying sometimes.

He lost his ability to perform simple tasks, partly because of physical impairment and partly because of mental impairment. When I arrived one day, he was sitting on the sofa with his underwear partly pulled up. "I need help," he muttered. I helped him pull up his underwear. Then, he started to put on his shoes without socks. I grabbed some socks to help him. By that time, he had already slipped on his shoes, so he took a sock and tried to put it on over his shoe.

When we got into the truck to go to lunch, he couldn't buckle his seat belt by himself.

I bought him a wheelchair, but he was too proud to use it most of the time.

I hired a caregiver to look after Trester and to cook and clean for him. The caregiver reported about mid-April that Trester had nearly stopped smoking. For someone who was a several-packs-a-day chain smoker for thirty or forty years, that was a dire sign. When I said goodbye one week, he had three cigarettes with him, but he seemed unable to light any or to decide on which one to smoke.

You might recall mention of an old, pink rocking chair that Trester had exiled from the living room to the workshop in 2005 because "they" told him not to sit in it anymore. It sat unused in the shop for perhaps five or more years. Trester spent much of his time in the workshop, sitting on a high wooden stool and cutting out pictures of houses that he taped into notebooks.

Then, he must have had a change of mind, because he started sitting in the pink chair more and more while in the shop. (He has gradually moved his time from sitting at the kitchen table or lying on the sofa to sitting in the shop.) At any rate, he had been sitting in the pink chair for perhaps a year or two when it occurred to me that a better chair might make him happier.

So, in mid-April, I brought him a nice recliner/rocker chair to replace the old pink chair. Just a few days later, his caregiver called me to say that the chair had caught on fire (from a cigarette, no doubt) and was completely burned up. Fortunately, the caregiver saw the smoke and put out the fire before the workshop (attached to the house) went up in flames. So then he was back in the pink rocker again.

By late April, Trester was so debilitated that would go to lunch with me but was no longer interested in going shopping at one of the dollar stores. He slept much of the day.

On a recent visit, he seemed to want to communicate a request but couldn't say it. After a few attempts, he managed to push out, in a barely understandable voice and a frustrated tone, "I can't talk!"

April 25, 2014

I drove out to take Trester his usual week's groceries and see him. When I walked into the living room, he was lying on the sofa as he often does. And, as I always do, I asked how he was doing.

"How are you feeling today?"

"Not good."

"Are you in pain?"
"Yes."
"Where is the pain?"
"They shot me eight times."
"Do you want to go to a doctor or the hospital?"
"Yes."

That "yes" was a shock. For the first time in years of my asking that question almost every week, Trester indicated that he was willing to get some medical help. I quickly got the wheel chair. His caregiver and I helped him get dressed (no easy task in itself), and put him in the chair, but he stood up and got out, heading for the bathroom. He apparently had an accident in his pants at this time.

Since Trester could not walk on his own and was resistant to riding in the wheel chair, I decided to call 911 and have him go to the hospital in an ambulance.

Soon four firemen and two paramedics arrived. I told them the details and my beliefs about Trester's stroke. The four firemen examined Trester and said, "There's no evidence of a stroke."

The two paramedics examined him and said, "There's no evidence of a stroke."

The firemen also put in their report that Trester had been lying in his feces possibly for weeks, thus involving social services. One of firemen gave Trester's caregiver a dirty, accusing look.

At the hospital, one of the doctors said he didn't think Trester had had a stroke. Another doctor said it was possible. A CAT scan was done, together with many other tests.

The diagnoses were:
- Stroke syndrome with right capsular infarct (blockage stroke, not bleeding stroke)
- Metabolic encephalopathy due to azotemia

(brain atrophy [degeneration] from poor kidney function)
- Atherosclerosis (plaque buildup in heart and brain arteries)
- Urinary tract infection
- Chronic Obstructive Pulmonary Disease (COPD) (breathing disorder caused by smoking)
- Uncontrolled hypertension (high blood pressure)
- Chronic kidney disease
- Sinus bradycardia (slow heartbeat)
- Paranoid schizophrenia
- Possible initial bronchitis and pneumonia from smoking

April 31, 2014 [at the hospital]

Blood pressure was 194/101 in his right arm and 158/87 in his left arm.

May 1, 2014 [at the hospital]

At 2 pm, Trester's blood pressure was 170/102. Trester was given an IV injection of Vasotec. At 4:45 pm, his blood pressure was 199/115 in his right arm and 203/110 in his left arm. The nurse added 20 mg of hydralazine by IV.

Trester was conscious but not very communicative. At one point he scowled at me and said, "What's wrong with you?"

May 2, 2014

The hospital decided that Trester should be discharged to a skilled nursing facility. Several days were needed to find a place that would take him, since he had only Medi-Cal insurance and had a record of schizophrenia. But a place in Riverside was found, and Trester was transported there.

During the day before transport, his blood pressure was 154/89 and 142/90.

May to July, 2014

At the skilled nursing facility, Trester became less and less able to eat and was losing weight. He could no longer talk. When I visited him, he sometimes seemed to recognize me and much of the time not. I took him chocolate candy and guava nectar canned juice, his favorite.

Near the end of July, he could no longer eat or drink the juice. Soon he was staring blankly into space. I thought he had had another stroke.

One morning around 2am the facility called and said Trester had labored breathing and asked if it was okay to put oxygen on him. Of course I said yes.

That evening when my wife and I visited him, they told us that they were treating Trester for a urinary tract infection, using IV antibiotics. I noticed that his fingers were gray. The facility had hooked Trester up to a pulse oximeter, and it registered 77 percent oxygen in Trester's blood. I called that to the attention of the nurse, and they began a series of tests that made them conclude that Trester should go to the hospital.

So Trester was taken to the hospital.

Another CAT scan revealed that Trester had indeed suffered another stroke. He was put on a ventilator (bipap) machine, hooked up to IV with more antibiotics and a potassium supplement, and put in DOU (Definitive Observation Unit, one step below ICU). He continued to decline and was moved to ICU (Intensive Care Unit), the after a few days, back to DOU.

August, 2014

After a few days in the hospital, the doctors (and there were six or seven) treating Trester decided that his prognosis was quite poor and he was sent back to the skilled nursing facility on hospice. The care given by the facility and the hospice company was outstanding. Everyone was kind and considerate. Trester had five or six people looking after him each day.

August 15, 2014

As my wife and I were getting ready to leave to visit Trester, we got a call from the facility that Trester had just breathed his last at 6:55 pm.

Trester's Funeral Service

Here is the text of the graveside service we did for Trester on August 22, 2014.

Trester Smith Harris, Jr.
August 30, 1948 – August 15, 2014

Bachelor's Degree in Economics
University of California, Santa Barbara

Juris Doctor, Law Degree
Pepperdine Law School

Licensed Attorney
California State Bar Association

Owner and Proprietor
Desert Hill Cactus Growers

Owner and Proprietor
Gordon's Tobacco

Welcome

Trester's Life

Trester accomplished much during his first 30 years, before he became ill. In addition to his university degree, law degree, admission to the California State Bar, and practicing law for a short time, Trester

- bought mountain property, built cabins, and sold them at a profit
- read and studied the Bible carefully
- studied psychology
- worked as a hypnotherapist, where he cured a woman of fear of freeway driving
- ran a nursery and mail order business, Desert Hill Cactus Growers
- ran a smoke shop, Gordon's Tobacco
- read extensively in classical economic theory
- ran for California State Assembly

✧✝✧

Eulogy and Reflections

Trester loved the world of nature. From age 10 or 11, he started collecting plants, eventually specializing in cactus and succulents. The shaded patio in the Inglewood home was filled with pots containing plants of all kinds. Trester bought seeds and plants, and his hobby was so well known that people gave him more plants and cuttings constantly.

When we moved to Corona, Trester filled his lath house with specimens of rare cacti and tropical plants, carefully nurturing them, feeding them with the best fertilizers and repotting them regularly.

Trester and I had a great childhood together. Since our house was six miles from town, we were fairly isolated, so we spent time with each other, down the hill on the property, building imaginary cities. I was Jim Carson and Trester was Ed Carson, brothers even in imagination. We built roads, stores, even Cinerama drive-in theaters, and planted little trees all around.

As we got old enough to drive, we spent a few weeks each summer, just the two of us, on driving vacations. We drove up to Canada, and across the US as far as New Mexico and Idaho. Trester especially liked Arizona, because we could collect the seed pods of many kinds of cactus plants, from the large Golden Barrel to the tiny mammalaria species. I remember one time we stopped at a cheap motel — we frequently chose cheap motels to make the money last longer — and the woman proprietor asked us if we were going to stay all night. Maybe that motel was too cheap. Anyway, we said yes and got a room. Trester spent much of the evening spreading out cactus seeds on paper towels, to dry and preserve them.

On another trip up to Crater Lake Oregon, we stopped by a six-dollar motel (thanks to the Auto Club book that lists prices) and checked in. We thought it odd that we could see the wall studs and the exterior shingles from inside the room. Not exactly insulated. But there was an oil heater there, so when we started to feel cool, we lit it. It worked by a drip system, with a dial ranging from 1 to 7. With no clue what that range represented, we set it on 3 or 4 and went to bed. Two or three hours later we woke up in a sauna. It must have been 200 degrees in the room. Frantically, we turned the heater off and opened the door for a few minutes. When the room was again endurable, we closed the door and went back to bed. But remember we had turned the heater off, not just down. So in another couple of hours, we awoke in a freezer. It must have been below zero in the room.

On those long drives across the states, Trester liked to talk about his favorite economic theories. He loved the Austrian school, and he read everything that his favorite economists wrote. I still remember some of their names: Friedrich Hayek, Ludwig von Mises, Eugen von Boehm-Bawerk, Murray Rothbard, Frederic Bastiat, and others. He would have been a great economics professor.

One of our favorite trips was to Hawaii, to the island of Maui. We flew over with our parents, I think it was about 1968 or 1970. Neither Trester nor I was 26 yet, so we couldn't rent a car ourselves, but dad rented a standard transmission, Datsun 210 and turned the keys over to us. I drove, even though I didn't know how to drive a stick shift. Stopping on a slope was pretty hairy. Anyway, we decided to take the road to Hana. The Lord was with us, because the way I drove on that road, if we had met another car coming in the opposite direction, there would have been some rearranged sheet metal and human body parts. We stopped frequently to take pictures—close ups of plants and wide shots of waterfalls. Trester kept exclaiming, "This is so neat!" He loved all the ferns and tropical flowers.

I mentioned pictures. Photography was a major interest of Trester, even after he became mentally ill. While he was still well, he took 35 millimeter slides. There were very few family pictures. Most of the dozens and dozens of 80-slide carousels are filled with pictures of plants and flowers. Trester liked photography so much that when he moved to Anaheim in the late 1970s, he bought some photography equipment so he could develop, enlarge, and print his own photos.

About 1970, Trester began to grow depressed, which in hindsight we have learned was the precursor to his schizophrenia. Unfortunately, we didn't really understand what he was going through, and at any rate our father didn't want Trester to see a psychiatrist because of the stigma attached. But Trester was a fighter, a stubborn fighter, and he fought the depression to the completion of his Bachelor's degree in economics from the University of California at Santa Barbara. Then, what we now think of as a heroic effort, he fought his depression all the way through law school, and finally earned his law degree, passed the bar exam, and became a licensed attorney. He practiced law for only a few months as his illness set in.

Trester moved to Anaheim for a while, where he had bought a tobacco business and tried to run it. By this time, Trester was seeing psychiatrists on his own, and taking the first generation of medications—stelazine and thorazine—whose chief side effect is sleepiness. That and his depression made it impossible to run the business for long. He moved back to Corona, where our mom took care of him until her passing in 1999.

So Tres was living alone in the Corona house. I took him his groceries each week and we went to lunch and shopping, where he started buying disposable cameras and taking pictures with them. Yes, even in his illness he remained interested in photography and in plants. I had the film developed for him at those one-hour photo places, mostly in grocery and drug stores. At the last count, he had somewhere between 40 and 50 photo albums filled with 4 by 6 prints of the neighborhood around where he lived. As the years passed, the disposable cameras and in-store one-hour photo processing services met the steamroller of digital cameras and cameras in phones. So I got Trester a digital camera. When he filled up a memory card with a thousand photos in just a few weeks, I swapped cards and took the full one home to print out for him.

Even though Trester suffered through physical, emotional, and psychic pain for the last 35 years of his life, tortured by a disease that made him think assassins were out to murder him and that war was going on all around him, and even though he fought the choking ghosts and enemies who insulted him over the radio, he remained a kind and grateful brother. I used to say that Trester is in there somewhere, and he would often break through the fog of his brain and say, "Thanks for helping."

God bless my brother. He was a true friend.

Scripture

For we know that if the earthly tent
which is our house
is torn down,
we have a building from God,
a house not made with hands,
eternal in the heavens.

For indeed in this house we groan,
longing to be clothed
with our dwelling from heaven;
inasmuch as we, having put it on,
shall not be found naked.

For indeed while we are in this tent,
we groan,
being burdened,
because we do not want to be unclothed,
but to be clothed,
in order that what is mortal
may be swallowed up by life.

—2 Corinthians 5:1-4

Prayer

Dear Lord,
We stand here before you,
and before the earthly remains of Trester,
whose body he's no doubt
so glad to be rid of at last.
If we were selfish,
we would be sad to see him go from among us,
but instead we rejoice
to know that he is at last set free
to live with you, enjoying a clear mind and
a healthy new body.
We look forward to the day
when we can join him in your kingdom,
where every tear will at last be wiped away.
O Lord, thank you for your goodness,
for giving us a savior who lets us live again.
In the name of Jesus we bless your holy name.
Amen.

Scripture

*Here on earth you will have
many trials and sorrows.
But take heart,
because I have overcome the world.*

—John 16:33b (NLT)

Psalm 23

The God of love my shepherd is,
And he that doth me feed:
While he is mine, and I am his,
What can I want or need?

He leads me to the tender grass,
Where I both feed and rest;
Then to the streams that gently pass:
In both I have the best.

Or if I stray, he doth convert
And bring my mind in frame:
And all this not for my desert,
But for his holy name.

Yea, in death's shady black abode
Well may I walk, not fear:
For thou art with me: and thy rod
To guide, thy staff to bear.

Nay, thou dost make me sit and dine,
Even in my enemy's sight:
My head with oil, my cup with wine
Runs over day and night.

Surely thy sweet and wondrous love
Shall measure all my days;
And as it never shall remove,
So neither shall my praise.

(George Herbert translation, c. 1633)

Benediction

May the God who brings delivery after suffering, joy after sorrow, and life after death, call us to love and to serve him so that we may one day join Trester in the Kingdom of the Lord forever. Amen.

Closing Thoughts

May this sad memoir touch your life and help your compassion to grow—not only for the mentally ill, but for all people who are challenged in some way. We complain about a flat tire or a broken fingernail or a bruised elbow, even though the thing is insignificant, remedied, and forgotten a few days later. At the same time, our brothers and sisters are suffering lifelong physical challenges, or permanent injuries or debilitations.

Our brains are the automobiles that take our minds from place to place. Some people have speedy, powerful automobiles that can take their minds to many places quickly and effortlessly. Others, like my brother, have defective, rattletrap cars, whose wobbly wheels want to careen off the road and crash into a ditch. Their lives are a constant struggle to steer back onto the road.

Let us be thankful, then, that God has given us helpful brains rather than contentious, errant brains. We might be driving an economy car that's not as sleek or powerful as what others are driving, but praise God it gets us where we need to go.

Thank you for reading this book. I hope it has proved beneficial to you and that you are a better person as a result. If so, it is one more victory, one more evidence that

Trester's life had meaning, purpose, and significance.

www.ingramcontent.com/pod-product-compliance
Lightning Source LLC
LaVergne TN
LVHW051823080426
835512LV00018B/2692